THE ONE-MINUTE BIBLE™

John R. Kohlenberger III, EDITOR

Benjamin Unseth, ASSOCIATE EDITOR

GARBORG'S

Bloomington, MN 55420

TABLE OF CONTENTS

A General Introduction to *The One-Minute Bible*™

The Bible is the greatest of all books. More than a book, it is in fact a collection of sixty-six books written over the span of sixteen centuries by kings and peasants, poets and prophets.

The books of the Law, Genesis through Deuteronomy, recount the early history of humanity and the great covenant at Sinai by which the living God of the universe bound himself to the nation of Israel. The historical books of Joshua through Esther highlight the covenant history of Israel, noting both Israel's successes and failures in keeping the covenant and God's patience and grace in enforcing its terms.

The books of poetry and wisdom, Job through Song of Songs, celebrate the God of Israel for his goodness, his holiness, and his accessibility to all who approach him on his terms. Wisdom offers timeless principles for a successful life in relation to God and his creation.

The prophets, Isaiah through Malachi, were the preachers of old. They proclaimed to the Israelites their failure to honor covenant obligations to their God, warned them of his impending righteous judgment, and offered hope to all nations of his coming salvation.

The Gospels, Matthew through John, tell of the life and teaching of Jesus the Messiah, the promised Savior of Israel and the nations. The book of Acts recounts the early history of the Christian church as the followers of Jesus take his message to the farthest corners of the globe.

The letters or epistles, Romans through Jude, were written by the first leaders of the church to Christian congregations and their leadership, offering encouragement, discipline, teaching, and hope. The book of Revelation tells of the end of this present world and of the establishment of the new heavens and new earth in which God will live with his people forever.

We hope *The One-Minute Bible*™ offers you a taste of God's Word that will not be fully satisfied by our bite-sized sampling. We encourage you to read daily from a full-text Bible, perhaps following one of the two annual reading schedules offered in the back of this book.

— THE EDITOR

A Special Introduction to *The One-Minute Bible*™

The One-Minute Bible™ draws on the timeless truths of God's Word from all eras of its history and from all forms of its literature. Always sensitive to context and historical application, the texts reproduced in these daily readings communicate in isolation the same message they present in their original location.

The One-Minute Bible™ offers 366 daily one-minute readings from the world's greatest literary treasure: the Holy Bible. Each day of the year, from January 1 through December 31, is indicated at the top of each page. Although this calendar can guide you through a one-year reading plan, please do not limit yourself to starting in January or limit your reading to one page a day!

One minute a day will allow you to survey the heart of the Bible in one year. If you want more, the related texts at the bottom of each page direct you to nearly 1,800 passages of Scripture that will further your understanding of the topics covered in that day's reading. Many of these texts are in *The One-Minute Bible*™–and you can find them by means of the Scripture Index on pages 413-420. However, we recommend that you look up these verses in a full-text Bible in case you want to read even more of the context than we suggest.

If you fall behind in the suggested daily reading program, don't worry! You can make up one week in seven minutes, half a month in fifteen. But again, don't be discouraged by failing to follow our schedule. If you get behind, simply jump back in where you left off and "Just Read It!"

Topical Headings and Organization

The One-Minute Bible™ begins with the first verse of Genesis and ends with the last verse of Revelation. Readings follow the general flow of biblical history, interlaced with several topical series, such as two weeks for Easter in April and a week for mothers in May. (A two-page table of contents follows this introduction.) Some readings reproduce an entire passage of Scripture, such as Psalm 2 on December 22. Often, several passages are combined to show the whole spectrum of biblical teaching on an important topic.

For example, in January 1, Genesis 1:1-2 introduces you to the Bible itself and to Creation in particular. John 1:1-5 introduces you to Jesus–the Word–through whom all things were created. Psalm 148:1-6 invites you to praise the Lord as the Creator. January 2 continues the Creation account, with five texts enlarging on the theme of light.

Blocks of text from different passages of Scripture are separated by a full space; their references are listed at the end of each reading. Half spaces indicate section breaks in poetry, such as after "Praise the Lord" on page 1. The text follows the wording and formatting of the New International Version of the Bible. On occasion, we have substituted proper nouns for pronouns to make our selection more clear. We want you to know when Jesus is speaking, so we inserted [Jesus said,] into such readings as Matthew 11:28-30 on March 24.

The 700 selected scriptures and 1,800 related texts were chosen to present the key themes of the Bible from each of its sixty-six books. Great care was taken to ensure that each text has the same meaning in *The One-Minute Bible*™ that it has in its larger context in the Holy Bible.

Indexes and Maps

The One-Minute Bible™ guides you through an overview of the Bible in daily one-minute readings. Immediately following the last reading are two daily reading schedules that will guide you through the entire Bible in a year. The morning and evening schedule outlines readings from both Old and New Testaments for each day of the year. The chronological schedule works through the Bible in historical order.

More than 450 key topics and personalities are indexed in the Topical Index found on pages 421-426. With this index you can find every reference to comfort, salvation, or the names of God found in *The One-Minute Bible*™. If you want to study any word or topic more thoroughly, we recommend *The NIV Exhaustive Concordance* (Zondervan, 1990) and *The NIV Nave's Topical Bible* (Zondervan, 1992), both edited by John R. Kohlenberger III. The Scripture Index, mentioned above, locates every text printed in *The One-Minute Bible.*™

Six maps show the land of Israel in Old and New Testament times and the world of the Bible in antiquity and today. Most of the countries, regions, and major cities mentioned in *The One-Minute Bible*™ can be located on these maps. For more thorough study of biblical geography and history, we recommend *The New Bible Dictionary* (Tyndale, 1982) and *The NIV Atlas of the Bible* (Zondervan, 1989).

— THE PUBLISHER

"Blessed Lord,
who hast caused
all Holy Scriptures
to be written for
our learning;

Grant that we may...
hear them, read, mark,
learn and inwardly
digest them."

Book of Common Prayer

Creation: *In the Beginning*

In the beginning God created the heavens and the earth. Now the earth was formless and empty, darkness was over the surface of the deep, and the Spirit of God was hovering over the waters.

In the beginning was the Word, and the Word was with God, and the Word was God. He was with God in the beginning.

Through him all things were made; without him nothing was made that has been made. In him was life, and that life was the light of men. The light shines in the darkness, but the darkness has not understood it.

Praise the LORD.

Praise the LORD from the heavens,
    praise him in the heights above.
Praise him, all his angels,
    praise him, all his heavenly hosts.
Praise him, sun and moon,
    praise him, all you shining stars.
Praise him, you highest heavens
    and you waters above the skies.
Let them praise the name of the LORD,
    for he commanded and they were created.
He set them in place for ever and ever;
    he gave a decree that will never pass away.

GENESIS 1:1-2; JOHN 1:1-5; PSALM 148:1-6

Related texts: PSALMS 102:25-28; 139:13-18; PROVERBS 8;
ISAIAH 40:12-31; 45:18-25; HEBREWS 11:1-3

1

Creation: *Let There Be Light*

THE ONE MINUTE BIBLE

And God said, "Let there be light," and there was light. God saw that the light was good, and he separated the light from the darkness. God called the light "day," and the darkness he called "night." And there was evening, and there was morning–the first day.

You are my lamp, O LORD;
    the LORD turns my darkness into light.

The LORD is my light and my salvation–
    whom shall I fear?
The LORD is the stronghold of my life–
    of whom shall I be afraid?

When Jesus spoke again to the people, he said, "I am the light of the world. Whoever follows me will never walk in darkness, but will have the light of life."

No longer will there be any curse. The throne of God and of the Lamb will be in the city, and his servants will serve him. They will see his face, and his name will be on their foreheads. There will be no more night. They will not need the light of a lamp or the light of the sun, for the Lord God will give them light. And they will reign for ever and ever.

GENESIS 1:3-5; 2 SAMUEL 22:29; PSALM 27:1; JOHN 8:12; REVELATION 22:3-5

Related texts: LEVITICUS 24:1-4; JOB 24:13-17; 38:8-20; JOHN 3:19-21; 1 JOHN 1:5-8

Creation: *The Sky Above*

And God said, "Let there be an expanse between the waters to separate water from water." So God made the expanse and separated the water under the expanse from the water above it. And it was so. God called the expanse "sky." And there was evening, and there was morning–the second day.

The heavens declare the glory of God;
    the skies proclaim the work of his hands.
Day after day they pour forth speech;
    night after night they display knowledge.
There is no speech or language
    where their voice is not heard.

I will praise you, O Lord, among the nations;
    I will sing of you among the peoples.
For great is your love, reaching to the heavens;
    your faithfulness reaches to the skies.

Be exalted, O God, above the heavens;
    let your glory be over all the earth.

But God made the earth by his power;
    he founded the world by his wisdom
    and stretched out the heavens by his understanding.
When he thunders, the waters in the heavens roar;
    he makes clouds rise from the ends of the earth.
He sends lightning with the rain
    and brings out the wind from his storehouses.

GENESIS 1:6-8; PSALMS 19:1-3; 57:9-11; JEREMIAH 10:12-13

THE ONE
MINUTE
BIBLE

Related texts: 1 CHRONICLES 16:23-31; JOB 38:22-38; PSALM 102:25-28; ACTS 1:1-12

Creation: *Land and Seas, Plants and Trees*

**THE ONE
MINUTE
BIBLE**

And God said, "Let the water under the sky be gathered to one place, and let dry ground appear." And it was so. God called the dry ground "land," and the gathered waters he called "seas." And God saw that it was good.

Then God said, "Let the land produce vegetation: seed-bearing plants and trees on the land that bear fruit with seed in it, according to their various kinds." And it was so. The land produced vegetation: plants bearing seed according to their kinds and trees bearing fruit with seed in it according to their kinds. And God saw that it was good. And there was evening, and there was morning–the third day.

"Should you not fear me?" declares the LORD.
    "Should you not tremble in my presence?
I made the sand a boundary for the sea,
    an everlasting barrier it cannot cross.
The waves may roll, but they cannot prevail;
    they may roar, but they cannot cross it.

He makes grass grow for the cattle,
    and plants for man to cultivate–
    bringing forth food from the earth:
wine that gladdens the heart of man,
    oil to make his face shine,
    and bread that sustains his heart.

GENESIS 1:9-13; JEREMIAH 5:22; PSALM 104:14-15

Related texts: JOB 12:7-12; 38:8-11; PSALM 104;
REVELATION 20:11–21:4; 22:1-3

Creation: *Sun, Moon and Stars*

**THE ONE
MINUTE
BIBLE**

And God said, "Let there be lights in the expanse of the sky to separate the day from the night, and let them serve as signs to mark seasons and days and years, and let them be lights in the expanse of the sky to give light on the earth." And it was so.

God made two great lights– the greater light to govern the day and the lesser light to govern the night. He also made the stars. God set them in the expanse of the sky to give light on the earth, to govern the day and the night, and to separate light from darkness. And God saw that it was good. And there was evening, and there was morning–the fourth day.

I did not see a temple in the city, because the Lord God Almighty and the Lamb are its temple. The city does not need the sun or the moon to shine on it, for the glory of God gives it light, and the Lamb is its lamp. The nations will walk by its light, and the kings of the earth will bring their splendor into it.

On no day will its gates ever be shut, for there will be no night there. The glory and honor of the nations will be brought into it. Nothing impure will ever enter it, nor will anyone who does what is shameful or deceitful, but only those whose names are written in the Lamb's book of life.

GENESIS 1:14-19; REVELATION 21:22-27

Related texts: NEHEMIAH 9:5-6; JOB 9:1-9; PSALMS 19:1-6; 104:19-23; PROVERBS 4:18-19; EPHESIANS 5:8-16

Creation: *All Creatures Great and Small*

**THE ONE
MINUTE
BIBLE**

And God said, "Let the water teem with living creatures, and let birds fly above the earth across the expanse of the sky." So God created the great creatures of the sea and every living and moving thing with which the water teems, according to their kinds, and every winged bird according to its kind. And God saw that it was good. God blessed them and said, "Be fruitful and increase in number and fill the water in the seas, and let the birds increase on the earth." And there was evening, and there was morning–the fifth day.

How many are your works, O LORD!
　　In wisdom you made them all;
　　the earth is full of your creatures.
There is the sea, vast and spacious,
　　teeming with creatures beyond number–
　　living things both large and small.
There the ships go to and fro,
　　and the leviathan, which you formed to frolic there.

These all look to you
　　to give them their food at the proper time.
When you give it to them,
　　they gather it up;
when you open your hand,
　　they are satisfied with good things.

GENESIS 1:20-23; PSALM 104:24-28

Related texts: PSALMS 104:11-18; 148:7-12; MATTHEW 6:25-33; 10:29-31; REVELATION 5:11-13

Creation: *The Cattle on a Thousand Hills*

THE ONE

MINUTE

BIBLE

And God said, "Let the land produce living creatures according to their kinds: livestock, creatures that move along the ground, and wild animals, each according to its kind." And it was so. God made the wild animals according to their kinds, the livestock according to their kinds, and all the creatures that move along the ground according to their kinds. And God saw that it was good.

I do not rebuke you for your sacrifices
    or your burnt offerings, which are ever before me.
I have no need of a bull from your stall
    or of goats from your pens,
for every animal of the forest is mine,
    and the cattle on a thousand hills.
I know every bird in the mountains,
    and the creatures of the field are mine.
If I were hungry I would not tell you,
    for the world is mine, and all that is in it.
Do I eat the flesh of bulls
    or drink the blood of goats?
Sacrifice thank offerings to God,
    fulfill your vows to the Most High,
and call upon me in the day of trouble;
    I will deliver you, and you will honor me.

GENESIS 1:24-25; PSALM 50:8-15

Related texts: GENESIS 9:1-3; PSALM 8; PROVERBS 12:10; ISAIAH 11:1-10; 65:17-25

**THE ONE
MINUTE
BIBLE**

Creation: *Mankind—The Image of God*

Then God said, "Let us make man in our image, in our likeness, and let them rule over the fish of the sea and the birds of the air, over the livestock, over all the earth, and over all the creatures that move along the ground."

So God created man in his own image,
   in the image of God he created him;
   male and female he created them.

God blessed them and said to them, "Be fruitful and increase in number; fill the earth and subdue it. Rule over the fish of the sea and the birds of the air and over every living creature that moves on the ground."

Then God said, "I give you every seed-bearing plant on the face of the whole earth and every tree that has fruit with seed in it. They will be yours for food. And to all the beasts of the earth and all the birds of the air and all the creatures that move on the ground–everything that has the breath of life in it–I give every green plant for food." And it was so.

God saw all that he had made, and it was very good. And there was evening, and there was morning–the sixth day.

GENESIS 1:26-31

Related texts: GENESIS 2:4-25; 9:6-7; PSALM 8; 1 CORINTHIANS 6:1-4; 2 CORINTHIANS 4:4-6; COLOSSIANS 1:9-20; 3:5-10

Creation: *God Rests*

**THE ONE
MINUTE
BIBLE**

Thus the heavens and the earth were completed in all their vast array.

By the seventh day God had finished the work he had been doing; so on the seventh day he rested from all his work. And God blessed the seventh day and made it holy, because on it he rested from all the work of creating that he had done.

> Remember the Sabbath day by keeping it holy. For in six days the LORD made the heavens and the earth, the sea, and all that is in them, but he rested on the seventh day. Therefore the LORD blessed the Sabbath day and made it holy.

One Sabbath Jesus was going through the grainfields, and as his disciples walked along, they began to pick some heads of grain. The Pharisees said to him, "Look, why are they doing what is unlawful on the Sabbath?"

He answered, "Have you never read what David did when he and his companions were hungry and in need? In the days of Abiathar the high priest, he entered the house of God and ate the consecrated bread, which is lawful only for priests to eat. And he also gave some to his companions."

Then he said to them, "The Sabbath was made for man, not man for the Sabbath. So the Son of Man is Lord even of the Sabbath."

GENESIS 2:1-3; EXODUS 20:8, 11; MARK 2:23-28

Related texts: EXODUS 16:11-30; PSALM 62:1-5; MATTHEW 11:25-30; MARK 6:30-32; HEBREWS 4:1-4

Adam and Eve: *The First Man and Woman*

**THE ONE
MINUTE
BIBLE**

The LORD God formed the man from the dust of the ground and breathed into his nostrils the breath of life, and the man became a living being.

The LORD God took the man and put him in the Garden of Eden to work it and take care of it. And the LORD God commanded the man, "You are free to eat from any tree in the garden; but you must not eat from the tree of the knowledge of good and evil, for when you eat of it you will surely die."

The LORD God said, "It is not good for the man to be alone. I will make a helper suitable for him."

But for Adam no suitable helper was found. So the LORD God caused the man to fall into a deep sleep; and while he was sleeping, he took one of the man's ribs and closed up the place with flesh. Then the LORD God made a woman from the rib he had taken out of the man, and he brought her to the man.

The man said,

> "This is now bone of my bones
> and flesh of my flesh;
> she shall be called 'woman,'
> for she was taken out of man."

For this reason a man will leave his father and mother and be united to his wife, and they will become one flesh.

The man and his wife were both naked, and they felt no shame.

GENESIS 2:7, 15-18, 20b-25

Related texts: GENESIS 1:26-29; MATTHEW 19:1-12; MARK 10:1-12; 1 CORINTHIANS 6:15–7:40

Rulers of God's Creation

O LORD, our Lord,
  how majestic is your name in all the earth!

You have set your glory
  above the heavens.
From the lips of children and infants
  you have ordained praise
because of your enemies,
  to silence the foe and the avenger.

When I consider your heavens,
  the work of your fingers,
the moon and the stars,
  which you have set in place,
what is man that you are mindful of him,
  the son of man that you care for him?
You made him a little lower than the heavenly beings
  and crowned him with glory and honor.

You made him ruler over the works of your hands;
  you put everything under his feet:
all flocks and herds,
  and the beasts of the field,
the birds of the air,
  and the fish of the sea,
  all that swim the paths of the seas.

O LORD, our Lord,
  how majestic is your name in all the earth!

PSALM 8

Related texts: GENESIS 1–2; MATTHEW 21:16; HEBREWS 2:5-9

The Fall of Mankind

**THE ONE
MINUTE
BIBLE**

Now the serpent was more crafty than any of the wild animals the LORD God had made. He said to the woman, "Did God really say, 'You must not eat from any tree in the garden'?"

The woman said to the serpent, "We may eat fruit from the trees in the garden, but God did say, 'You must not eat fruit from the tree that is in the middle of the garden, and you must not touch it, or you will die.'"

"You will not surely die," the serpent said to the woman. "For God knows that when you eat of it your eyes will be opened, and you will be like God, knowing good and evil."

When the woman saw that the fruit of the tree was good for food and pleasing to the eye, and also desirable for gaining wisdom, she took some and ate it. She also gave some to her husband, who was with her, and he ate it. Then the eyes of both of them were opened, and they realized they were naked; so they sewed fig leaves together and made coverings for themselves.

Then the man and his wife heard the sound of the LORD God as he was walking in the garden in the cool of the day, and they hid from the LORD God among the trees of the garden.

GENESIS 3:1-8

Related texts: EZEKIEL 28:13-19; ROMANS 5:12-19; 1 TIMOTHY 2:11-15; JAMES 1:12-15

God Judges the First Sin

THE ONE
MINUTE
BIBLE

But the LORD God called to the man, "Where are you?"

He answered, "I heard you in the garden, and I was afraid because I was naked; so I hid."

And he said, "Who told you that you were naked? Have you eaten from the tree that I commanded you not to eat from?"

The man said, "The woman you put here with me–she gave me some fruit from the tree, and I ate it."

Then the LORD God said to the woman, "What is this you have done?"

The woman said, "The serpent deceived me, and I ate."

So the LORD God said to the serpent, "Because you have done this,

"Cursed are you above all the livestock
and all the wild animals!
You will crawl on your belly
and you will eat dust
all the days of your life.
And I will put enmity
between you and the woman,
and between your offspring and hers;
he will crush your head,
and you will strike his heel."

To the woman he said,

"I will greatly increase your pains in childbearing;
with pain you will give birth to children.
Your desire will be for your husband,
and he will rule over you."

Therefore, there is now no condemnation for those who are in Christ Jesus.

GENESIS 3:9-16; ROMANS 8:1

Related texts: DEUTERONOMY 32:1-6; ROMANS 3:9-18;
REVELATION 12:9; 20:1-3, 7-15; 22:1-3

God Exiles Adam and Eve from the Garden

**THE ONE
MINUTE
BIBLE**

To Adam the LORD God said, "Because you listened to your wife and ate from the tree about which I commanded you, 'You must not eat of it,'

"Cursed is the ground because of you;
through painful toil you will eat of it
all the days of your life.
It will produce thorns and thistles for you,
and you will eat the plants of the field.
By the sweat of your brow
you will eat your food
until you return to the ground,
since from it you were taken;
for dust you are
and to dust you will return."

Adam named his wife Eve, because she would become the mother of all the living.

The LORD God made garments of skin for Adam and his wife and clothed them. And the LORD God said, "The man has now become like one of us, knowing good and evil. He must not be allowed to reach out his hand and take also from the tree of life and eat, and live forever." So the LORD God banished him from the Garden of Eden to work the ground from which he had been taken. After he drove the man out, he placed on the east side of the Garden of Eden cherubim and a flaming sword flashing back and forth to guard the way to the tree of life.

For as in Adam all die, so in Christ all will be made alive.

GENESIS 3:17-24; 1 CORINTHIANS 15:22

Related texts: GENESIS 18:16-33; PSALM 50; ROMANS 8:18-25; REVELATION 22

Death in Adam, Life in Christ

Therefore, just as sin entered the world through one man, and death through sin, and in this way death came to all men, because all sinned–for before the law was given, sin was in the world. But sin is not taken into account when there is no law. Nevertheless, death reigned from the time of Adam to the time of Moses, even over those who did not sin by breaking a command, as did Adam, who was a pattern of the one to come.

But the gift is not like the trespass. For if the many died by the trespass of the one man, how much more did God's grace and the gift that came by the grace of the one man, Jesus Christ, overflow to the many!

Again, the gift of God is not like the result of the one man's sin: The judgment followed one sin and brought condemnation, but the gift followed many trespasses and brought justification. For if, by the trespass of the one man, death reigned through that one man, how much more will those who receive God's abundant provision of grace and of the gift of righteousness reign in life through the one man, Jesus Christ.

For the wages of sin is death, but the gift of God is eternal life in Christ Jesus our Lord.

ROMANS 5:12-17; 6:23

Related texts: GENESIS 3; ROMANS 5:18–6:23; EPHESIANS 2:1-10; COLOSSIANS 3:1-17

Cain and Abel: The First Murder

**THE ONE
MINUTE
BIBLE**

Adam lay with his wife Eve, and she became pregnant and gave birth to Cain. She said, "With the help of the LORD I have brought forth a man." Later she gave birth to his brother Abel.

Now Abel kept flocks, and Cain worked the soil. In the course of time Cain brought some of the fruits of the soil as an offering to the LORD. But Abel brought fat portions from some of the firstborn of his flock. The LORD looked with favor on Abel and his offering, but on Cain and his offering he did not look with favor. So Cain was very angry, and his face was downcast.

Then the LORD said to Cain, "Why are you angry? Why is your face downcast? If you do what is right, will you not be accepted? But if you do not do what is right, sin is crouching at your door; it desires to have you, but you must master it."

Now Cain said to his brother Abel, "Let's go out to the field." And while they were in the field, Cain attacked his brother Abel and killed him.

Then the LORD said to Cain, "Where is your brother Abel?"

"I don't know," he replied. "Am I my brother's keeper?"

The LORD said, "What have you done? Listen! Your brother's blood cries out to me from the ground. Now you are under a curse and driven from the ground, which opened its mouth to receive your brother's blood from your hand. When you work the ground, it will no longer yield its crops for you. You will be a restless wanderer on the earth."

GENESIS 4:1-12

Related texts: EXODUS 20:13; MATTHEW 5:21-26; HEBREWS 11:4; 1 JOHN 3:11-12

Noah: The Righteous Man

This is the account of Noah.

Noah was a righteous man, blameless among the people of his time, and he walked with God. Noah had three sons: Shem, Ham and Japheth.

Now the earth was corrupt in God's sight and was full of violence. God saw how corrupt the earth had become, for all the people on earth had corrupted their ways. So God said to Noah, "I am going to put an end to all people, for the earth is filled with violence because of them. I am surely going to destroy both them and the earth. So make yourself an ark of cypress wood; make rooms in it and coat it with pitch inside and out.

I am going to bring floodwaters on the earth to destroy all life under the heavens, every creature that has the breath of life in it. Everything on earth will perish. But I will establish my covenant with you, and you will enter the ark–you and your sons and your wife and your sons' wives with you. You are to bring into the ark two of all living creatures, male and female, to keep them alive with you. You are to take every kind of food that is to be eaten and store it away as food for you and for them."

Noah did everything just as God commanded him.

GENESIS 6:9-14, 17-19, 21-22

**THE ONE
MINUTE
BIBLE**

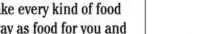

Related texts: PSALMS 29; 36; HEBREWS 11:1-7; 1 PETER 3:18-22

The Great Flood

**THE ONE
MINUTE
BIBLE**

Noah was six hundred years old when the floodwaters came on the earth. And Noah and his sons and his wife and his sons' wives entered the ark to escape the waters of the flood. Pairs of clean and unclean animals, of birds and of all creatures that move along the ground, male and female, came to Noah and entered the ark, as God had commanded Noah. And after the seven days the floodwaters came on the earth.

In the six hundredth year of Noah's life, on the seventeenth day of the second month—on that day all the springs of the great deep burst forth, and the floodgates of the heavens were opened.

For forty days the flood kept coming on the earth, and as the waters increased they lifted the ark high above the earth. The waters rose and increased greatly on the earth, and the ark floated on the surface of the water. They rose greatly on the earth, and all the high mountains under the entire heavens were covered. Every living thing on the face of the earth was wiped out; men and animals and the creatures that move along the ground and the birds of the air were wiped from the earth. Only Noah was left, and those with him in the ark.

By faith Noah, when warned about things not yet seen, in holy fear built an ark to save his family. By his faith he condemned the world and became heir of the righteousness that comes by faith.

GENESIS 7:6-11, 17-19, 23; HEBREWS 11:7

Related texts: PSALM 93; NAHUM 1:1-8; MATTHEW 24:36-42;
LUKE 17:26-36; 2 PETER 2:4-9

After the Flood

**THE ONE
MINUTE
BIBLE**

But God remembered Noah and all the wild animals and the livestock that were with him in the ark, and he sent a wind over the earth, and the waters receded.

After forty days Noah opened the window he had made in the ark and sent out a raven, and it kept flying back and forth until the water had dried up from the earth. Then he sent out a dove to see if the water had receded from the surface of the ground.

But the dove could find no place to set its feet because there was water over all the surface of the earth; so it returned to Noah in the ark. He waited seven more days and again sent out the dove from the ark. When the dove returned to him in the evening, there in its beak was a freshly plucked olive leaf! Then Noah knew that the water had receded from the earth.

So Noah came out, together with his sons and his wife and his sons' wives.

Then Noah built an altar to the LORD and, taking some of all the clean animals and clean birds, he sacrificed burnt offerings on it. The LORD smelled the pleasing aroma and said in his heart: "Never again will I curse the ground because of man, even though every inclination of his heart is evil from childhood. And never again will I destroy all living creatures, as I have done."

GENESIS 8:1, 6-9a, 10-11, 18, 20-21

Related texts: GENESIS 9; 2 PETER 3:1-14; REVELATION 21:1-4

God Calls Abraham

**THE ONE
MINUTE
BIBLE**

The Lord had said to Abraham, "Leave your country, your people and your father's household and go to the land I will show you.

"I will make you into a great nation
   and I will bless you;
I will make your name great,
   and you will be a blessing.
I will bless those who bless you,
   and whoever curses you I will curse;
and all peoples on earth
   will be blessed through you."

So Abraham left, as the Lord had told him; and Lot went with him. Abraham was seventy-five years old when he set out from Haran. He took his wife Sarah, his nephew Lot, all the possessions they had accumulated and the people they had acquired in Haran, and they set out for the land of Canaan, and they arrived there.

Abraham traveled through the land as far as the site of the great tree of Moreh at Shechem. At that time the Canaanites were in the land. The Lord appeared to Abraham and said, "To your offspring I will give this land." So he built an altar there to the Lord who had appeared to him.

Genesis 12:1-7

Related texts: Psalm 67; Acts 7:2-5; Hebrews 6:13-16; 11:8-10

God Promises Abraham a Son

**THE ONE
MINUTE
BIBLE**

After this, the word of the LORD came to Abraham in a vision:

> "Do not be afraid, Abraham.
> I am your shield,
> your very great reward."

But Abraham said, "O Sovereign LORD, what can you give me since I remain childless and the one who will inherit my estate is Eliezer of Damascus?" And Abraham said, "You have given me no children; so a servant in my household will be my heir."

Then the word of the LORD came to him: "This man will not be your heir, but a son coming from your own body will be your heir." He took him outside and said, "Look up at the heavens and count the stars—if indeed you can count them." Then he said to him, "So shall your offspring be."

Abraham believed the LORD, and he credited it to him as righteousness.

The words "it was credited to him" were written not for Abraham alone, but also for us, to whom God will credit righteousness—for us who believe in him who raised Jesus our Lord from the dead. He was delivered over to death for our sins and was raised to life for our justification.

GENESIS 15:1-6; ROMANS 4:23-25

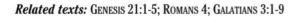

Related texts: GENESIS 21:1-5; ROMANS 4; GALATIANS 3:1-9

**THE ONE
MINUTE
BIBLE**

Ishmael and Isaac: Abraham's Sons

Now Sarah, Abraham's wife, had borne him no children. But she had an Egyptian maidservant named Hagar; so she said to Abraham, "The LORD has kept me from having children. Go, sleep with my maidservant; perhaps I can build a family through her."

Abraham agreed to what Sarah said. So after Abraham had been living in Canaan ten years, Sarah his wife took her Egyptian maidservant Hagar and gave her to her husband to be his wife. He slept with Hagar, and she conceived.

So Hagar bore Abraham a son, and Abraham gave the name Ishmael to the son she had borne. Abraham was eighty-six years old when Hagar bore him Ishmael.

Now the LORD was gracious to Sarah as he had said, and the LORD did for Sarah what he had promised. Sarah became pregnant and bore a son to Abraham in his old age, at the very time God had promised him. Abraham gave the name Isaac to the son Sarah bore him. When his son Isaac was eight days old, Abraham circumcised him, as God commanded him. Abraham was a hundred years old when his son Isaac was born to him.

By faith Abraham, even though he was past age— and Sarah herself was barren—was enabled to become a father because he considered him faithful who had made the promise.

GENESIS 16:1-4a, 15-16; 21:1-5; HEBREWS 11:11

Related texts: GENESIS 21:6-21; ACTS 7:1-8; ROMANS 4; GALATIANS 4:22-31

Abraham Offers Isaac As a Sacrifice

Some time later God tested Abraham. He said to him, "Abraham!"

"Here I am," he replied.

Then God said, "Take your son, your only son, Isaac, whom you love, and go to the region of Moriah. Sacrifice him there as a burnt offering on one of the mountains I will tell you about."

When they reached the place God had told him about, Abraham built an altar there and arranged the wood on it. He bound his son Isaac and laid him on the altar, on top of the wood. Then he reached out his hand and took the knife to slay his son. But the angel of the LORD called out to him from heaven, "Abraham! Abraham!"

"Here I am," he replied.

"Do not lay a hand on the boy," he said. "Do not do anything to him. Now I know that you fear God, because you have not withheld from me your son, your only son."

Abraham looked up and there in a thicket he saw a ram caught by its horns. He went over and took the ram and sacrificed it as a burnt offering instead of his son. So Abraham called that place The LORD Will Provide. And to this day it is said, "On the mountain of the LORD it will be provided."

This is love: not that we loved God, but that he loved us and sent his Son as an atoning sacrifice for our sins.

GENESIS 22:1-2, 9-14; 1 JOHN 4:10

**THE ONE
MINUTE
BIBLE**

Esau and Jacob: Isaac's Sons

**THE ONE
MINUTE
BIBLE**

This is the account of Abraham's son Isaac.

Abraham became the father of Isaac, and Isaac was forty years old when he married Rebekah daughter of Bethuel the Aramean from Paddan Aram and sister of Laban the Aramean.

Isaac prayed to the LORD on behalf of his wife, because she was barren. The LORD answered his prayer, and his wife Rebekah became pregnant. The babies jostled each other within her, and she said, "Why is this happening to me?" So she went to inquire of the LORD. The LORD said to her,

"Two nations are in your womb,
    and two peoples from within you will be separated;
one people will be stronger than the other,
    and the older will serve the younger."

When the time came for her to give birth, there were twin boys in her womb. The first to come out was red, and his whole body was like a hairy garment; so they named him Esau. After this, his brother came out, with his hand grasping Esau's heel; so he was named Jacob. Isaac was sixty years old when Rebekah gave birth to them.

The boys grew up, and Esau became a skillful hunter, a man of the open country, while Jacob was a quiet man, staying among the tents. Isaac, who had a taste for wild game, loved Esau, but Rebekah loved Jacob.

GENESIS 25:19-28

Related texts: 1 SAMUEL 1; MALACHI 1:1-5; ROMANS 9

Esau Sells His Inheritance to Jacob

**THE ONE
MINUTE
BIBLE**

Once when Jacob was cooking some stew, Esau came in from the open country, famished. He said to Jacob, "Quick, let me have some of that red stew! I'm famished!" (That is why he was also called Edom.)

Jacob replied, "First sell me your birthright."

"Look, I am about to die," Esau said. "What good is the birthright to me?"

But Jacob said, "Swear to me first." So he swore an oath to him, selling his birthright to Jacob.

Then Jacob gave Esau some bread and some lentil stew. He ate and drank, and then got up and left.

So Esau despised his birthright.

"I have loved you," says the LORD.

"But you ask, 'How have you loved us?'

"Was not Esau Jacob's brother?" the LORD says. "Yet I have loved Jacob, but Esau I have hated, and I have turned his mountains into a wasteland and left his inheritance to the desert jackals."

See that no one is sexually immoral, or is godless like Esau, who for a single meal sold his inheritance rights as the oldest son. Afterward, as you know, when he wanted to inherit this blessing, he was rejected. He could bring about no change of mind, though he sought the blessing with tears.

GENESIS 25:29-34; MALACHI 1:2-3; HEBREWS 12:16-17

Related texts: GENESIS 27–36; PSALM 60; OBADIAH

Joseph the Dreamer: Jacob's Favorite Son

**THE ONE
MINUTE
BIBLE**

Joseph, a young man of seventeen, was tending the flocks with his brothers, the sons of Bilhah and the sons of Zilpah, his father's wives, and he brought their father a bad report about them.

Now Jacob loved Joseph more than any of his other sons, because he had been born to him in his old age; and he made a richly ornamented robe for him. When his brothers saw that their father loved him more than any of them, they hated him and could not speak a kind word to him.

Joseph had a dream, and when he told it to his brothers, they hated him all the more. He said to them, "Listen to this dream I had: We were binding sheaves of grain out in the field when suddenly my sheaf rose and stood upright, while your sheaves gathered around mine and bowed down to it."

Then he had another dream, and he told it to his brothers. "Listen," he said, "I had another dream, and this time the sun and moon and eleven stars were bowing down to me."

When he told his father as well as his brothers, his father rebuked him and said, "What is this dream you had? Will your mother and I and your brothers actually come and bow down to the ground before you?" His brothers were jealous of him, but his father kept the matter in mind.

GENESIS 37:2b-7, 9-11

Related texts: GENESIS 28:10-19; 41:1-45; JOEL 2:28-32; MATTHEW 1:18–2:22

Jacob Moves His Family to Egypt

**THE ONE
MINUTE
BIBLE**

Then God gave Abraham the covenant of circumcision. And Abraham became the father of Isaac and circumcised him eight days after his birth. Later Isaac became the father of Jacob, and Jacob became the father of the twelve patriarchs.

Because the patriarchs were jealous of Joseph, they sold him as a slave into Egypt. But God was with him and rescued him from all his troubles. He gave Joseph wisdom and enabled him to gain the goodwill of Pharaoh king of Egypt; so he made him ruler over Egypt and all his palace.

Then a famine struck all Egypt and Canaan, bringing great suffering, and our fathers could not find food. When Jacob heard that there was grain in Egypt, he sent our fathers on their first visit. On their second visit, Joseph told his brothers who he was, and Pharaoh learned about Joseph's family. After this, Joseph sent for his father Jacob and his whole family, seventy-five in all. Then Jacob went down to Egypt, where he and our fathers died.

Jacob lived in Egypt seventeen years, and the years of his life were a hundred and forty-seven.

ACTS 7:8-15; GENESIS 47:28

Related texts: GENESIS 37–50; PSALM 46; MATTHEW 8:5-13; MARK 12:24-27

Joseph: God Intended it for Good

**THE ONE
MINUTE
BIBLE**

When Joseph's brothers saw that their father was dead, they said, "What if Joseph holds a grudge against us and pays us back for all the wrongs we did to him?" So they sent word to Joseph, saying, "Your father left these instructions before he died: 'This is what you are to say to Joseph: I ask you to forgive your brothers the sins and the wrongs they committed in treating you so badly.' Now please forgive the sins of the servants of the God of your father." When their message came to him, Joseph wept.

His brothers then came and threw themselves down before him. "We are your slaves," they said.

But Joseph said to them, "Don't be afraid. Am I in the place of God? You intended to harm me, but God intended it for good to accomplish what is now being done, the saving of many lives. So then, don't be afraid. I will provide for you and your children." And he reassured them and spoke kindly to them.

Then Joseph said to his brothers, "I am about to die. But God will surely come to your aid and take you up out of this land to the land he promised on oath to Abraham, Isaac and Jacob."

And we know that in all things God works for the good of those who love him, who have been called according to his purpose.

GENESIS 50:15-21, 24; ROMANS 8:28

Related texts: GENESIS 37–50; EXODUS 1; 13:17-19; JOSHUA 24:32; PSALM 105:7-25; HEBREWS 11:21-22

Job: Blameless and Blessed

In the land of Uz there lived a man whose name was Job. This man was blameless and upright; he feared God and shunned evil. He was the greatest man among all the people of the East.

One day the angels came to present themselves before the LORD, and Satan also came with them. The LORD said to Satan, "Where have you come from?"

Satan answered the LORD, "From roaming through the earth and going back and forth in it."

Then the LORD said to Satan, "Have you considered my servant Job? There is no one on earth like him; he is blameless and upright, a man who fears God and shuns evil."

"Does Job fear God for nothing?" Satan replied. "Have you not put a hedge around him and his household and everything he has? You have blessed the work of his hands, so that his flocks and herds are spread throughout the land. But stretch out your hand and strike everything he has, and he will surely curse you to your face."

The LORD said to Satan, "Very well, then, everything he has is in your hands, but on the man himself do not lay a finger."

Then Satan went out from the presence of the LORD.

JOB 1:1, 3b, 6-12

**THE ONE
MINUTE
BIBLE**

Related texts: JOB 28; PROVERBS 1:7; 8:13; 9:10; PHILIPPIANS 2:14-15; 1 PETER 5:8-11

Job Loses His Wealth and His Children

**THE ONE
MINUTE
BIBLE**

One day when Job's sons and daughters were feasting and drinking wine at the oldest brother's house, a messenger came to Job and said, "The oxen were plowing and the donkeys were grazing nearby, and the Sabeans attacked and carried them off. They put the servants to the sword, and I am the only one who has escaped to tell you!"

While he was still speaking, another messenger came and said, "The fire of God fell from the sky and burned up the sheep and the servants, and I am the only one who has escaped to tell you!"

While he was still speaking, another messenger came and said, "The Chaldeans formed three raiding parties and swept down on your camels and carried them off. They put the servants to the sword, and I am the only one who has escaped to tell you!"

While he was still speaking, yet another messenger came and said, "Your sons and daughters were feasting and drinking wine at the oldest brother's house, when suddenly a mighty wind swept in from the desert and struck the four corners of the house. It collapsed on them and they are dead, and I am the only one who has escaped to tell you!"

At this, Job got up and tore his robe and shaved his head. Then he fell to the ground in worship and said:

"Naked I came from my mother's womb,
and naked I will depart.
The LORD gave and the LORD has taken away;
may the name of the LORD be praised."

In all this, Job did not sin by charging God with wrongdoing.

JOB 1:13-22

Related texts: HABAKKUK 3:17-19; 1 THESSALONIANS 5:16-18; REVELATION 7:13-17

Job Loses His Health

**THE ONE
MINUTE
BIBLE**

On another day the angels came to present
themselves before the LORD, and Satan also came with
them to present himself before him. And the LORD said
to Satan, "Where have you come from?"

Satan answered the LORD, "From roaming through
the earth and going back and forth in it."

Then the LORD said to Satan, "Have you considered
my servant Job? There is no one on earth like him; he is
blameless and upright, a man who fears God and shuns
evil. And he still maintains his integrity, though you
incited me against him to ruin him without any reason."

"Skin for skin!" Satan replied. "A man will give all
he has for his own life. But stretch out your hand and
strike his flesh and bones, and he will surely curse you
to your face."

The LORD said to Satan, "Very well, then, he is in
your hands; but you must spare his life."

So Satan went out from the presence of the LORD
and afflicted Job with painful sores from the soles of his
feet to the top of his head. Then Job took a piece of
broken pottery and scraped himself with it as he sat
among the ashes.

His wife said to him, "Are you still holding on to
your integrity? Curse God and die!"

He replied, "You are talking like a foolish woman.
Shall we accept good from God, and not trouble?"

In all this, Job did not sin in what he said.

JOB 2:1-10

Related texts: JOB 19:25-27; PROVERBS 11:2-6; PHILIPPIANS 3:7-11

*A thorough knowledge of the
Bible is worth more than
a college education.*
Theodore Roosevelt (1858-1919)
UNITED STATES PRESIDENT

I am a man of one book.
St. Thomas Aquinas (1227-1274)
ITALIAN THEOLOGIAN/PHILOSOPHER

*The man of one book is
always formidable; but when
that book is the Bible he
is irresistible.*
William Mackergo Taylor (1829-1895)
SCOTTISH CLERGYMAN

Is Suffering Always Punishment?

When Job's three friends, Eliphaz the Temanite, Bildad the Shuhite and Zophar the Naamathite, heard about all the troubles that had come upon him, they set out from their homes and met together by agreement to go and sympathize with him and comfort him. When they saw him from a distance, they could hardly recognize him; they began to weep aloud, and they tore their robes and sprinkled dust on their heads. Then they sat on the ground with him for seven days and seven nights. No one said a word to him, because they saw how great his suffering was.

Then Eliphaz the Temanite replied:

"Consider now: Who, being innocent, has
 ever perished?
 Where were the upright ever destroyed?
As I have observed, those who plow evil
 and those who sow trouble reap it.
At the breath of God they are destroyed;
 at the blast of his anger they perish.

"But if it were I, I would appeal to God;
 I would lay my cause before him.

"Blessed is the man whom God corrects;
 so do not despise the discipline of the
 Almighty.
For he wounds, but he also binds up;
 he injures, but his hands also heal.

"We have examined this, and it is true.
 So hear it and apply it to yourself."

JOB 2:11-13; 4:1, 7-9; 5:8, 17-18, 27

Related texts: JOB 4–5; 8; 11; 15; 18; 20; 22; 25; 32–37;
HEBREWS 12:5-11

Job Protests His Innocence

**THE ONE
MINUTE
BIBLE**

Then Job replied:

> "How long will you torment me
>> and crush me with words?
> Ten times now you have reproached me;
>> shamelessly you attack me.
> If it is true that I have gone astray,
>> my error remains my concern alone.
> If indeed you would exalt yourselves above me
>> and use my humiliation against me,
> then know that God has wronged me
>> and drawn his net around me.

> "Though I cry, 'I've been wronged!' I get
>> no response;
>> though I call for help, there is no justice."

And Job continued his discourse:

> "As surely as God lives, who has denied me justice,
>> the Almighty, who has made me taste bitterness
>>> of soul,
> as long as I have life within me,
>> the breath of God in my nostrils,
> my lips will not speak wickedness,
>> and my tongue will utter no deceit.
> I will never admit you are in the right;
>> till I die, I will not deny my integrity.
> I will maintain my righteousness and never let
>> go of it;
>> my conscience will not reproach me as long
>>> as I live."

JOB 19:1-7; 27:1-6

Related texts: JOB 3; 6–7; 9–10; 12–14; 16–17; 19; 21; 23–24; 26–31;

PSALM 7; LUKE 18:1-8

God Answers Job

Then the LORD answered Job out of the storm. He said:

> "Who is this that darkens my counsel
>> with words without knowledge?
> Brace yourself like a man;
>> I will question you,
>> and you shall answer me.

> "Where were you when I laid the earth's foundation?
>> Tell me, if you understand.
> Who marked off its dimensions? Surely you know!
>> Who stretched a measuring line across it?
> On what were its footings set,
>> or who laid its cornerstone—
> while the morning stars sang together
>> and all the angels shouted for joy?"

The LORD said to Job:

> "Will the one who contends with the Almighty
>> correct him?
>> Let him who accuses God answer him!"

Then Job answered the LORD:

> "I am unworthy—how can I reply to you?
>> I put my hand over my mouth.
> I spoke once, but I have no answer—
>> twice, but I will say no more."

Then the LORD spoke to Job out of the storm:

> "Brace yourself like a man;
>> I will question you,
>> and you shall answer me.

> "Would you discredit my justice?
>> Would you condemn me to justify yourself?"

JOB 38:1-7; 40:1-8

THE ONE MINUTE BIBLE

Related texts: PSALM 30; JOB 38–41; HABAKKUK 1:1–2:1; ROMANS 9–10

37

God Vindicates and Restores Job

**THE ONE
MINUTE
BIBLE**

Then Job replied to the LORD:

> "I know that you can do all things;
>> no plan of yours can be thwarted.
> [You asked,] 'Who is this that obscures my counsel
>> without knowledge?'
>> Surely I spoke of things I did not understand,
>> things too wonderful for me to know.
>
> ["You said,] 'Listen now, and I will speak;
>> I will question you,
>> and you shall answer me.'
> My ears had heard of you
>> but now my eyes have seen you.
> Therefore I despise myself
>> and repent in dust and ashes."

After the LORD had said these things to Job, he said to Eliphaz the Temanite, "I am angry with you and your two friends, because you have not spoken of me what is right, as my servant Job has. So now take seven bulls and seven rams and go to my servant Job and sacrifice a burnt offering for yourselves. My servant Job will pray for you, and I will accept his prayer and not deal with you according to your folly. You have not spoken of me what is right, as my servant Job has." So Eliphaz the Temanite, Bildad the Shuhite and Zophar the Naamathite did what the LORD told them; and the LORD accepted Job's prayer.

After Job had prayed for his friends, the LORD made him prosperous again and gave him twice as much as he had before.

JOB 42:1-10

Related texts: PSALMS 17; 37; MATTHEW 5:1-6; JAMES 5:11

The Beatitudes: *Poor in Spirit*

Now when Jesus saw the crowds, he went up on a mountainside and sat down. His disciples came to him, and he began to teach them, saying:

"Blessed are the poor in spirit,
for theirs is the kingdom of heaven."

**THE ONE
MINUTE
BIBLE**

The sacrifices of God are a broken spirit;
a broken and contrite heart,
O God, you will not despise.

For this is what the high and lofty One says—
he who lives forever, whose name is holy:
"I live in a high and holy place,
but also with him who is contrite and lowly in spirit,
to revive the spirit of the lowly
and to revive the heart of the contrite."

My brothers, as believers in our glorious Lord Jesus Christ, don't show favoritism. Suppose a man comes into your meeting wearing a gold ring and fine clothes, and a poor man in shabby clothes also comes in. If you show special attention to the man wearing fine clothes and say, "Here's a good seat for you," but say to the poor man, "You stand there" or "Sit on the floor by my feet," have you not discriminated among yourselves and become judges with evil thoughts?

Listen, my dear brothers: Has not God chosen those who are poor in the eyes of the world to be rich in faith and to inherit the kingdom he promised those who love him?

MATTHEW 5:1-3; PSALM 51:17; ISAIAH 57:15; JAMES 2:1-5

Related texts: JOB 34:17-19; ISAIAH 57:15-19; 66:2; LUKE 6:20;
ACTS 10:34-35; EPHESIANS 6:5-9

The Beatitudes: *Those Who Mourn*

**THE ONE
MINUTE
BIBLE**

Blessed are those who mourn,
    for they will be comforted.

The Spirit of the Sovereign Lord is on me,
    because the Lord has anointed me
    to preach good news to the poor.
He has sent me to bind up the brokenhearted,
    to proclaim freedom for the captives
    and release from darkness for the prisoners,
to proclaim the year of the Lord's favor
    and the day of vengeance of our God,
to comfort all who mourn,
    and provide for those who grieve in Zion—
to bestow on them a crown of beauty
    instead of ashes,
the oil of gladness
    instead of mourning,
and a garment of praise
    instead of a spirit of despair.
They will be called oaks of righteousness,
    a planting of the Lord
    for the display of his splendor.

And I heard a loud voice from the throne saying, "Now the dwelling of God is with men, and he will live with them. They will be his people, and God himself will be with them and be their God. He will wipe every tear from their eyes. There will be no more death or mourning or crying or pain, for the old order of things has passed away."

Matthew 5:4; Isaiah 61:1-3; Revelation 21:3-4

Related texts: Nehemiah 8:1-12; Ecclesiastes 3:1-8; Psalm 119:49-50;
Luke 6:21; 2 Corinthians 1:3-7; 7:8-11

The Beatitudes: *The Meek*

Blessed are the meek,
    for they will inherit the earth.

Do not fret because of evil men
    or be envious of those who do wrong;
for like the grass they will soon wither,
    like green plants they will soon die away.

Trust in the LORD and do good;
    dwell in the land and enjoy safe pasture.
Delight yourself in the LORD
    and he will give you the desires of your heart.

Commit your way to the LORD;
    trust in him and he will do this:
He will make your righteousness shine like the dawn,
    the justice of your cause like the noonday sun.

Be still before the LORD and wait patiently for him;
    do not fret when men succeed in their ways,
    when they carry out their wicked schemes.

Refrain from anger and turn from wrath;
    do not fret—it leads only to evil.
For evil men will be cut off,
    but those who hope in the LORD will inherit the land.

A little while, and the wicked will be no more;
    though you look for them, they will not be found.
But the meek will inherit the land
    and enjoy great peace.

MATTHEW 5:5; PSALM 37:1-11

Related texts: PSALMS 25:12-13; 37:12-40; MATTHEW 11:25-30;
GALATIANS 5:19-23; 2 CORINTHIANS 10:1-5; 1 PETER 3:8-9

The Beatitudes: *Hungry for Righteousness*

**THE ONE
MINUTE
BIBLE**

Blessed are those who hunger and thirst for
      righteousness,
   for they will be filled.

As the deer pants for streams of water,
   so my soul pants for you, O God.
My soul thirsts for God, for the living God.
   When can I go and meet with God?

    Jesus answered, "Everyone who drinks this water
will be thirsty again, but whoever drinks the water I give
him will never thirst. Indeed, the water I give him will
become in him a spring of water welling up to eternal
life."

    Then Jesus declared, "I am the bread of life. He
who comes to me will never go hungry, and he who
believes in me will never be thirsty."

    On the last and greatest day of the Feast, Jesus
stood and said in a loud voice, "If anyone is thirsty, let
him come to me and drink. Whoever believes in me, as
the Scripture has said, streams of living water will flow
from within him." By this he meant the Spirit, whom
those who believed in him were later to receive. Up to
that time the Spirit had not been given, since Jesus had
not yet been glorified.

    The Spirit and the bride say, "Come!" And let him
who hears say, "Come!" Whoever is thirsty, let him
come; and whoever wishes, let him take the free gift of
the water of life.

MATTHEW 5:6; PSALM 42:1-2; JOHN 4:13-14; 6:35; 7:37-39;
REVELATION 22:17

Related texts: PSALMS 107:1-9; 146; ISAIAH 55:1-2; LUKE 6:21;
REVELATION 7:16-17

The Beatitudes: *The Merciful*

Blessed are the merciful,
>   for they will be shown mercy.

>   For the LORD your God is a merciful God; he will not
abandon or destroy you or forget the covenant with your
forefathers, which he confirmed to them by oath.

I lift up my eyes to you,
>   to you whose throne is in heaven.
As the eyes of slaves look to the hand of their master,
>   as the eyes of a maid look to the hand of her
>   mistress,
so our eyes look to the LORD our God,
>   till he shows us his mercy.
Have mercy on us, O LORD, have mercy on us,
>   for we have endured much contempt.
We have endured much ridicule from the proud,
>   much contempt from the arrogant.

For I desire mercy, not sacrifice,
>   and acknowledgment of God rather than burnt
>   offerings.

He has showed you, O man, what is good.
>   And what does the LORD require of you?
To act justly and to love mercy
>   and to walk humbly with your God.

>   Speak and act as those who are going to be judged
by the law that gives freedom, because judgment
without mercy will be shown to anyone who has not
been merciful. Mercy triumphs over judgment!

MATTHEW 5:7; DEUTERONOMY 4:31; PSALM 123:1-4; HOSEA 6:6;
MICAH 6:8; JAMES 2:12-13

Related texts: PSALM 6; MICAH 7:18-19; ZECHARIAH 7:9-10;
LUKE 6:27-38; 10:25-37; JUDE 1:20-23

The Beatitudes: *The Pure in Heart*

**THE ONE
MINUTE
BIBLE**

Blessed are the pure in heart,
for they will see God.

Who may ascend the hill of the LORD?
Who may stand in his holy place?
He who has clean hands and a pure heart,
who does not lift up his soul to an idol
or swear by what is false.
He will receive blessing from the LORD
and vindication from God his Savior.

Create in me a pure heart, O God,
and renew a steadfast spirit within me.

Flee the evil desires of youth, and pursue
righteousness, faith, love and peace, along with those
who call on the Lord out of a pure heart.

Therefore, brothers, since we have confidence to
enter the Most Holy Place by the blood of Jesus, by a
new and living way opened for us through the curtain,
that is, his body, and since we have a great priest over
the house of God, let us draw near to God with a sincere
heart in full assurance of faith, having our hearts
sprinkled to cleanse us from a guilty conscience and
having our bodies washed with pure water.

MATTHEW 5:8; PSALMS 24:3-5; 51:10; 2 TIMOTHY 2:22;
HEBREWS 10:19-22

Related texts: 2 CHRONICLES 30:13-20; PROVERBS 20:5-11; MARK 7:1-23;
HEBREWS 3; 12:14-29

The Beatitudes: *The Peacemakers*

Blessed are the peacemakers,
for they will be called sons of God.

Come, my children, listen to me;
I will teach you the fear of the LORD.
Whoever of you loves life
and desires to see many good days,
keep your tongue from evil
and your lips from speaking lies.
Turn from evil and do good;
seek peace and pursue it.

Consider the blameless, observe the upright;
there is a future for the man of peace.
But all sinners will be destroyed;
the future of the wicked will be cut off.

"There is no peace," says the LORD, "for the wicked."

If it is possible, as far as it depends on you, live at peace with everyone.

The wisdom that comes from heaven is first of all pure; then peace-loving, considerate, submissive, full of mercy and good fruit, impartial and sincere. Peacemakers who sow in peace raise a harvest of righteousness.

MATTHEW 5:9; PSALMS 34:11-14; 37:37-38; ISAIAH 48:22;
ROMANS 12:18; JAMES 3:17

**THE ONE
MINUTE
BIBLE**

Related texts: ISAIAH 9:6-7; JOHN 1:1-13; ROMANS 8:9-23;
GALATIANS 3:26–4:7; 1 JOHN 3:1-11

**THE ONE
MINUTE
BIBLE**

The Beatitudes: *The Persecuted Righteous*

Blessed are those who are persecuted because of righteousness,
   for theirs is the kingdom of heaven.

Blessed are you when people insult you, persecute you and falsely say all kinds of evil against you because of me. Rejoice and be glad, because great is your reward in heaven, for in the same way they persecuted the prophets who were before you.

But the LORD is with me like a mighty warrior;
   so my persecutors will stumble and not prevail.
They will fail and be thoroughly disgraced;
   their dishonor will never be forgotten.

For it is commendable if a man bears up under the pain of unjust suffering because he is conscious of God. But how is it to your credit if you receive a beating for doing wrong and endure it? But if you suffer for doing good and you endure it, this is commendable before God. To this you were called, because Christ suffered for you, leaving you an example, that you should follow in his steps.

That is why, for Christ's sake, I delight in weaknesses, in insults, in hardships, in persecutions, in difficulties. For when I am weak, then I am strong.

MATTHEW 5:10-12; JEREMIAH 20:11; 1 PETER 2:19-21;
2 CORINTHIANS 12:10

Related texts: JOB 36:15-17; ISAIAH 53; 1 PETER 1:3-9; 4:12-19

Unconditional Love

Who shall separate us from the love of Christ? Shall trouble or hardship or persecution or famine or nakedness or danger or sword? As it is written:

"For your sake we face death all day long;
we are considered as sheep to be slaughtered."

No, in all these things we are more than conquerors through him who loved us. For I am convinced that neither death nor life, neither angels nor demons, neither the present nor the future, nor any powers, neither height nor depth, nor anything else in all creation, will be able to separate us from the love of God that is in Christ Jesus our Lord.

And so we know and rely on the love God has for us. God is love. Whoever lives in love lives in God, and God in him. In this way, love is made complete among us so that we will have confidence on the day of judgment, because in this world we are like him. There is no fear in love. But perfect love drives out fear, because fear has to do with punishment. The one who fears is not made perfect in love.

We love because he first loved us.

ROMANS 8:35-39; 1 JOHN 4:16-19

Related texts: DEUTERONOMY 7:7-11; 10:14-15; JOHN 3:16-19;
ROMANS 5:8-11; EPHESIANS 2:4-10

The Greatest Is Love

**THE ONE
MINUTE
BIBLE**

If I speak in the tongues of men and of angels, but have not love, I am only a resounding gong or a clanging cymbal. If I have the gift of prophecy and can fathom all mysteries and all knowledge, and if I have a faith that can move mountains, but have not love, I am nothing. If I give all I possess to the poor and surrender my body to the flames, but have not love, I gain nothing.

Love is patient, love is kind. It does not envy, it does not boast, it is not proud. It is not rude, it is not self-seeking, it is not easily angered, it keeps no record of wrongs. Love does not delight in evil but rejoices with the truth. It always protects, always trusts, always hopes, always perseveres.

Love never fails.

And now these three remain: faith, hope and love. But the greatest of these is love.

Place me like a seal over your heart,
    like a seal on your arm;
for love is as strong as death,
    its jealousy unyielding as the grave.
It burns like blazing fire,
    like a mighty flame.
Many waters cannot quench love;
    rivers cannot wash it away.
If one were to give
    all the wealth of his house for love,
    it would be utterly scorned.

Husbands, love your wives, just as Christ loved the church and gave himself up for her.

1 CORINTHIANS 13:1-8a, 13; SONG OF SONGS 8:6-7; EPHESIANS 5:25

Related texts: DEUTERONOMY 6:1-5; PSALM 136; JOHN 15:9-17; 1 JOHN 3

Israelites Oppressed in Egypt

These are the names of the sons of Israel who went to Egypt with Jacob, each with his family: Reuben, Simeon, Levi and Judah; Issachar, Zebulun and Benjamin; Dan and Naphtali; Gad and Asher. The descendants of Jacob numbered seventy in all; Joseph was already in Egypt.

Now Joseph and all his brothers and all that generation died, but the Israelites were fruitful and multiplied greatly and became exceedingly numerous, so that the land was filled with them.

Then a new king, who did not know about Joseph, came to power in Egypt. "Look," he said to his people, "the Israelites have become much too numerous for us. Come, we must deal shrewdly with them or they will become even more numerous and, if war breaks out, will join our enemies, fight against us and leave the country."

So they put slave masters over them to oppress them with forced labor, and they built Pithom and Rameses as store cities for Pharaoh. But the more they were oppressed, the more they multiplied and spread; so the Egyptians came to dread the Israelites and worked them ruthlessly.

Then Pharaoh gave this order to all his people: "Every boy that is born you must throw into the Nile, but let every girl live."

EXODUS 1:1-13, 22

**THE ONE
MINUTE
BIBLE**

Related texts: PSALM 105:23-25; ACTS 7:9-34; 1 CORINTHIANS 7:21-23; GALATIANS 3:26-28

The Birth of Moses

**THE ONE
MINUTE
BIBLE**

Now a man of the house of Levi married a Levite woman, and she became pregnant and gave birth to a son. When she saw that he was a fine child, she hid him for three months. But when she could hide him no longer, she got a papyrus basket for him and coated it with tar and pitch. Then she placed the child in it and put it among the reeds along the bank of the Nile. His sister stood at a distance to see what would happen to him.

Then Pharaoh's daughter went down to the Nile to bathe, and her attendants were walking along the river bank. She saw the basket among the reeds and sent her slave girl to get it. She opened it and saw the baby. He was crying, and she felt sorry for him. "This is one of the Hebrew babies," she said.

Then his sister asked Pharaoh's daughter, "Shall I go and get one of the Hebrew women to nurse the baby for you?"

"Yes, go," she answered. And the girl went and got the baby's mother. Pharaoh's daughter said to her, "Take this baby and nurse him for me, and I will pay you." So the woman took the baby and nursed him. When the child grew older, she took him to Pharaoh's daughter and he became her son. She named him Moses, saying, "I drew him out of the water."

EXODUS 2:1-10

Related texts: ISAIAH 49:13-19; ACTS 7:20-22; HEBREWS 11:23

Moses Flees from Egypt

THE ONE
MINUTE
BIBLE

One day, after Moses had grown up, he went out to where his own people were and watched them at their hard labor. He saw an Egyptian beating a Hebrew, one of his own people. Glancing this way and that and seeing no one, he killed the Egyptian and hid him in the sand. The next day he went out and saw two Hebrews fighting. He asked the one in the wrong, "Why are you hitting your fellow Hebrew?"

The man said, "Who made you ruler and judge over us? Are you thinking of killing me as you killed the Egyptian?" Then Moses was afraid and thought, "What I did must have become known."

When Pharaoh heard of this, he tried to kill Moses, but Moses fled from Pharaoh and went to live in Midian.

During that long period, the king of Egypt died. The Israelites groaned in their slavery and cried out, and their cry for help because of their slavery went up to God. God heard their groaning and he remembered his covenant with Abraham, with Isaac and with Jacob. So God looked on the Israelites and was concerned about them.

The LORD provided redemption for his people;
    he ordained his covenant forever—
    holy and awesome is his name.

EXODUS 2:11-15a, 23-25; PSALM 111:9

Related texts: NUMBERS 32:23; ACTS 7:23-29; HEBREWS 11:24-27

The LORD Appears to Moses

**THE ONE
MINUTE
BIBLE**

Now Moses was tending the flock of Jethro his father-in-law, the priest of Midian, and he led the flock to the far side of the desert and came to Horeb, the mountain of God. There the angel of the LORD appeared to him in flames of fire from within a bush. Moses saw that though the bush was on fire it did not burn up. So Moses thought, "I will go over and see this strange sight—why the bush does not burn up."

When the LORD saw that he had gone over to look, God called to him from within the bush, "Moses! Moses!"

And Moses said, "Here I am."

"Do not come any closer," God said. "Take off your sandals, for the place where you are standing is holy ground." Then he said, "I am the God of your father, the God of Abraham, the God of Isaac and the God of Jacob." At this, Moses hid his face, because he was afraid to look at God.

The LORD said, "I have indeed seen the misery of my people in Egypt. I have heard them crying out because of their slave drivers, and I am concerned about their suffering. So I have come down to rescue them from the hand of the Egyptians and to bring them up out of that land into a good and spacious land, a land flowing with milk and honey.

"So now, go. I am sending you to Pharaoh to bring my people the Israelites out of Egypt."

EXODUS 3:1-8a, 10

Related texts: ISAIAH 6; ACTS 7:30-35; REVELATION 15:2-4

The LORD Reveals His Name to Moses

**THE ONE
MINUTE
BIBLE**

But Moses said to God, "Who am I, that I should go to Pharaoh and bring the Israelites out of Egypt?"

And God said, "I will be with you. And this will be the sign to you that it is I who have sent you: When you have brought the people out of Egypt, you will worship God on this mountain."

Moses said to God, "Suppose I go to the Israelites and say to them, 'The God of your fathers has sent me to you,' and they ask me, 'What is his name?' Then what shall I tell them?"

God said to Moses, "I AM WHO I AM. This is what you are to say to the Israelites: 'I AM has sent me to you.'"

God also said to Moses, "Say to the Israelites, 'The LORD, the God of your fathers—the God of Abraham, the God of Isaac and the God of Jacob—has sent me to you.' This is my name forever, the name by which I am to be remembered from generation to generation."

God also said to Moses, "I am the LORD. I appeared to Abraham, to Isaac and to Jacob as God Almighty, but by my name the LORD I did not make myself known to them."

EXODUS 3:11-15; 6:2-3

Related texts: EXODUS 20:7: JOHN 6:35; 8:12, 58; 10:7, 11; 11:25; 14:6; 15:1; REVELATION 1:8

The Names of God: *The Lord*

**THE ONE
MINUTE
BIBLE**

The Lord is a refuge for the oppressed,
a stronghold in times of trouble.
Those who know your name will trust in you,
for you, Lord, have never forsaken those who
seek you.

You shall not misuse the name of the Lord your God, for
the Lord will not hold anyone guiltless who misuses
his name.

I will proclaim the name of the Lord.
Oh, praise the greatness of our God!
He is the Rock, his works are perfect,
and all his ways are just.
A faithful God who does no wrong,
upright and just is he.

Give thanks to the Lord, call on his name;
make known among the nations what he has done.
Sing to him, sing praise to him;
tell of all his wonderful acts.
Glory in his holy name;
let the hearts of those who seek the Lord rejoice.

The name of the Lord is a strong tower;
the righteous run to it and are safe.

No one is like you, O Lord;
you are great,
and your name is mighty in power.

Psalm 9:9-10; Exodus 20:7; Deuteronomy 32:3-4;
1 Chronicles 16:8-10; Proverbs 18:10; Jeremiah 10:6

Related texts: Exodus 15:1-3; Isaiah 42:5-9; Colossians 3:16-17;
Hebrews 13:15

The Names of God: *The Sovereign LORD*

How great you are, O Sovereign LORD! There is no one like you, and there is no God but you, as we have heard with our own ears. And who is like your people Israel—the one nation on earth that God went out to redeem as a people for himself, and to make a name for himself, and to perform great and awesome wonders by driving out nations and their gods from before your people, whom you redeemed from Egypt? You have established your people Israel as your very own forever, and you, O LORD, have become their God.

Our God is a God who saves;
    from the Sovereign LORD comes escape from death.

For you have been my hope, O Sovereign LORD,
    my confidence since my youth.

Those who are far from you will perish;
    you destroy all who are unfaithful to you.
But as for me, it is good to be near God.
    I have made the Sovereign LORD my refuge;
    I will tell of all your deeds.

2 SAMUEL 7:22-24; PSALMS 68:20; 71:5; 73:27-28

Related texts: ISAIAH 50:4-11; ACTS 4:23-35; EPHESIANS 5:19-20

The Names of God: *The Lord Almighty*

**THE ONE
MINUTE
BIBLE**

Lift up your heads, O you gates;
  be lifted up, you ancient doors,
  that the King of glory may come in.
Who is this King of glory?
  The Lord strong and mighty,
  the Lord mighty in battle.
Lift up your heads, O you gates;
  lift them up, you ancient doors,
  that the King of glory may come in.
Who is he, this King of glory?
  The Lord Almighty—
  he is the King of glory. *Selah*

And I saw what looked like a sea of glass mixed
with fire and, standing beside the sea, those who had
been victorious over the beast and his image and over
the number of his name. They held harps given them by
God and sang the song of Moses the servant of God and
the song of the Lamb:

  "Great and marvelous are your deeds,
    Lord God Almighty.
  Just and true are your ways,
    King of the ages.
  Who will not fear you, O Lord,
    and bring glory to your name?
  For you alone are holy.
  All nations will come
    and worship before you,
  for your righteous acts have been revealed."

PSALM 24:7-10; REVELATION 15:2-4

Related texts: 1 SAMUEL 17:39-51; ISAIAH 54:5; REVELATION 4:1-8

Names of God: *The Almighty*

So listen to me, you men of understanding.
  Far be it from God to do evil,
    from the Almighty to do wrong.
He repays a man for what he has done;
  he brings upon him what his conduct deserves.
It is unthinkable that God would do wrong,
  that the Almighty would pervert justice.

The Almighty is beyond our reach and exalted in power;
  in his justice and great righteousness, he does
        not oppress.
Therefore, men revere him,
  for does he not have regard for all the wise in heart?

He who dwells in the shelter of the Most High
  will rest in the shadow of the Almighty.
I will say of the LORD, "He is my refuge and my fortress,
  my God, in whom I trust."
Surely he will save you from the fowler's snare
  and from the deadly pestilence.
He will cover you with his feathers,
  and under his wings you will find refuge;
    his faithfulness will be your shield and rampart.

  "I am the Alpha and the Omega," says the Lord
God, "who is, and who was, and who is to come, the
Almighty."

JOB 34:10-12; 37:23-24; PSALM 91:1-4; REVELATION 1:8

Related texts: GENESIS 17:1; 28:3; 35:11; 43:14; 48:3; 49:25;
EXODUS 6:2-4; REVELATION 21:22-27

**THE ONE
MINUTE
BIBLE**

February 24

Names of God: *The Lord*

For the LORD your God is God of gods and Lord of lords, the great God, mighty and awesome, who shows no partiality and accepts no bribes. He defends the cause of the fatherless and the widow, and loves the alien, giving him food and clothing.

O LORD, our Lord,
    how majestic is your name in all the earth!

Lord, you have been our dwelling place
    throughout all generations.
Before the mountains were born
    or you brought forth the earth and the world,
    from everlasting to everlasting you are God.

That if you confess with your mouth, "Jesus is Lord," and believe in your heart that God raised him from the dead, you will be saved. For it is with your heart that you believe and are justified, and it is with your mouth that you confess and are saved. As the Scripture says, "Anyone who trusts in him will never be put to shame." For there is no difference between Jew and Gentile—the same Lord is Lord of all and richly blesses all who call on him, for, "Everyone who calls on the name of the Lord will be saved."

So then, just as you received Christ Jesus as Lord, continue to live in him, rooted and built up in him, strengthened in the faith as you were taught, and overflowing with thankfulness.

DEUTERONOMY 10:17-18; PSALMS 8:9; 90:1-2; ROMANS 10:9-13;
COLOSSIANS 2:6-7

Related texts: JOB 28; PSALMS 8; 86; 110; DANIEL 9:1-19;
PHILIPPIANS 2:5-11

58

Names of God: *The Most High*

THE ONE
MINUTE
BIBLE

My shield is God Most High,
who saves the upright in heart.

God is our refuge and strength,
an ever-present help in trouble.
Therefore we will not fear, though the earth give way
and the mountains fall into the heart of the sea,
though its waters roar and foam
and the mountains quake with their surging. *Selah*
There is a river whose streams make glad the city of God,
the holy place where the Most High dwells.
God is within her, she will not fall;
God will help her at break of day.
Nations are in uproar, kingdoms fall;
he lifts his voice, the earth melts.
The Lord Almighty is with us;
the God of Jacob is our fortress. *Selah*

Clap your hands, all you nations;
shout to God with cries of joy.
How awesome is the Lord Most High,
the great King over all the earth!

It is good to praise the Lord
and make music to your name, O Most High,
to proclaim your love in the morning
and your faithfulness at night,
to the music of the ten-stringed lyre
and the melody of the harp.
For you make me glad by your deeds, O Lord;
I sing for joy at the works of your hands.
How great are your works, O Lord,
how profound your thoughts!

PSALMS 7:10; 46:1-7; 47:1-2; 92:1-5

Related texts: GENESIS 14:18-24; PSALMS 7; 9:1-2; 91; LUKE 1:26-38

Names of God: *The Creator*

**THE ONE
MINUTE
BIBLE**

Remember your Creator
in the days of your youth,
before the days of trouble come
and the years approach when you will say,
"I find no pleasure in them"—
before the sun and the light
and the moon and the stars grow dark,
and the clouds return after the rain;
when the keepers of the house tremble,
and the strong men stoop,
when the grinders cease because they are few,
and those looking through the windows grow dim;
when the doors to the street are closed
and the sound of grinding fades;
when men rise up at the sound of birds,
but all their songs grow faint;
when men are afraid of heights
and of dangers in the streets;
when the almond tree blossoms
and the grasshopper drags himself along
and desire no longer is stirred.
Then man goes to his eternal home
and mourners go about the streets.

Remember him—before the silver cord is severed,
or the golden bowl is broken;
before the pitcher is shattered at the spring,
or the wheel broken at the well,
and the dust returns to the ground it came from,
and the spirit returns to God who gave it.

Ecclesiastes 12:1-7

Related texts: Genesis 1; 14:18-24; Ecclesiastes 12:9-14;
Isaiah 40:27-31; Revelation 4:11

Names of God: *Everlasting God, King Eternal*

Why do you say, O Jacob,
 and complain, O Israel,
"My way is hidden from the LORD;
 my cause is disregarded by my God"?
Do you not know?
 Have you not heard?
The LORD is the everlasting God,
 the Creator of the ends of the earth.
He will not grow tired or weary,
 and his understanding no one can fathom.
He gives strength to the weary
 and increases the power of the weak.
Even youths grow tired and weary,
 and young men stumble and fall;
but those who hope in the LORD
 will renew their strength.
They will soar on wings like eagles;
 they will run and not grow weary,
 they will walk and not be faint.

    Here is a trustworthy saying that deserves full
acceptance: Christ Jesus came into the world to save
sinners—of whom I am the worst. But for that very
reason I was shown mercy so that in me, the worst of
sinners, Christ Jesus might display his unlimited
patience as an example for those who would believe on
him and receive eternal life. Now to the King eternal,
immortal, invisible, the only God, be honor and glory for
ever and ever. Amen.

ISAIAH 40:27-31; 1 TIMOTHY 1:15-17

Related texts: DEUTERONOMY 33:27; PSALM 90:1-2; ROMANS 16:25-27;
HEBREWS 9:14

Names of God: *The Holy One*

**THE ONE
MINUTE
BIBLE**

Yet you are enthroned as the Holy One;
    you are the praise of Israel.
In you our fathers put their trust;
    they trusted and you delivered them.
They cried to you and were saved;
    in you they trusted and were not disappointed.

The fear of the LORD is the beginning of wisdom,
    and knowledge of the Holy One is understanding.
For through me your days will be many,
    and years will be added to your life.
If you are wise, your wisdom will reward you;
    if you are a mocker, you alone will suffer.

Our Redeemer—the LORD Almighty is his name—
    is the Holy One of Israel.

    In the synagogue there was a man possessed by a demon, an evil spirit. He cried out at the top of his voice, "Ha! What do you want with us, Jesus of Nazareth? Have you come to destroy us? I know who you are—the Holy One of God!"
    "Be quiet!" Jesus said sternly. "Come out of him!" Then the demon threw the man down before them all and came out without injuring him.
    All the people were amazed and said to each other, "What is this teaching? With authority and power he gives orders to evil spirits and they come out!"

PSALM 22:3-5; PROVERBS 9:10-12; ISAIAH 47:4; LUKE 4:33-36

Related texts: PSALM 16; ISAIAH 40:25-31; 54:5; ACTS 2:22-39

Names of God: *Judge*

The LORD reigns forever;
   he has established his throne for judgment.
He will judge the world in righteousness;
   he will govern the peoples with justice.

O LORD, the God who avenges,
   O God who avenges, shine forth.
Rise up, O Judge of the earth;
   pay back to the proud what they deserve.

A shoot will come up from the stump of Jesse;
   from his roots a Branch will bear fruit.
The Spirit of the LORD will rest on him—
   the Spirit of wisdom and of understanding,
   the Spirit of counsel and of power,
   the Spirit of knowledge and of the fear of the LORD—
   and he will delight in the fear of the LORD.

He will not judge by what he sees with his eyes,
   or decide by what he hears with his ears;
but with righteousness he will judge the needy,
   with justice he will give decisions for the poor
      of the earth.
He will strike the earth with the rod of his mouth;
   with the breath of his lips he will slay the wicked.
Righteousness will be his belt
   and faithfulness the sash around his waist.

For the LORD is our judge,
   the LORD is our lawgiver,
the LORD is our king;
   it is he who will save us.

PSALMS 9:7-8; 94:1-2; ISAIAH 11:1-5; 33:22

**THE ONE
MINUTE
BIBLE**

Related texts: JUDGES 11:27; PSALMS 7; 82; 96; JOHN 5:25-30;
ACTS 10:34-43; JAMES 4:11-12; REVELATION 19:11-16

*All human history as described in
the Bible, may be summarized in one phrase,
God in Search of Man. There are no words in
the world more knowing, more disclosing and
more indispensable, words both stern and
graceful, heart-rending and healing.*
Abraham Joshua Heschel (1907-   )
AMERICAN THEOLOGIAN

*I was dazzled by the revelation of the truth
and obtained complete answers to the
questions: What is the meaning of my life?
And the meaning of other people's lives?*
Leo Tolstoy (1828-1910)
RUSSIAN NOVELIST
(On studying the Gospels)

*Prayer, in its turn, needs to be sustained
by reading the Holy Scripture.*
Francois Fenelon (1651-1715)
FRENCH ROMAN CATHOLIC BISHOP

Names of God: *King*

**THE ONE
MINUTE
BIBLE**

The Lord sits enthroned over the flood;
  the Lord is enthroned as King forever.
The Lord gives strength to his people;
  the Lord blesses his people with peace.

I am the Lord, your Holy One,
  Israel's Creator, your King.

  So Pilate asked Jesus, "Are you the king of the
Jews?"
  "Yes, it is as you say," Jesus replied.

  I saw heaven standing open and there before me
was a white horse, whose rider is called Faithful and
True. With justice he judges and makes war. His eyes
are like blazing fire, and on his head are many crowns.
He has a name written on him that no one knows but he
himself. He is dressed in a robe dipped in blood, and his
name is the Word of God. The armies of heaven were
following him, riding on white horses and dressed in
fine linen, white and clean. Out of his mouth comes a
sharp sword with which to strike down the nations. "He
will rule them with an iron scepter." He treads the
winepress of the fury of the wrath of God Almighty. On
his robe and on his thigh he has this name written:
KING OF KINGS AND LORD OF LORDS.

PSALM 29:10-11; ISAIAH 43:15; LUKE 23:3; REVELATION 19:11-16

Related texts: PSALMS 47; 95:1-7; ISAIAH 44:6-8; JEREMIAH 10:6-10;
MATTHEW 21:1-5; 1 TIMOTHY 1:17; 6:15

Names of God: *The Mighty One*

THE ONE
MINUTE
BIBLE

Although you have been forsaken and hated,
    with no one traveling through,
I will make you the everlasting pride
    and the joy of all generations.
You will drink the milk of nations
    and be nursed at royal breasts.
Then you will know that I, the Lord, am your Savior,
    your Redeemer, the Mighty One of Jacob.

And Mary said:

    "My soul glorifies the Lord
        and my spirit rejoices in God my Savior,
    for he has been mindful
        of the humble state of his servant.
    From now on all generations will call me blessed,
        for the Mighty One has done great things
            for me—
        holy is his name.
    His mercy extends to those who fear him,
        from generation to generation.
    He has performed mighty deeds with his arm;
        he has scattered those who are proud in their
            inmost thoughts.
    He has brought down rulers from their thrones
        but has lifted up the humble.
    He has filled the hungry with good things
        but has sent the rich away empty.
    He has helped his servant Israel,
        remembering to be merciful
    to Abraham and his descendants forever,
        even as he said to our fathers."

ISAIAH 60:15-16; LUKE 1:46-55

Related texts: JOSHUA 22:22; PSALMS 50; 132; ISAIAH 49:24-26;
MARK 14:60-62

Names of God: *Redeemer*

I know that my Redeemer lives,
and that in the end he will stand upon the earth.
And after my skin has been destroyed,
yet in my flesh I will see God;
I myself will see him
with my own eyes—I, and not another.
How my heart yearns within me!

Who can discern his errors?
Forgive my hidden faults.
Keep your servant also from willful sins;
may they not rule over me.
Then will I be blameless,
innocent of great transgression.
May the words of my mouth and the meditation
of my heart
be pleasing in your sight,
O Lord, my Rock and my Redeemer.

This is what the Lord says—
Israel's King and Redeemer, the Lord Almighty:
I am the first and I am the last;
apart from me there is no God.
Who then is like me? Let him proclaim it.
Let him declare and lay out before me
what has happened since I established my ancient
people,
and what is yet to come—
yes, let him foretell what will come.
Do not tremble, do not be afraid.
Did I not proclaim this and foretell it long ago?
You are my witnesses. Is there any God besides me?
No, there is no other Rock; I know not one.

JOB 19:25-27; PSALM 19:12-14; ISAIAH 44:6-8

Related texts: ISAIAH 44:24-28; 54; LUKE 24:13-36; GALATIANS 4:4-5;
TITUS 2:11-14

**THE ONE
MINUTE
BIBLE**

Names of God: *Refuge*

The L‍ORD is a refuge for the oppressed,
    a stronghold in times of trouble.
Those who know your name will trust in you,
    for you, L‍ORD, have never forsaken those who seek you.

Hear my cry, O God;
    listen to my prayer.

From the ends of the earth I call to you,
    I call as my heart grows faint;
    lead me to the rock that is higher than I.
For you have been my refuge,
    a strong tower against the foe.

I long to dwell in your tent forever
    and take refuge in the shelter of your wings. *Selah*

You are my refuge and my shield;
    I have put my hope in your word.

O L‍ORD, my strength and my fortress,
    my refuge in time of distress,
to you the nations will come
    from the ends of the earth and say,
"Our fathers possessed nothing but false gods,
    worthless idols that did them no good.
Do men make their own gods?
    Yes, but they are not gods!"

"Therefore I will teach them—
    this time I will teach them
    my power and might.
Then they will know
    that my name is the L‍ORD."

PSALMS 9:9-10; 61:1-4; 119:114; JEREMIAH 16:19-21

Related texts: 2 SAMUEL 22:3, 31; PSALMS 46; 59:16-17; 71; 91;
ISAIAH 25:1-5

Names of God: *Rock*

**THE ONE
MINUTE
BIBLE**

Listen, O heavens, and I will speak;
    hear, O earth, the words of my mouth.
Let my teaching fall like rain
    and my words descend like dew,
like showers on new grass,
    like abundant rain on tender plants.
I will proclaim the name of the LORD.
    Oh, praise the greatness of our God!
He is the Rock, his works are perfect,
    and all his ways are just.
A faithful God who does no wrong,
    upright and just is he.

Then Hannah prayed and said:

    "My heart rejoices in the LORD;
        in the LORD my horn is lifted high.
    My mouth boasts over my enemies,
        for I delight in your deliverance.

    "There is no one holy like the LORD;
        there is no one besides you;
        there is no Rock like our God."

The LORD is my rock, my fortress and my deliverer;
    my God is my rock, in whom I take refuge.
    He is my shield and the horn of my salvation, my
        stronghold.
I call to the LORD, who is worthy of praise,
    and I am saved from my enemies.

DEUTERONOMY 32:1-4; 1 SAMUEL 2:1-2; PSALM 18:2-3

Related texts: DEUTERONOMY 32; 2 SAMUEL 22; PSALM 62;
ROMANS 9:30-33; 1 CORINTHIANS 10:1-4; 1 PETER 2:1-8

Names of God: *Savior*

**THE ONE
MINUTE
BIBLE**

Why are you downcast, O my soul?
  Why so disturbed within me?
Put your hope in God,
  for I will yet praise him,
  my Savior and my God.

"You are my witnesses," declares the LORD,
  "and my servant whom I have chosen,
so that you may know and believe me
  and understand that I am he.
Before me no god was formed,
  nor will there be one after me.
I, even I, am the LORD,
  and apart from me there is no savior.
I have revealed and saved and proclaimed—
  I, and not some foreign god among you.
You are my witnesses," declares the LORD, "that I
    am God.
  Yes, and from ancient days I am he.
No one can deliver out of my hand.
  When I act, who can reverse it?"

For the grace of God that brings salvation has
appeared to all men. It teaches us to say "No" to
ungodliness and worldly passions, and to live self-
controlled, upright and godly lives in this present age,
while we wait for the blessed hope—the glorious
appearing of our great God and Savior, Jesus Christ,
who gave himself for us to redeem us from all
wickedness and to purify for himself a people that are
his very own, eager to do what is good.

PSALM 42:11; ISAIAH 43:10-13; TITUS 2:11-14

Related texts: PSALM 68:19-20; MICAH 7:1-7; HABAKKUK 3:16-19;
LUKE 1:47-55; 2:8-20; JOHN 4:40-42; ACTS 5:29-32

Names of God: *Shepherd*

The LORD is my shepherd, I shall not be in want.

See, the Sovereign LORD comes with power,
   and his arm rules for him.
See, his reward is with him,
   and his recompense accompanies him.
He tends his flock like a shepherd:
   He gathers the lambs in his arms
and carries them close to his heart;
   he gently leads those that have young.

   May the God of peace, who through the blood of the
eternal covenant brought back from the dead our Lord
Jesus, that great Shepherd of the sheep, equip you with
everything good for doing his will, and may he work in us
what is pleasing to him, through Jesus Christ, to whom
be glory for ever and ever. Amen.

Therefore,
   "they are before the throne of God
      and serve him day and night in his temple;
   and he who sits on the throne will spread his tent
         over them.
   Never again will they hunger;
      never again will they thirst.
   The sun will not beat upon them,
      nor any scorching heat.
   For the Lamb at the center of the throne will be
         their shepherd;
      he will lead them to springs of living water.
   And God will wipe away every tear from their eyes."

PSALM 23:1; ISAIAH 40:10-11; HEBREWS 13:20-21; REVELATION 7:15-17

Related texts: PSALMS 23; 80:1-7; EZEKIEL 34; MICAH 5:2-5;
JOHN 10:11-15; 1 PETER 2:21-25; 5:1-4

The Fruit of the Spirit

**THE ONE
MINUTE
BIBLE**

The acts of the sinful nature are obvious: sexual immorality, impurity and debauchery; idolatry and witchcraft; hatred, discord, jealousy, fits of rage, selfish ambition, dissensions, factions and envy; drunkenness, orgies, and the like. I warn you, as I did before, that those who live like this will not inherit the kingdom of God.

But the fruit of the Spirit is love, joy, peace, patience, kindness, goodness, faithfulness, gentleness and self-control. Against such things there is no law.

For you were once darkness, but now you are light in the Lord. Live as children of light (for the fruit of the light consists in all goodness, righteousness and truth) and find out what pleases the Lord. Have nothing to do with the fruitless deeds of darkness, but rather expose them.

No good tree bears bad fruit, nor does a bad tree bear good fruit. Each tree is recognized by its own fruit. People do not pick figs from thornbushes, or grapes from briers. The good man brings good things out of the good stored up in his heart, and the evil man brings evil things out of the evil stored up in his heart. For out of the overflow of his heart his mouth speaks.

GALATIANS 5:19-23; EPHESIANS 5:8-11; LUKE 6:43-45

Related texts: PSALMS 1; 112; ISAIAH 27:2-3; JOHN 15:1-16; ROMANS 7:1-6

The Fruit of the Spirit: *Love*

I love you, O LORD, my strength.

"The most important [commandment]," answered Jesus, "is this: 'Hear, O Israel, the Lord our God, the Lord is one. Love the Lord your God with all your heart and with all your soul and with all your mind and with all your strength.' The second is this: 'Love your neighbor as yourself.' There is no commandment greater than these."

"A new command I give you: Love one another. As I have loved you, so you must love one another. By this all men will know that you are my disciples, if you love one another."

"You have heard that it was said, 'Love your neighbor and hate your enemy.' But I tell you: Love your enemies and pray for those who persecute you, that you may be sons of your Father in heaven. He causes his sun to rise on the evil and the good, and sends rain on the righteous and the unrighteous. If you love those who love you, what reward will you get? Are not even the tax collectors doing that?"

Therefore, as God's chosen people, holy and dearly loved, clothe yourselves with compassion, kindness, humility, gentleness and patience. Bear with each other and forgive whatever grievances you may have against one another. Forgive as the Lord forgave you. And over all these virtues put on love, which binds them all together in perfect unity.

PSALM 18:1; MARK 12:29-31; JOHN 13:34-35; MATTHEW 5:43-46;
COLOSSIANS 3:12-14

Related texts: DEUTERONOMY 6:4-6; JOHN 14-15; 21:15-17;
1 CORINTHIANS 13; 1 JOHN 4:7-21; 1 PETER 4:7-8

God Is Love

**THE ONE
MINUTE
BIBLE**

Then the Lᴏʀᴅ came down in the cloud and stood there with him and proclaimed his name, the Lᴏʀᴅ. And he passed in front of Moses, proclaiming, "The Lᴏʀᴅ, the Lᴏʀᴅ, the compassionate and gracious God, slow to anger, abounding in love and faithfulness, maintaining love to thousands, and forgiving wickedness, rebellion and sin. Yet he does not leave the guilty unpunished; he punishes the children and their children for the sin of the fathers to the third and fourth generation."

The Lᴏʀᴅ loves righteousness and justice;
the earth is full of his unfailing love.

For God so loved the world that he gave his one and only Son, that whoever believes in him shall not perish but have eternal life.

But God demonstrates his own love for us in this: While we were still sinners, Christ died for us.
For I am convinced that neither death nor life, neither angels nor demons, neither the present nor the future, nor any powers, neither height nor depth, nor anything else in all creation, will be able to separate us from the love of God that is in Christ Jesus our Lord.

God is love. Whoever lives in love lives in God, and God in him.

Exᴏᴅᴜs 34:5-7; Psᴀʟᴍ 33:5; Jᴏʜɴ 3:16;
Rᴏᴍᴀɴs 5:8; 8:38-39; 1 Jᴏʜɴ 4:16b

Related texts: Psᴀʟᴍ 136; Jᴇʀᴇᴍɪᴀʜ 31:3-6; Zᴇᴘʜᴀɴɪᴀʜ 3:16-17;
1 Jᴏʜɴ 4:7-21

The Fruit of the Spirit: *Joy*

Sing joyfully to the LORD, you righteous;
    it is fitting for the upright to praise him.
Praise the LORD with the harp;
    make music to him on the ten-stringed lyre.
Sing to him a new song;
    play skillfully, and shout for joy.
For the word of the LORD is right and true;
    he is faithful in all he does.

When the righteous prosper, the city rejoices;
    when the wicked perish, there are shouts of joy.

Though the fig tree does not bud
    and there are no grapes on the vines,
though the olive crop fails
    and the fields produce no food,
though there are no sheep in the pen
    and no cattle in the stalls,
yet I will rejoice in the LORD,
    I will be joyful in God my Savior.

THE ONE MINUTE BIBLE

May the God of hope fill you with all joy and peace as you trust in him, so that you may overflow with hope by the power of the Holy Spirit.

Rejoice in the Lord always. I will say it again: Rejoice!

Dear friends, do not be surprised at the painful trial you are suffering, as though something strange were happening to you. But rejoice that you participate in the sufferings of Christ, so that you may be overjoyed when his glory is revealed.

PSALM 33:1-4; PROVERBS 11:10; HABAKKUK 3:17-18; ROMANS 15:13;
PHILIPPIANS 4:4; 1 PETER 4:12

Related texts: NEHEMIAH 8:1-12; PSALMS 28:6-9; 30:4-5; ISAIAH 61

God Is Joyful

**THE ONE
MINUTE
BIBLE**

May the glory of the LORD endure forever;
   may the LORD rejoice in his works—
he who looks at the earth, and it trembles,
   who touches the mountains, and they smoke.
I will sing to the LORD all my life;
   I will sing praise to my God as long as I live.
May my meditation be pleasing to him,
   as I rejoice in the LORD.

On that day they will say to Jerusalem,
   "Do not fear, O Zion;
   do not let your hands hang limp.
The LORD your God is with you,
   he is mighty to save.
He will take great delight in you,
   he will quiet you with his love,
   he will rejoice over you with singing."

Let us fix our eyes on Jesus, the author and
perfecter of our faith, who for the joy set before him
endured the cross, scorning its shame, and sat down at
the right hand of the throne of God. Consider him who
endured such opposition from sinful men, so that you
will not grow weary and lose heart.

PSALM 104:31-34; ZEPHANIAH 3:16-17; HEBREWS 12:2-3

Related texts: 1 CHRONICLES 16:23-33; NEHEMIAH 8:1-12; PSALM 21:1-7;
ISAIAH 62:4-7

The Fruit of the Spirit: *Peace*

The LORD bless you
    and keep you;
the LORD make his face shine upon you
    and be gracious to you;
the LORD turn his face toward you
    and give you peace.

Great peace have they who love your law,
    and nothing can make them stumble.

You will keep in perfect peace
    him whose mind is steadfast,
    because he trusts in you.
Trust in the LORD forever,
    for the LORD, the LORD, is the Rock eternal.

      Peace I leave with you; my peace I give you. I do not give to you as the world gives. Do not let your hearts be troubled and do not be afraid.

      Do not be anxious about anything, but in everything, by prayer and petition, with thanksgiving, present your requests to God. And the peace of God, which transcends all understanding, will guard your hearts and your minds in Christ Jesus.

      Let the peace of Christ rule in your hearts, since as members of one body you were called to peace. And be thankful.

NUMBERS 6:24-26; PSALM 119:165; ISAIAH 26:3-4; JOHN 14:27;
PHILIPPIANS 4:6-7; COLOSSIANS 3:15

**THE ONE
MINUTE
BIBLE**

Related texts: PROVERBS 12:20; ISAIAH 32:17; 57:21; MICAH 4:1-5;
LUKE 2:13-14; ROMANS 8:1-6

God Is Peaceful

**THE ONE
MINUTE
BIBLE**

The LORD gives strength to his people;
  the LORD blesses his people with peace.

For to us a child is born,
  to us a son is given,
  and the government will be on his shoulders.
And he will be called
  Wonderful Counselor, Mighty God,
  Everlasting Father, Prince of Peace.
Of the increase of his government and peace
  there will be no end.
He will reign on David's throne
  and over his kingdom,
establishing and upholding it
  with justice and righteousness
  from that time on and forever.
The zeal of the LORD Almighty
  will accomplish this.

Therefore, since we have been justified through faith, we have peace with God through our Lord Jesus Christ, through whom we have gained access by faith into this grace in which we now stand. And we rejoice in the hope of the glory of God.

May God himself, the God of peace, sanctify you through and through. May your whole spirit, soul and body be kept blameless at the coming of our Lord Jesus Christ.

Now may the Lord of peace himself give you peace at all times and in every way. The Lord be with all of you.

PSALM 29:11; ISAIAH 9:6-7; ROMANS 5:1-2; 1 THESSALONIANS 5:23;
2 THESSALONIANS 3:16

Related texts: ECCLESIASTES 3:1-8; ROMANS 15:33; 16:20;
2 CORINTHIANS 13:11; PHILIPPIANS 4:6-9

The Fruit of the Spirit: *Patience*

**THE ONE
MINUTE
BIBLE**

Be still before the LORD and wait patiently for him;
    do not fret when men succeed in their ways,
    when they carry out their wicked schemes.

Refrain from anger and turn from wrath;
    do not fret—it leads only to evil.
For evil men will be cut off,
    but those who hope in the LORD will inherit the land.

I waited patiently for the LORD;
    he turned to me and heard my cry.
He lifted me out of the slimy pit,
    out of the mud and mire;
he set my feet on a rock
    and gave me a firm place to stand.
He put a new song in my mouth,
    a hymn of praise to our God.
Many will see and fear
    and put their trust in the LORD.

A patient man has great understanding,
    but a quick-tempered man displays folly.

Love is patient, love is kind. It does not envy, it does not boast, it is not proud.

Be patient, then, brothers, until the Lord's coming. See how the farmer waits for the land to yield its valuable crop and how patient he is for the autumn and spring rains. You too, be patient and stand firm, because the Lord's coming is near.

PSALMS 37:7-9; 40:1-3; PROVERBS 14:29; 1 CORINTHIANS 13:4; JAMES 5:7-8

Related texts: PROVERBS 15:18; 16:32; 19:11; 25:15; ECCLESIASTES 7:8; ROMANS 12:9-12

God Is Patient

**THE ONE
MINUTE
BIBLE**

Here is a trustworthy saying that deserves full acceptance: Christ Jesus came into the world to save sinners—of whom I am the worst. But for that very reason I was shown mercy so that in me, the worst of sinners, Christ Jesus might display his unlimited patience as an example for those who would believe on him and receive eternal life.

The Lord is not slow in keeping his promise, as some understand slowness. He is patient with you, not wanting anyone to perish, but everyone to come to repentance.

But the day of the Lord will come like a thief. The heavens will disappear with a roar; the elements will be destroyed by fire, and the earth and everything in it will be laid bare.

Since everything will be destroyed in this way, what kind of people ought you to be? You ought to live holy and godly lives as you look forward to the day of God and speed its coming. That day will bring about the destruction of the heavens by fire, and the elements will melt in the heat. But in keeping with his promise we are looking forward to a new heaven and a new earth, the home of righteousness.

So then, dear friends, since you are looking forward to this, make every effort to be found spotless, blameless and at peace with him. Bear in mind that our Lord's patience means salvation, just as our dear brother Paul also wrote you with the wisdom that God gave him.

1 TIMOTHY 1:15-16; 2 PETER 3:9-15

Related texts: ISAIAH 7:13; 65:17-25; ROMANS 2:1-4; 3:21-28; 1 PETER 3:18-20; REVELATION 21:1-8

The Fruit of the Spirit: *Kindness*

A kindhearted woman gains respect,
  but ruthless men gain only wealth.

A kind man benefits himself,
  but a cruel man brings trouble on himself.

He who despises his neighbor sins,
  but blessed is he who is kind to the needy.

He who oppresses the poor shows contempt for
      their Maker,
  but whoever is kind to the needy honors God.

He who is kind to the poor lends to the LORD,
  and he will reward him for what he has done.

Be kind and compassionate to one another,
forgiving each other, just as in Christ God forgave you.

Therefore, as God's chosen people, holy and dearly
loved, clothe yourselves with compassion, kindness,
humility, gentleness and patience. Bear with each other
and forgive whatever grievances you may have against
one another. Forgive as the Lord forgave you. And over
all these virtues put on love, which binds them all
together in perfect unity.

PROVERBS 11:16-17; 14:21, 31; 19:17; EPHESIANS 4:32;
COLOSSIANS 3:12-14

Related texts: RUTH 1:1–3:10; PROVERBS 14:21; 1 THESSALONIANS 5:15

God Is Kind

**THE ONE
MINUTE
BIBLE**

I will tell of the kindnesses of the LORD,
    the deeds for which he is to be praised,
    according to all the LORD has done for us—
yes, the many good things he has done
    for the house of Israel,
    according to his compassion and many kindnesses.

This is what the LORD says:

"Let not the wise man boast of his wisdom
    or the strong man boast of his strength
    or the rich man boast of his riches,
but let him who boasts boast about this:
    that he understands and knows me,
that I am the LORD, who exercises kindness,
    justice and righteousness on earth,
    for in these I delight,"

declares the LORD.

At one time we too were foolish, disobedient,
deceived and enslaved by all kinds of passions and
pleasures. We lived in malice and envy, being hated and
hating one another. But when the kindness and love of
God our Savior appeared, he saved us, not because of
righteous things we had done, but because of his mercy.

ISAIAH 63:7; JEREMIAH 9:23-24; TITUS 3:3-5a

Related texts: ISAIAH 53:1-8; ROMANS 2:1-8; 11:11-24

The Fruit of the Spirit: *Goodness*

**THE ONE
MINUTE
BIBLE**

A good man obtains favor from the LORD,
    but the LORD condemns a crafty man.

I know that there is nothing better for men than to
be happy and do good while they live. That everyone
may eat and drink, and find satisfaction in all his toil—
this is the gift of God.

No good tree bears bad fruit, nor does a bad tree
bear good fruit. Each tree is recognized by its own fruit.
People do not pick figs from thornbushes, or grapes
from briers. The good man brings good things out of the
good stored up in his heart, and the evil man brings evil
things out of the evil stored up in his heart. For out of
the overflow of his heart his mouth speaks.

Let us not become weary in doing good, for at the
proper time we will reap a harvest if we do not give up.
Therefore, as we have opportunity, let us do good to all
people, especially to those who belong to the family of
believers.

For we are God's workmanship, created in Christ
Jesus to do good works, which God prepared in advance
for us to do.

Dear friend, do not imitate what is evil but what is
good. Anyone who does what is good is from God.
Anyone who does what is evil has not seen God.

PROVERBS 12:2; ECCLESIASTES 3:12; LUKE 6:43-45; GALATIANS 6:9-10;
EPHESIANS 2:10; 3 JOHN 11

Related texts: PSALM 34:8-14; PROVERBS 3:27; 11:27; 1 PETER 2:12-15

God Is Good

**THE ONE
MINUTE
BIBLE**

Taste and see that the LORD is good;
  blessed is the man who takes refuge in him.

I will praise you forever for what you have done;
  in your name I will hope, for your name is good.
  I will praise you in the presence of your saints.

Surely God is good to Israel,
  to those who are pure in heart.

For the LORD is good and his love endures forever;
  his faithfulness continues through all generations.

Give thanks to the LORD, for he is good;
  his love endures forever.

You are good, and what you do is good;
  teach me your decrees.

Praise the LORD, for the LORD is good;
  sing praise to his name, for that is pleasant.

The LORD is good to all;
  he has compassion on all he has made.

PSALMS 34:8; 52:9; 73:1; 100:5; 118:29; 119:68; 135:3; 145:9

Related texts: 2 CHRONICLES 6:41; PSALM 84:9-12; MARK 10:17-18;
86 | ROMANS 8:18-28; 3 JOHN 11

The Fruit of the Spirit: *Faithfulness*

**THE ONE
MINUTE
BIBLE**

But be sure to fear the LORD and serve him
faithfully with all your heart; consider what great things
he has done for you.

To the faithful you show yourself faithful,
    to the blameless you show yourself blameless,
to the pure you show yourself pure,
    but to the crooked you show yourself shrewd.
You save the humble,
    but your eyes are on the haughty to bring them low.

Love the LORD, all his saints!
    The LORD preserves the faithful,
    but the proud he pays back in full.
Be strong and take heart,
    all you who hope in the LORD.

Here is a trustworthy saying:
    If we died with him,
        we will also live with him;
    if we endure,
        we will also reign with him.
    If we disown him,
        he will also disown us;
    if we are faithless,
        he will remain faithful,
        for he cannot disown himself.

1 SAMUEL 12:24; 2 SAMUEL 22:26-28; PSALM 31:23-24; 2 TIMOTHY 2:11-13

Related texts: PSALM 101; PROVERBS 3:1-4; MATTHEW 24:45-51; 25:14-30

God Is Faithful

**THE ONE
MINUTE
BIBLE**

Know therefore that the Lord your God is God; he is the faithful God, keeping his covenant of love to a thousand generations of those who love him and keep his commands. But

those who hate him he will repay to their face by
destruction;
he will not be slow to repay to their face those
who hate him.

I will sing of the Lord's great love forever;
with my mouth I will make your faithfulness known
through all generations.
I will declare that your love stands firm forever,
that you established your faithfulness in heaven
itself.

Yet this I call to mind
and therefore I have hope:
Because of the Lord's great love we are not consumed,
for his compassions never fail.
They are new every morning;
great is your faithfulness.

So, if you think you are standing firm, be careful that you don't fall! No temptation has seized you except what is common to man. And God is faithful; he will not let you be tempted beyond what you can bear. But when you are tempted, he will also provide a way out so that you can stand up under it.

If we confess our sins, he is faithful and just and will forgive us our sins and purify us from all unrighteousness.

Deuteronomy 7:9-10; Psalm 89:1-2; Lamentations 3:21-23;
1 Corinthians 10:12-13; 1 John 1:9

Related texts: Deuteronomy 31:30–32:4; 2 Thessalonians 3:3;
2 Timothy 2:11-13; Revelation 19:11-16

The Fruit of the Spirit: *Gentleness*

A gentle answer turns away wrath,
   but a harsh word stirs up anger.

Through patience a ruler can be persuaded,
   and a gentle tongue can break a bone.

**THE ONE
MINUTE
BIBLE**

   Be completely humble and gentle; be patient,
bearing with one another in love. Make every effort to
keep the unity of the Spirit through the bond of peace.

   Rejoice in the Lord always. I will say it again:
Rejoice! Let your gentleness be evident to all. The Lord
is near. Do not be anxious about anything, but in
everything, by prayer and petition, with thanksgiving,
present your requests to God. And the peace of God,
which transcends all understanding, will guard your
hearts and your minds in Christ Jesus.

   Who is going to harm you if you are eager to do
good? But even if you should suffer for what is right,
you are blessed. "Do not fear what they fear; do not be
frightened." But in your hearts set apart Christ as Lord.
Always be prepared to give an answer to everyone who
asks you to give the reason for the hope that you have.
But do this with gentleness and respect, keeping a clear
conscience, so that those who speak maliciously against
your good behavior in Christ may be ashamed of their
slander.

PROVERBS 15:1; 25:15; EPHESIANS 4:2-3; PHILIPPIANS 4:4-7;
1 PETER 3:13-16

Related texts: ISAIAH 8:12-15; 1 TIMOTHY 6:3-11; 2 TIMOTHY 2:24-25;
1 PETER 3:1-6

God Is Gentle

**THE ONE
MINUTE
BIBLE**

See, the Sovereign LORD comes with power,
    and his arm rules for him.
See, his reward is with him,
    and his recompense accompanies him.
He tends his flock like a shepherd:
    He gathers the lambs in his arms
and carries them close to his heart;
    he gently leads those that have young.

Rejoice greatly, O Daughter of Zion!
    Shout, Daughter of Jerusalem!
See, your king comes to you,
    righteous and having salvation,
    gentle and riding on a donkey,
    on a colt, the foal of a donkey.

[Jesus said,] "Come to me, all you who are weary
and burdened, and I will give you rest. Take my yoke
upon you and learn from me, for I am gentle and
humble in heart, and you will find rest for your souls.
For my yoke is easy and my burden is light."

ISAIAH 40:10-11; ZECHARIAH 9:9; MATTHEW 11:28-30

Related texts: 1 KINGS 19:9-12; 2 CORINTHIANS 10:1; MATTHEW 21:1-12

The Fruit of the Spirit: *Self-Control*

Like a city whose walls are broken down
  is a man who lacks self-control.

You must teach what is in accord with sound doctrine. Teach the older men to be temperate, worthy of respect, self-controlled, and sound in faith, in love and in endurance.

Likewise, teach the older women to be reverent in the way they live, not to be slanderers or addicted to much wine, but to teach what is good. Then they can train the younger women to love their husbands and children, to be self-controlled and pure, to be busy at home, to be kind, and to be subject to their husbands, so that no one will malign the word of God.

Similarly, encourage the young men to be self-controlled.

For this very reason, make every effort to add to your faith goodness; and to goodness, knowledge; and to knowledge, self-control; and to self-control, perseverance; and to perseverance, godliness; and to godliness, brotherly kindness; and to brotherly kindness, love. For if you possess these qualities in increasing measure, they will keep you from being ineffective and unproductive in your knowledge of our Lord Jesus Christ.

PROVERBS 25:28; TITUS 2:1-6; 2 PETER 1:5-8

Related texts: PROVERBS 1:1-7; 23:23; 1 THESSALONIANS 5:5-10;
2 TIMOTHY 1:7; TITUS 2:11-14; 1 PETER 4:7

**THE ONE
MINUTE
BIBLE**

God Is Slow to Anger

The LORD is compassionate and gracious,
 slow to anger, abounding in love.
He will not always accuse,
 nor will he harbor his anger forever;
he does not treat us as our sins deserve
 or repay us according to our iniquities.
For as high as the heavens are above the earth,
 so great is his love for those who fear him;
as far as the east is from the west,
 so far has he removed our transgressions from us.

The LORD is gracious and compassionate,
 slow to anger and rich in love.
The LORD is good to all;
 he has compassion on all he has made.

The LORD is a jealous and avenging God;
 the LORD takes vengeance and is filled with wrath.
The LORD takes vengeance on his foes
 and maintains his wrath against his enemies.
The LORD is slow to anger and great in power;
 the LORD will not leave the guilty unpunished.
His way is in the whirlwind and the storm,
 and clouds are the dust of his feet.

PSALMS 103:8-12; 145:8-9; NAHUM 1:2-3

Related texts: EXODUS 34:5-7; PSALM 86:15-17; JOEL 2:12-14;
JONAH 3–4; 2 PETER 3:8-15

God Sends Moses to Egypt

God also said to Moses, "Say to the Israelites, 'The LORD, the God of your fathers—the God of Abraham, the God of Isaac and the God of Jacob—has sent me to you.' This is my name forever, the name by which I am to be remembered from generation to generation.

"Go, assemble the elders of Israel and say to them, 'The LORD, the God of your fathers—the God of Abraham, Isaac and Jacob—appeared to me and said: I have watched over you and have seen what has been done to you in Egypt. And I have promised to bring you up out of your misery in Egypt into the land of the Canaanites, Hittites, Amorites, Perizzites, Hivites and Jebusites—a land flowing with milk and honey.'

"The elders of Israel will listen to you. Then you and the elders are to go to the king of Egypt and say to him, 'The LORD, the God of the Hebrews, has met with us. Let us take a three-day journey into the desert to offer sacrifices to the LORD our God.' But I know that the king of Egypt will not let you go unless a mighty hand compels him. So I will stretch out my hand and strike the Egyptians with all the wonders that I will perform among them. After that, he will let you go.

"And I will make the Egyptians favorably disposed toward this people, so that when you leave you will not go empty-handed. Every woman is to ask her neighbor and any woman living in her house for articles of silver and gold and for clothing, which you will put on your sons and daughters. And so you will plunder the Egyptians."

EXODUS 3:15-22

THE ONE MINUTE BIBLE

Related texts: GENESIS 13:12-17; 15:12-16; HAGGAI 2:4-8; ACTS 7:30-36

Moses Confronts Pharaoh

**THE ONE
MINUTE
BIBLE**

The LORD said to Moses, "When you return to Egypt, see that you perform before Pharaoh all the wonders I have given you the power to do. But I will harden his heart so that he will not let the people go. Then say to Pharaoh, 'This is what the LORD says: Israel is my firstborn son, and I told you, "Let my son go, so he may worship me." But you refused to let him go; so I will kill your firstborn son.'"

The LORD said to Aaron, "Go into the desert to meet Moses." So he met Moses at the mountain of God and kissed him. Then Moses told Aaron everything the LORD had sent him to say, and also about all the miraculous signs he had commanded him to perform.

Moses and Aaron brought together all the elders of the Israelites, and Aaron told them everything the LORD had said to Moses. He also performed the signs before the people, and they believed. And when they heard that the LORD was concerned about them and had seen their misery, they bowed down and worshiped.

Afterward Moses and Aaron went to Pharaoh and said, "This is what the LORD, the God of Israel, says: 'Let my people go, so that they may hold a festival to me in the desert.'"

Pharaoh said, "Who is the LORD, that I should obey him and let Israel go? I do not know the LORD and I will not let Israel go."

EXODUS 4:21-23, 27-31; 5:1-2

Related texts: EXODUS 1:8-13; 9:13-16; PROVERBS 29:1-2; JOHN 10:33-38

God Hardens Pharaoh's Heart

**THE ONE
MINUTE
BIBLE**

Then the LORD said to Moses, "See, I have made you like God to Pharaoh, and your brother Aaron will be your prophet. You are to say everything I command you, and your brother Aaron is to tell Pharaoh to let the Israelites go out of his country. But I will harden Pharaoh's heart, and though I multiply my miraculous signs and wonders in Egypt, he will not listen to you. Then I will lay my hand on Egypt and with mighty acts of judgment I will bring out my divisions, my people the Israelites. And the Egyptians will know that I am the LORD when I stretch out my hand against Egypt and bring the Israelites out of it."

The LORD said to Moses and Aaron, "When Pharaoh says to you, 'Perform a miracle,' then say to Aaron, 'Take your staff and throw it down before Pharaoh,' and it will become a snake."

So Moses and Aaron went to Pharaoh and did just as the LORD commanded. Aaron threw his staff down in front of Pharaoh and his officials, and it became a snake. Pharaoh then summoned wise men and sorcerers, and the Egyptian magicians also did the same things by their secret arts: Each one threw down his staff and it became a snake. But Aaron's staff swallowed up their staffs. Yet Pharaoh's heart became hard and he would not listen to them, just as the LORD had said.

EXODUS 7:1-5, 8-13

Related texts: EXODUS 8:7, 18-19; ROMANS 9:14-21; 2 TIMOTHY 3:8-9

The Plagues Against Egypt

**THE ONE
MINUTE
BIBLE**

O my people, hear my teaching;
    listen to the words of my mouth.
I will open my mouth in parables,
    I will utter hidden things, things from of old—
what we have heard and known,
    what our fathers have told us.
We will not hide them from their children;
    we will tell the next generation
the praiseworthy deeds of the LORD,
    his power, and the wonders he has done.

The day he displayed his miraculous signs in Egypt,
    his wonders in the region of Zoan.
He turned their rivers to blood;
    they could not drink from their streams.
He sent swarms of flies that devoured them,
    and frogs that devastated them.
He gave their crops to the grasshopper,
    their produce to the locust.
He destroyed their vines with hail
    and their sycamore-figs with sleet.
He gave over their cattle to the hail,
    their livestock to bolts of lightning.
He unleashed against them his hot anger,
    his wrath, indignation and hostility—
    a band of destroying angels.
He prepared a path for his anger;
    he did not spare them from death
    but gave them over to the plague.
He struck down all the firstborn of Egypt,
    the firstfruits of manhood in the tents of Ham.

PSALM 78:1-4, 43-51

Related texts: EXODUS 7:15–10:29; DEUTERONOMY 4:32-38;
1 SAMUEL 4:2-8; ACTS 7:30-36

God Kills the Firstborn in Egypt

Now the LORD had said to Moses, "I will bring one more plague on Pharaoh and on Egypt. After that, he will let you go from here, and when he does, he will drive you out completely. Tell the people that men and women alike are to ask their neighbors for articles of silver and gold." (The LORD made the Egyptians favorably disposed toward the people, and Moses himself was highly regarded in Egypt by Pharaoh's officials and by the people.)

So Moses said, "This is what the LORD says: 'About midnight I will go throughout Egypt. Every firstborn son in Egypt will die, from the firstborn son of Pharaoh, who sits on the throne, to the firstborn son of the slave girl, who is at her hand mill, and all the firstborn of the cattle as well. There will be loud wailing throughout Egypt— worse than there has ever been or ever will be again. But among the Israelites not a dog will bark at any man or animal.' Then you will know that the LORD makes a distinction between Egypt and Israel. All these officials of yours will come to me, bowing down before me and saying, 'Go, you and all the people who follow you!' After that I will leave." Then Moses, hot with anger, left Pharaoh.

The LORD had said to Moses, "Pharaoh will refuse to listen to you—so that my wonders may be multiplied in Egypt." Moses and Aaron performed all these wonders before Pharaoh, but the LORD hardened Pharaoh's heart, and he would not let the Israelites go out of his country.

EXODUS 11:1-10

Related texts: EXODUS 4:22-23; PSALMS 105:23-38; 135:8-9; 136:10-12; ROMANS 9:14-21; HEBREWS 11:28

I never omit to read it, and every day with the same pleasure.... The soul can never go astray with this book for its guide.
Napoleon Bonaparte (1769-1821)
EMPEROR OF FRANCE

It ain't those parts of the Bible that I can't understand that bother me, it is the parts that I do understand.
Mark Twain (1835-1910)
AMERICAN AUTHOR

No sciences are better attested than the religion of the Bible.
Sir Isaac Newton (1642-1727)
ENGLISH SCIENTIST

The First Passover

**THE ONE
MINUTE
BIBLE**

Then Moses summoned all the elders of Israel and said to them, "Go at once and select the animals for your families and slaughter the Passover lamb. Take a bunch of hyssop, dip it into the blood in the basin and put some of the blood on the top and on both sides of the doorframe. Not one of you shall go out the door of his house until morning. When the LORD goes through the land to strike down the Egyptians, he will see the blood on the top and sides of the doorframe and will pass over that doorway, and he will not permit the destroyer to enter your houses and strike you down.

"Obey these instructions as a lasting ordinance for you and your descendants. When you enter the land that the LORD will give you as he promised, observe this ceremony. And when your children ask you, 'What does this ceremony mean to you?' then tell them, 'It is the Passover sacrifice to the LORD, who passed over the houses of the Israelites in Egypt and spared our homes when he struck down the Egyptians.'" Then the people bowed down and worshiped. The Israelites did just what the LORD commanded Moses and Aaron.

EXODUS 12:21-28

Related texts: NUMBERS 9:1-14; DEUTERONOMY 16:1-8; 2 CHRONICLES 30; 1 CORINTHIANS 5:6-8

The Prophecy of the Suffering Servant

**THE ONE
MINUTE
BIBLE**

See, my servant will act wisely;
    he will be raised and lifted up and highly exalted.

He was despised and rejected by men,
    a man of sorrows, and familiar with suffering.
Like one from whom men hide their faces
    he was despised, and we esteemed him not.

Surely he took up our infirmities
    and carried our sorrows,
yet we considered him stricken by God,
    smitten by him, and afflicted.
But he was pierced for our transgressions,
    he was crushed for our iniquities;
the punishment that brought us peace was upon him,
    and by his wounds we are healed.
We all, like sheep, have gone astray,
    each of us has turned to his own way;
and the LORD has laid on him
    the iniquity of us all.

He was oppressed and afflicted,
    yet he did not open his mouth;
he was led like a lamb to the slaughter,
    and as a sheep before her shearers is silent,
    so he did not open his mouth.

Yet it was the LORD's will to crush him and cause him
      to suffer,
    and though the LORD makes his life a guilt offering,
he will see his offspring and prolong his days,
    and the will of the LORD will prosper in his hand.

ISAIAH 52:13; 53:3-7, 10

Related texts: PSALM 22; MARK 10:45; ACTS 8:26-39; 1 PETER 2:21-25

Jesus: The Lamb of God

The next day John saw Jesus coming toward him and said, "Look, the Lamb of God, who takes away the sin of the world! This is the one I meant when I said, 'A man who comes after me has surpassed me because he was before me.' I myself did not know him, but the reason I came baptizing with water was that he might be revealed to Israel."

Then John gave this testimony: "I saw the Spirit come down from heaven as a dove and remain on him. I would not have known him, except that the one who sent me to baptize with water told me, 'The man on whom you see the Spirit come down and remain is he who will baptize with the Holy Spirit.' I have seen and I testify that this is the Son of God."

Then I looked and heard the voice of many angels, numbering thousands upon thousands, and ten thousand times ten thousand. They encircled the throne and the living creatures and the elders. In a loud voice they sang:

"Worthy is the Lamb, who was slain,
to receive power and wealth and wisdom and strength and honor and glory and praise!"

JOHN 1:29-34; REVELATION 5:11-12

Related texts: GENESIS 22:1-19; HEBREWS 9:11-28; 1 PETER 1:18-20; REVELATION 5–7; 21:9–22:4

Jesus Predicts His Resurrection

**THE ONE
MINUTE
BIBLE**

Jesus called them together and said, "You know that those who are regarded as rulers of the Gentiles lord it over them, and their high officials exercise authority over them. Not so with you. Instead, whoever wants to become great among you must be your servant, and whoever wants to be first must be slave of all. For even the Son of Man did not come to be served, but to serve, and to give his life as a ransom for many."

Once when Jesus was praying in private and his disciples were with him, he asked them, "Who do the crowds say I am?"

They replied, "Some say John the Baptist; others say Elijah; and still others, that one of the prophets of long ago has come back to life."

"But what about you?" he asked. "Who do you say I am?"

Peter answered, "The Christ of God."

Jesus strictly warned them not to tell this to anyone. And he said, "The Son of Man must suffer many things and be rejected by the elders, chief priests and teachers of the law, and he must be killed and on the third day be raised to life."

MARK 10:42-45; LUKE 9:18-22

Related texts: PSALM 16; MATTHEW 12:38-41; MARK 10:32-34;
LUKE 24:13-32; ACTS 2:14-40

Jesus' Triumphal Entry

**THE ONE
MINUTE
BIBLE**

As they approached Jerusalem and came to Bethphage on the Mount of Olives, Jesus sent two disciples, saying to them, "Go to the village ahead of you, and at once you will find a donkey tied there, with her colt by her. Untie them and bring them to me. If anyone says anything to you, tell him that the Lord needs them, and he will send them right away."

This took place to fulfill what was spoken through the prophet:

"Say to the Daughter of Zion,
'See, your king comes to you,
gentle and riding on a donkey,
on a colt, the foal of a donkey.'"

The disciples went and did as Jesus had instructed them. They brought the donkey and the colt, placed their cloaks on them, and Jesus sat on them. A very large crowd spread their cloaks on the road, while others cut branches from the trees and spread them on the road. The crowds that went ahead of him and those that followed shouted,

"Hosanna to the Son of David!"

"Blessed is he who comes in the name of the Lord!"

"Hosanna in the highest!"

When Jesus entered Jerusalem, the whole city was stirred and asked, "Who is this?"

The crowds answered, "This is Jesus, the prophet from Nazareth in Galilee."

MATTHEW 21:1-11

Related texts: PSALM 118; ZECHARIAH 9:9; MARK 11:1-11; LUKE 19:28-40; JOHN 12:12-16

Jesus Cleanses the Temple

**THE ONE
MINUTE
BIBLE**

As Jesus approached Jerusalem and saw the city, he wept over it and said, "If you, even you, had only known on this day what would bring you peace—but now it is hidden from your eyes. The days will come upon you when your enemies will build an embankment against you and encircle you and hem you in on every side. They will dash you to the ground, you and the children within your walls. They will not leave one stone on another, because you did not recognize the time of God's coming to you."

Jesus entered the temple area and drove out all who were buying and selling there. He overturned the tables of the money changers and the benches of those selling doves. "It is written," he said to them, "'My house will be called a house of prayer,' but you are making it a 'den of robbers.'"

The blind and the lame came to him at the temple, and he healed them. But when the chief priests and the teachers of the law saw the wonderful things he did and the children shouting in the temple area, "Hosanna to the Son of David," they were indignant.

"Do you hear what these children are saying?" they asked him.

"Yes," replied Jesus, "have you never read,

"'From the lips of children and infants
    you have ordained praise'?"

LUKE 19:41-44; MATTHEW 21:12-16

Related texts: PSALM 8; ISAIAH 56; JEREMIAH 7:9-11; MARK 11:15-18; JOHN 2:13-17

Whose Son Is the Messiah?

THE ONE
MINUTE
BIBLE

While the Pharisees were gathered together, Jesus asked them, "What do you think about the Christ? Whose son is he?"

"The son of David," they replied.

He said to them, "How is it then that David, speaking by the Spirit, calls him 'Lord'? For he says,

"'The Lord said to my Lord:

"Sit at my right hand
until I put your enemies
under your feet."'

If then David calls him 'Lord,' how can he be his son?" No one could say a word in reply, and from that day on no one dared to ask him any more questions.

After six days Jesus took Peter, James and John with him and led them up a high mountain, where they were all alone. There he was transfigured before them.

Then a cloud appeared and enveloped them, and a voice came from the cloud: "This is my Son, whom I love. Listen to him!"

We did not follow cleverly invented stories when we told you about the power and coming of our Lord Jesus Christ, but we were eyewitnesses of his majesty. For he received honor and glory from God the Father when the voice came to him from the Majestic Glory, saying, "This is my Son, whom I love; with him I am well pleased."

MATTHEW 22:41-46; MARK 9:2, 7; 2 PETER 1:16-17

Related texts: PSALM 110; MATTHEW 27:45-54; MARK 1:9-11;
LUKE 9:28-36; ACTS 2

The Last Supper

**THE ONE
MINUTE
BIBLE**

Then came the day of Unleavened Bread on which the Passover lamb had to be sacrificed. Jesus sent Peter and John, saying, "Go and make preparations for us to eat the Passover."

When the hour came, Jesus and his apostles reclined at the table. And he said to them, "I have eagerly desired to eat this Passover with you before I suffer. For I tell you, I will not eat it again until it finds fulfillment in the kingdom of God."

After taking the cup, he gave thanks and said, "Take this and divide it among you. For I tell you I will not drink again of the fruit of the vine until the kingdom of God comes."

And he took bread, gave thanks and broke it, and gave it to them, saying, "This is my body given for you; do this in remembrance of me."

In the same way, after the supper he took the cup, saying, "This cup is the new covenant in my blood, which is poured out for you. But the hand of him who is going to betray me is with mine on the table. The Son of Man will go as it has been decreed, but woe to that man who betrays him."

LUKE 22:7-8, 14-22

Related texts: JEREMIAH 31:31-36; MATTHEW 26:17-30; MARK 14:12-26; REVELATION 19:4-9

Jesus Is Betrayed

**THE ONE
MINUTE
BIBLE**

When he had finished praying, Jesus left with his disciples and crossed the Kidron Valley. On the other side there was an olive grove, and he and his disciples went into it.

Now Judas, who betrayed him, knew the place, because Jesus had often met there with his disciples. So Judas came to the grove, guiding a detachment of soldiers and some officials from the chief priests and Pharisees. They were carrying torches, lanterns and weapons.

Jesus, knowing all that was going to happen to him, went out and asked them, "Who is it you want?"

"Jesus of Nazareth," they replied.

"I am he," Jesus said. (And Judas the traitor was standing there with them.) When Jesus said, "I am he," they drew back and fell to the ground.

Again he asked them, "Who is it you want?"

And they said, "Jesus of Nazareth."

"I told you that I am he," Jesus answered. "If you are looking for me, then let these men go." This happened so that the words he had spoken would be fulfilled: "I have not lost one of those you gave me."

JOHN 18:1-9

Related texts: GENESIS 37; MATTHEW 26:47-56; MARK 14:43-50; LUKE 22:47-54; JOHN 6:35-40; 17:1-12

Jesus Is Condemned to Death

THE ONE
MINUTE
BIBLE

The chief priests and the whole Sanhedrin were looking for false evidence against Jesus so that they could put him to death. But they did not find any, though many false witnesses came forward.

Finally two came forward and declared, "This fellow said, 'I am able to destroy the temple of God and rebuild it in three days.'"

Then the high priest stood up and said to Jesus, "Are you not going to answer? What is this testimony that these men are bringing against you?" But Jesus remained silent.

The high priest said to him, "I charge you under oath by the living God: Tell us if you are the Christ, the Son of God."

"Yes, it is as you say," Jesus replied. "But I say to all of you: In the future you will see the Son of Man sitting at the right hand of the Mighty One and coming on the clouds of heaven."

Then the high priest tore his clothes and said, "He has spoken blasphemy! Why do we need any more witnesses? Look, now you have heard the blasphemy. What do you think?"

"He is worthy of death," they answered.

Then they spit in his face and struck him with their fists. Others slapped him and said, "Prophesy to us, Christ. Who hit you?"

MATTHEW 26:59-68

Related texts: LEVITICUS 24:13-16; DANIEL 7:13-14; MARK 14:55-65; LUKE 23:63-71

Jesus Is Crucified

**THE ONE
MINUTE
BIBLE**

They brought Jesus to the place called Golgotha (which means The Place of the Skull). Then they offered him wine mixed with myrrh, but he did not take it. And they crucified him. Dividing up his clothes, they cast lots to see what each would get.

It was the third hour when they crucified him. The written notice of the charge against him read: THE KING OF THE JEWS. They crucified two robbers with him, one on his right and one on his left. Those who passed by hurled insults at him, shaking their heads and saying, "So! You who are going to destroy the temple and build it in three days, come down from the cross and save yourself!"

In the same way the chief priests and the teachers of the law mocked him among themselves. "He saved others," they said, "but he can't save himself! Let this Christ, this King of Israel, come down now from the cross, that we may see and believe." Those crucified with him also heaped insults on him.

With a loud cry, Jesus breathed his last.

The curtain of the temple was torn in two from top to bottom. And when the centurion, who stood there in front of Jesus, heard his cry and saw how he died, he said, "Surely this man was the Son of God!"

MARK 15:22-32, 37-39

Related texts: PSALM 22; ISAIAH 53; MATTHEW 27:33-56; LUKE 23:26-48; JOHN 3:13-16; 19:16-37

Alive Again!

**THE ONE
MINUTE
BIBLE**

After the Sabbath, at dawn on the first day of the week, Mary Magdalene and the other Mary went to look at the tomb.

There was a violent earthquake, for an angel of the Lord came down from heaven and, going to the tomb, rolled back the stone and sat on it. His appearance was like lightning, and his clothes were white as snow. The guards were so afraid of him that they shook and became like dead men.

The angel said to the women, "Do not be afraid, for I know that you are looking for Jesus, who was crucified. He is not here; he has risen, just as he said. Come and see the place where he lay. Then go quickly and tell his disciples: 'He has risen from the dead and is going ahead of you into Galilee. There you will see him.' Now I have told you."

So the women hurried away from the tomb, afraid yet filled with joy, and ran to tell his disciples. Suddenly Jesus met them. "Greetings," he said. They came to him, clasped his feet and worshiped him. Then Jesus said to them, "Do not be afraid. Go and tell my brothers to go to Galilee; there they will see me."

MATTHEW 28:1-10

Related texts: PSALM 16:8-11; MARK 16:1-8; LUKE 24:1-10; JOHN 20:1-18; 1 CORINTHIANS 15

The All-Importance of the Resurrection

But if it is preached that Christ has been raised from the dead, how can some of you say that there is no resurrection of the dead? If there is no resurrection of the dead, then not even Christ has been raised. And if Christ has not been raised, our preaching is useless and so is your faith. More than that, we are then found to be false witnesses about God, for we have testified about God that he raised Christ from the dead. But he did not raise him if in fact the dead are not raised. For if the dead are not raised, then Christ has not been raised either. And if Christ has not been raised, your faith is futile; you are still in your sins. Then those also who have fallen asleep in Christ are lost. If only for this life we have hope in Christ, we are to be pitied more than all men.

But Christ has indeed been raised from the dead, the firstfruits of those who have fallen asleep. For since death came through a man, the resurrection of the dead comes also through a man. For as in Adam all die, so in Christ all will be made alive.

1 CORINTHIANS 15:12-22

THE ONE MINUTE BIBLE

Related texts: JOB 19:23-27; 1 CORINTHIANS 15:23-58; ROMANS 6:1-11; ACTS 2:22-36

Jesus Christ: Our Passover

THE ONE MINUTE BIBLE

Your boasting is not good. Don't you know that a little yeast works through the whole batch of dough? Get rid of the old yeast that you may be a new batch without yeast—as you really are. For Christ, our Passover lamb, has been sacrificed. Therefore let us keep the Festival, not with the old yeast, the yeast of malice and wickedness, but with bread without yeast, the bread of sincerity and truth.

Since you call on a Father who judges each man's work impartially, live your lives as strangers here in reverent fear. For you know that it was not with perishable things such as silver or gold that you were redeemed from the empty way of life handed down to you from your forefathers, but with the precious blood of Christ, a lamb without blemish or defect. He was chosen before the creation of the world, but was revealed in these last times for your sake. Through him you believe in God, who raised him from the dead and glorified him, and so your faith and hope are in God.

Now that you have purified yourselves by obeying the truth so that you have sincere love for your brothers, love one another deeply, from the heart.

1 CORINTHIANS 5:6-8; 1 PETER 1:17-22

Related texts: EXODUS 12–13; JOHN 1:19-36; HEBREWS 2:11-18; REVELATION 13:8

The Israelites Leave Egypt

**THE ONE
MINUTE
BIBLE**

At midnight the LORD struck down all the firstborn in Egypt, from the firstborn of Pharaoh, who sat on the throne, to the firstborn of the prisoner, who was in the dungeon, and the firstborn of all the livestock as well. Pharaoh and all his officials and all the Egyptians got up during the night, and there was loud wailing in Egypt, for there was not a house without someone dead.

During the night Pharaoh summoned Moses and Aaron and said, "Up! Leave my people, you and the Israelites! Go, worship the LORD as you have requested. Take your flocks and herds, as you have said, and go. And also bless me."

The Egyptians urged the people to hurry and leave the country. "For otherwise," they said, "we will all die!" So the people took their dough before the yeast was added, and carried it on their shoulders in kneading troughs wrapped in clothing. The Israelites did as Moses instructed and asked the Egyptians for articles of silver and gold and for clothing. The LORD had made the Egyptians favorably disposed toward the people, and they gave them what they asked for; so they plundered the Egyptians.

By day the LORD went ahead of them in a pillar of cloud to guide them on their way and by night in a pillar of fire to give them light, so that they could travel by day or night. Neither the pillar of cloud by day nor the pillar of fire by night left its place in front of the people.

EXODUS 12:29-36; 13:21-22

Related texts: DEUTERONOMY 16:1-8; PSALM 78:41-52; 105:26-38; 2 THESSALONIANS 1:5-10

Pharaoh Pursues the Israelites

**THE ONE
MINUTE
BIBLE**

The Egyptians—all Pharaoh's horses and chariots, horsemen and troops—pursued the Israelites and overtook them as they camped by the sea near Pi Hahiroth, opposite Baal Zephon.

As Pharaoh approached, the Israelites looked up, and there were the Egyptians, marching after them. They were terrified and cried out to the LORD. They said to Moses, "Was it because there were no graves in Egypt that you brought us to the desert to die? What have you done to us by bringing us out of Egypt? Didn't we say to you in Egypt, 'Leave us alone; let us serve the Egyptians'? It would have been better for us to serve the Egyptians than to die in the desert!"

Moses answered the people, "Do not be afraid. Stand firm and you will see the deliverance the LORD will bring you today. The Egyptians you see today you will never see again. The LORD will fight for you; you need only to be still."

Then the LORD said to Moses, "Why are you crying out to me? Tell the Israelites to move on. Raise your staff and stretch out your hand over the sea to divide the water so that the Israelites can go through the sea on dry ground. I will harden the hearts of the Egyptians so that they will go in after them. And I will gain glory through Pharaoh and all his army, through his chariots and his horsemen. The Egyptians will know that I am the LORD when I gain glory through Pharaoh, his chariots and his horsemen."

EXODUS 14:9-18

Related texts: PSALM 37:7; 46:10; ISAIAH 59:1; ROMANS 9:14-24; HEBREWS 11:1-2

Crossing the Red Sea

Then Moses stretched out his hand over the sea, and all that night the LORD drove the sea back with a strong east wind and turned it into dry land. The waters were divided, and the Israelites went through the sea on dry ground, with a wall of water on their right and on their left.

The Egyptians pursued them, and all Pharaoh's horses and chariots and horsemen followed them into the sea. During the last watch of the night the LORD looked down from the pillar of fire and cloud at the Egyptian army and threw it into confusion. He made the wheels of their chariots come off so that they had difficulty driving. And the Egyptians said, "Let's get away from the Israelites! The LORD is fighting for them against Egypt."

Then the LORD said to Moses, "Stretch out your hand over the sea so that the waters may flow back over the Egyptians and their chariots and horsemen." Moses stretched out his hand over the sea, and at daybreak the sea went back to its place. The Egyptians were fleeing toward it, and the LORD swept them into the sea. The water flowed back and covered the chariots and horsemen—the entire army of Pharaoh that had followed the Israelites into the sea. Not one of them survived.

EXODUS 14:21-28

Related texts: PSALMS 114; 136:13-15; DEUTERONOMY 11:1-4; JOSHUA 24:5-7; HEBREWS 11:23-29

The LORD Is a Warrior

**THE ONE
MINUTE
BIBLE**

That day the LORD saved Israel from the hands of the Egyptians, and Israel saw the Egyptians lying dead on the shore. And when the Israelites saw the great power the LORD displayed against the Egyptians, the people feared the LORD and put their trust in him and in Moses his servant.

Then Moses and the Israelites sang this song to the LORD:

"I will sing to the LORD,
    for he is highly exalted.
The horse and its rider
    he has hurled into the sea.
The LORD is my strength and my song;
    he has become my salvation.
He is my God, and I will praise him,
    my father's God, and I will exalt him.
The LORD is a warrior;
    the LORD is his name.
Pharaoh's chariots and his army
    he has hurled into the sea.
The best of Pharaoh's officers
    are drowned in the Red Sea.
"Who among the gods is like you, O LORD?
    Who is like you—
        majestic in holiness,
        awesome in glory,
        working wonders?
"In your unfailing love you will lead
    the people you have redeemed.
In your strength you will guide them
    to your holy dwelling.
The LORD will reign
    for ever and ever."

EXODUS 14:30-31; 15:1-4, 11, 13, 18

Related texts: PSALM 136; EPHESIANS 5:19-20; REVELATION 15:2-4

God's Care in the Desert

Give thanks to the LORD, call on his name;
    make known among the nations what he has done.
Sing to him, sing praise to him;
    tell of all his wonderful acts.
Glory in his holy name;
    let the hearts of those who seek the LORD rejoice.
Look to the LORD and his strength;
    seek his face always.

Remember the wonders he has done,
    his miracles, and the judgments he pronounced,
O descendants of Abraham his servant,
    O sons of Jacob, his chosen ones.

He brought out Israel, laden with silver and gold,
    and from among their tribes no one faltered.
Egypt was glad when they left,
    because dread of Israel had fallen on them.
He spread out a cloud as a covering,
    and a fire to give light at night.
They asked, and he brought them quail
    and satisfied them with the bread of heaven.
He opened the rock, and water gushed out;
    like a river it flowed in the desert.
For he remembered his holy promise
    given to his servant Abraham.
He brought out his people with rejoicing,
    his chosen ones with shouts of joy;
he gave them the lands of the nations,
    and they fell heir to what others had toiled for—
that they might keep his precepts
    and observe his laws.
Praise the LORD.

PSALM 105:1-6, 37-48

Related texts: GENESIS 15; EXODUS 15:19–18:27; JOHN 6; ACTS 7:36-38;
1 CORINTHIANS 10:1-4

God Makes a Covenant With Israel

**THE ONE
MINUTE
BIBLE**

In the third month after the Israelites left Egypt—on the very day—they came to the Desert of Sinai. After they set out from Rephidim, they entered the Desert of Sinai, and Israel camped there in the desert in front of the mountain.

Then Moses went up to God, and the LORD called to him from the mountain and said, "This is what you are to say to the house of Jacob and what you are to tell the people of Israel: 'You yourselves have seen what I did to Egypt, and how I carried you on eagles' wings and brought you to myself. Now if you obey me fully and keep my covenant, then out of all nations you will be my treasured possession. Although the whole earth is mine, you will be for me a kingdom of priests and a holy nation.' These are the words you are to speak to the Israelites."

So Moses went back and summoned the elders of the people and set before them all the words the LORD had commanded him to speak. The people all responded together, "We will do everything the LORD has said." So Moses brought their answer back to the LORD.

The LORD said to Moses, "I am going to come to you in a dense cloud, so that the people will hear me speaking with you and will always put their trust in you." Then Moses told the LORD what the people had said.

EXODUS 19:1-9

Related texts: DEUTERONOMY 4:1-20; JEREMIAH 31:31-34; HEBREWS 8

The Ten Commandments: *No Other Gods*

THE ONE
MINUTE
BIBLE

> I am the LORD your God, who brought you out of
>   Egypt out of the land of slavery.
> You shall have no other gods before me.

Sing to the LORD, all the earth;
    proclaim his salvation day after day.
Declare his glory among the nations,
    his marvelous deeds among all peoples.
For great is the LORD and most worthy of praise;
    he is to be feared above all gods.
For all the gods of the nations are idols,
    but the LORD made the heavens.
Splendor and majesty are before him;
    strength and joy in his dwelling place.
Ascribe to the LORD, O families of nations,
    ascribe to the LORD glory and strength,
    ascribe to the LORD the glory due his name.
Bring an offering and come before him;
    worship the LORD in the splendor of his holiness.
Tremble before him, all the earth!
    The world is firmly established; it cannot be moved.
Let the heavens rejoice, let the earth be glad;
    let them say among the nations, "The LORD reigns!"

EXODUS 20:2-3; 1 CHRONICLES 16:23-31

Related texts: EXODUS 18:8-10; DEUTERONOMY 4:32-39; 5:1-21; 13:1-16;
ISAIAH 37:15-20; EPHESIANS 4:4-6

The Ten Commandments: *No Idols*

**THE ONE
MINUTE
BIBLE**

You shall not make for yourself an idol in the
form of anything in heaven above or on the
earth beneath or in the waters below. You shall
not bow down to them or worship them; for I,
the LORD your God, am a jealous God, punishing
the children for the sin of the fathers to the
third and fourth generation of those who
hate me, but showing love to a thousand
[generations] of those who love me and keep
my commandments.

Not to us, O LORD, not to us
but to your name be the glory,
because of your love and faithfulness.

Why do the nations say,
"Where is their God?"
Our God is in heaven;
he does whatever pleases him.
But their idols are silver and gold,
made by the hands of men.
They have mouths, but cannot speak,
eyes, but they cannot see;
they have ears, but cannot hear,
noses, but they cannot smell;
they have hands, but cannot feel,
feet, but they cannot walk;
nor can they utter a sound with their throats.
Those who make them will be like them,
and so will all who trust in them.

EXODUS 20:4-6; PSALM 115:1-8

Related texts: DEUTERONOMY 7; ISAIAH 44:6-19; JEREMIAH 10:1-16;
16:19-21; MATTHEW 6:19-24; 1 JOHN 5:21

The Ten Commandments: *God's Name*

You shall not misuse the name of the LORD your
God, for the LORD will not hold anyone guiltless
who misuses his name.

Now the son of an Israelite mother and an Egyptian
father went out among the Israelites, and a fight broke
out in the camp between him and an Israelite. The son
of the Israelite woman blasphemed the Name with a
curse; so they brought him to Moses. (His mother's
name was Shelomith, the daughter of Dibri the Danite.)
They put him in custody until the will of the LORD should
be made clear to them.

Then the LORD said to Moses: "Take the blasphemer
outside the camp. All those who heard him are to lay
their hands on his head, and the entire assembly is to
stone him. Say to the Israelites: 'If anyone curses his
God, he will be held responsible; anyone who
blasphemes the name of the LORD must be put to death.
The entire assembly must stone him. Whether an alien
or native-born, when he blasphemes the Name, he must
be put to death.'"

The name of the LORD is a strong tower;
the righteous run to it and are safe.

EXODUS 20:7; LEVITICUS 24:10-16; PROVERBS 18:10

Related texts: EXODUS 3:13-15; PSALMS 20; 86:5-12; ACTS 4:5-12

The Ten Commandments: *The Sabbath*

**THE ONE
MINUTE
BIBLE**

Remember the Sabbath day by keeping it holy. Six days you shall labor and do all your work, but the seventh day is a Sabbath to the LORD your God. On it you shall not do any work, neither you, nor your son or daughter, nor your manservant or maidservant, nor your animals, nor the alien within your gates. For in six days the LORD made the heavens and the earth, the sea, and all that is in them, but he rested on the seventh day. Therefore the LORD blessed the Sabbath day and made it holy.

Going on from that place, Jesus went into their synagogue, and a man with a shriveled hand was there. Looking for a reason to accuse Jesus, they asked him, "Is it lawful to heal on the Sabbath?"

He said to them, "If any of you has a sheep and it falls into a pit on the Sabbath, will you not take hold of it and lift it out? How much more valuable is a man than a sheep! Therefore it is lawful to do good on the Sabbath."

Then he said to the man, "Stretch out your hand." So he stretched it out and it was completely restored, just as sound as the other.

EXODUS 20:8-11; MATTHEW 12:9-13

Related texts: GENESIS 2:1-3; EXODUS 16:11-30; PSALM 62:1-5;
MARK 2:23-28; HEBREWS 4:1-4

124

The Ten Commandments: *Parents*

Honor your father and your mother, so that you may live long in the land the LORD your God is giving you.

Anyone who attacks his father or his mother must be put to death.

If anyone curses his father or mother, he must be put to death. He has cursed his father or his mother, and his blood will be on his own head.

The proverbs of Solomon:
A wise son brings joy to his father,
but a foolish son grief to his mother.

Listen to your father, who gave you life,
and do not despise your mother when she is old.
Buy the truth and do not sell it;
get wisdom, discipline and understanding.
The father of a righteous man has great joy;
he who has a wise son delights in him.
May your father and mother be glad;
may she who gave you birth rejoice!

Children, obey your parents in the Lord, for this is right. "Honor your father and mother"—which is the first commandment with a promise—"that it may go well with you and that you may enjoy long life on the earth."

EXODUS 20:12; 21:15; LEVITICUS 20:9; PROVERBS 10:1; 23:22-25;
EPHESIANS 6:1-3

THE ONE MINUTE BIBLE

Related texts: MALACHI 4:5-6; COLOSSIANS 3:20-21; 2 TIMOTHY 3:1-5;
TITUS 1:6-9

The Ten Commandments: *Murder*

**THE ONE
MINUTE
BIBLE**

You shall not murder.

Whoever sheds the blood of man,
    by man shall his blood be shed;
for in the image of God
    has God made man.

[Jesus said,] "You have heard that it was said to the people long ago, 'Do not murder, and anyone who murders will be subject to judgment.' But I tell you that anyone who is angry with his brother will be subject to judgment. Again, anyone who says to his brother, 'Raca,' is answerable to the Sanhedrin. But anyone who says, 'You fool!' will be in danger of the fire of hell."

This is the message you heard from the beginning: We should love one another. Do not be like Cain, who belonged to the evil one and murdered his brother. And why did he murder him? Because his own actions were evil and his brother's were righteous. Do not be surprised, my brothers, if the world hates you. We know that we have passed from death to life, because we love our brothers. Anyone who does not love remains in death. Anyone who hates his brother is a murderer, and you know that no murderer has eternal life in him.

This is how we know what love is: Jesus Christ laid down his life for us. And we ought to lay down our lives for our brothers.

EXODUS 20:13; GENESIS 9:6; MATTHEW 5:21-22; 1 JOHN 3:11-16

Related texts: GENESIS 4:1-16; NUMBERS 35:9-34; MATTHEW 15:10-20; JOHN 8:42-44; ROMANS 1:28-32

The Ten Commandments: *Adultery*

**THE ONE
MINUTE
BIBLE**

You shall not commit adultery.

Why be captivated, my son, by an adulteress?
    Why embrace the bosom of another man's wife?
For a man's ways are in full view of the LORD,
    and he examines all his paths.
The evil deeds of a wicked man ensnare him;
    the cords of his sin hold him fast.
He will die for lack of discipline,
    led astray by his own great folly.

[Jesus said,] "You have heard that it was said, 'Do not commit adultery.' But I tell you that anyone who looks at a woman lustfully has already committed adultery with her in his heart."

Do you not know that the wicked will not inherit the kingdom of God? Do not be deceived: Neither the sexually immoral nor idolaters nor adulterers nor male prostitutes nor homosexual offenders nor thieves nor the greedy nor drunkards nor slanderers nor swindlers will inherit the kingdom of God. And that is what some of you were. But you were washed, you were sanctified, you were justified in the name of the Lord Jesus Christ and by the Spirit of our God.

Marriage should be honored by all, and the marriage bed kept pure, for God will judge the adulterer and all the sexually immoral.

EXODUS 20:14; PROVERBS 5:20-23; MATTHEW 5:27-28;
1 CORINTHIANS 6:9-11; HEBREWS 13:4

Related texts: PROVERBS 5:1-19; 6:20-35; ROMANS 1:18-27;
EPHESIANS 4:17-24; COLOSSIANS 3:1-7; 1 THESSALONIANS 4:3-8

The Ten Commandments: *Stealing*

**THE ONE
MINUTE
BIBLE**

You shall not steal.

Do not trust in extortion
    or take pride in stolen goods;
though your riches increase,
    do not set your heart on them.
One thing God has spoken,
    two things have I heard:
that you, O God, are strong,
    and that you, O Lord, are loving.
Surely you will reward each person
    according to what he has done.

Command those who are rich in this present world not to be arrogant nor to put their hope in wealth, which is so uncertain, but to put their hope in God, who richly provides us with everything for our enjoyment. Command them to do good, to be rich in good deeds, and to be generous and willing to share. In this way they will lay up treasure for themselves as a firm foundation for the coming age, so that they may take hold of the life that is truly life.

He who has been stealing must steal no longer, but must work, doing something useful with his own hands, that he may have something to share with those in need.

EXODUS 20:15; PSALM 62:10-12; 1 TIMOTHY 6:17-19; EPHESIANS 4:28

Related texts: PROVERBS 1:10-19; 10:2; ISAIAH 10:1-4; MALACHI 3:6-12; TITUS 2:9-10

The Ten Commandments: *False Testimony*

> You shall not give false testimony against your
> neighbor.

If a malicious witness takes the stand to accuse a
man of a crime, the two men involved in the dispute
must stand in the presence of the LORD before the
priests and the judges who are in office at the time. The
judges must make a thorough investigation, and if the
witness proves to be a liar, giving false testimony
against his brother, then do to him as he intended to do
to his brother. You must purge the evil from among you.
The rest of the people will hear of this and be afraid,
and never again will such an evil thing be done among
you.

LORD, who may dwell in your sanctuary?
    Who may live on your holy hill?
He whose walk is blameless
    and who does what is righteous,
who speaks the truth from his heart
    and has no slander on his tongue,
who does his neighbor no wrong
    and casts no slur on his fellowman,
who despises a vile man
    but honors those who fear the LORD,
who keeps his oath
    even when it hurts,
who lends his money without usury
    and does not accept a bribe against the innocent.
He who does these things
    will never be shaken.

EXODUS 20:16; DEUTERONOMY 19:16-20; PSALM 15

Related texts: PROVERBS 12:17-18; 25:18; ISAIAH 29:19-21;
MATTHEW 15:10-20; MARK 14:53-64

The Ten Commandments: *Coveting*

**THE ONE
MINUTE
BIBLE**

You shall not covet your neighbor's house. You
shall not covet your neighbor's wife, or his
manservant or maidservant, his ox or donkey, or
anything that belongs to your neighbor.

Let no debt remain outstanding, except the
continuing debt to love one another, for he who loves
his fellowman has fulfilled the law. The commandments,
"Do not commit adultery," "Do not murder," "Do not
steal," "Do not covet," and whatever other
commandment there may be, are summed up in this
one rule: "Love your neighbor as yourself." Love does no
harm to its neighbor. Therefore love is the fulfillment of
the law.

But godliness with contentment is great gain. For
we brought nothing into the world, and we can take
nothing out of it. But if we have food and clothing, we
will be content with that.

Keep your lives free from the love of money and be
content with what you have, because God has said,

"Never will I leave you;
never will I forsake you."

EXODUS 20:17; ROMANS 13:8-10; 1 TIMOTHY 6:6-8; HEBREWS 13:5

Related texts: DEUTERONOMY 31:6; PROVERBS 1:10-19;
PHILIPPIANS 4:11-12; 1 TIMOTHY 6:9-11; JAMES 4:1-3; 1 JOHN 2:15-17

*When I read...the Holy Scriptures...
all seems luminous, a single
word opens up infinite horizons
to my soul.*
St. Terese of Lisieux (1873-1897)
FRENCH NUN

*The highest earthly enjoyments
are but a shadow of the joy I
find in reading God's word.*
Lady Jane Grey (1537-1554)
QUEEN OF ENGLAND FOR NINE DAYS

*The most stupendous book, the most
sublime literature, even apart from
its sacred character, in the history
of the world.*
Blanche Mary Kelly (1881-1966)
AMERICAN AUTHOR

The Greatest Commandment

Hear, O Israel: The LORD our God, the LORD is one. Love the LORD your God with all your heart and with all your soul and with all your strength. These commandments that I give you today are to be upon your hearts. Impress them on your children. Talk about them when you sit at home and when you walk along the road, when you lie down and when you get up. Tie them as symbols on your hands and bind them on your foreheads. Write them on the doorframes of your houses and on your gates.

Do not seek revenge or bear a grudge against one of your people, but love your neighbor as yourself. I am the LORD.

When an alien lives with you in your land, do not mistreat him. The alien living with you must be treated as one of your native-born. Love him as yourself, for you were aliens in Egypt. I am the LORD your God.

"Teacher, which is the greatest commandment in the Law?"

Jesus replied: "'Love the Lord your God with all your heart and with all your soul and with all your mind.' This is the first and greatest commandment. And the second is like it: 'Love your neighbor as yourself.' All the Law and the Prophets hang on these two commandments."

DEUTERONOMY 6:4-9; LEVITICUS 19:18, 33-34; MATTHEW 22:36-40

THE ONE MINUTE BIBLE

Related texts: MICAH 6:8; MARK 12:28-31; LUKE 10:25-37; ACTS 4:32-35; ROMANS 13:8-10; 2 CORINTHIANS 8:13-15

The Law: *Widows, Orphans and Foreigners*

THE ONE MINUTE BIBLE

Do not take advantage of a widow or an orphan. If you do and they cry out to me, I will certainly hear their cry. My anger will be aroused, and I will kill you with the sword; your wives will become widows and your children fatherless.

Do not deprive the alien or the fatherless of justice, or take the cloak of the widow as a pledge. Remember that you were slaves in Egypt and the LORD your God redeemed you from there. That is why I command you to do this.

When you are harvesting in your field and you overlook a sheaf, do not go back to get it. Leave it for the alien, the fatherless and the widow, so that the LORD your God may bless you in all the work of your hands. When you beat the olives from your trees, do not go over the branches a second time. Leave what remains for the alien, the fatherless and the widow. When you harvest the grapes in your vineyard, do not go over the vines again. Leave what remains for the alien, the fatherless and the widow. Remember that you were slaves in Egypt. That is why I command you to do this.

Religion that God our Father accepts as pure and faultless is this: to look after orphans and widows in their distress and to keep oneself from being polluted by the world.

EXODUS 22:22-24; DEUTERONOMY 24:17-22; JAMES 1:27

Related texts: DEUTERONOMY 10:17-20; PSALMS 68:5; 146:9; 1 TIMOTHY 5:3-16

The Law: *Restitution*

If a man steals an ox or a sheep and slaughters it or sells it, he must pay back five head of cattle for the ox and four sheep for the sheep.

If a thief is caught breaking in and is struck so that he dies, the defender is not guilty of bloodshed; but if it happens after sunrise, he is guilty of bloodshed.

A thief must certainly make restitution, but if he has nothing, he must be sold to pay for his theft.

If the stolen animal is found alive in his possession—whether ox or donkey or sheep—he must pay back double.

If a man grazes his livestock in a field or vineyard and lets them stray and they graze in another man's field, he must make restitution from the best of his own field or vineyard.

If a fire breaks out and spreads into thornbushes so that it burns shocks of grain or standing grain or the whole field, the one who started the fire must make restitution.

If a man gives his neighbor silver or goods for safekeeping and they are stolen from the neighbor's house, the thief, if he is caught, must pay back double. But if the thief is not found, the owner of the house must appear before the judges to determine whether he has laid his hands on the other man's property. In all cases of illegal possession of an ox, a donkey, a sheep, a garment, or any other lost property about which somebody says, "This is mine," both parties are to bring their cases before the judges. The one whom the judges declare guilty must pay back double to his neighbor.

EXODUS 22:1-9

THE ONE MINUTE BIBLE

Related texts: NUMBERS 5:5-8; MATTHEW 5:23,24; LUKE 19:1-10; 1 CORINTHIANS 6:1-11

**THE ONE
MINUTE
BIBLE**

The Law: *Eye for Eye*

If men who are fighting hit a pregnant woman and she gives birth prematurely but there is no serious injury, the offender must be fined whatever the woman's husband demands and the court allows. But if there is serious injury, you are to take life for life, eye for eye, tooth for tooth, hand for hand, foot for foot, burn for burn, wound for wound, bruise for bruise.

If anyone takes the life of a human being, he must be put to death. Anyone who takes the life of someone's animal must make restitution—life for life. If anyone injures his neighbor, whatever he has done must be done to him: fracture for fracture, eye for eye, tooth for tooth. As he has injured the other, so he is to be injured. Whoever kills an animal must make restitution, but whoever kills a man must be put to death. You are to have the same law for the alien and the native-born. I am the LORD your God.

[Jesus said,] "You have heard that it was said, 'Eye for eye, and tooth for tooth.' But I tell you, Do not resist an evil person. If someone strikes you on the right cheek, turn to him the other also."

EXODUS 21:22-25; LEVITICUS 24:17-22; MATTHEW 5:38-39

Related texts: EXODUS 21:22-25; DEUTERONOMY 19:16-21; PSALM 103:8-12; MATTHEW 5:38-42

The Law: *Capital Punishment*

Anyone who strikes a man and kills him shall surely be put to death.

Anyone who attacks his father or his mother must be put to death.

Anyone who kidnaps another and either sells him or still has him when he is caught must be put to death.

Do not allow a sorceress to live.

Anyone who has sexual relations with an animal must be put to death.

Whoever sacrifices to any god other than the LORD must be destroyed.

Observe the Sabbath, because it is holy to you. Anyone who desecrates it must be put to death; whoever does any work on that day must be cut off from his people.

If anyone curses his father or mother, he must be put to death. He has cursed his father or his mother, and his blood will be on his own head.

If a man commits adultery with another man's wife—with the wife of his neighbor—both the adulterer and the adulteress must be put to death.

If a man sleeps with his father's wife, he has dishonored his father. Both the man and the woman must be put to death; their blood will be on their own heads.

If a man sleeps with his daughter-in-law, both of them must be put to death. What they have done is a perversion; their blood will be on their own heads.
If a man lies with a man as one lies with a woman, both of them have done what is detestable. They must be put to death; their blood will be on their own heads.

EXODUS 21:12, 15-16; 22:18-20; 31:14; LEVITICUS 20:9-13

Related texts: GENESIS 9:6; LEVITICUS 24:17-22; DEUTERONOMY 24:16; MATTHEW 21:33-44

The Law: *Clean and Unclean*

THE ONE
MINUTE
BIBLE

The LORD said to Moses and Aaron, "Say to the Israelites: 'Of all the animals that live on land, these are the ones you may eat: You may eat any animal that has a split hoof completely divided and that chews the cud.

"'Of all the creatures living in the water of the seas and the streams, you may eat any that have fins and scales. But all creatures in the seas or streams that do not have fins and scales—whether among all the swarming things or among all the other living creatures in the water—you are to detest. And since you are to detest them, you must not eat their meat and you must detest their carcasses.

"'All flying insects that walk on all fours are to be detestable to you. There are, however, some winged creatures that walk on all fours that you may eat: those that have jointed legs for hopping on the ground.

"'I am the LORD your God; consecrate yourselves and be holy, because I am holy. Do not make yourselves unclean by any creature that moves about on the ground. I am the LORD who brought you up out of Egypt to be your God; therefore be holy, because I am holy.'"

LEVITICUS 11:1-3, 9-11, 20-21, 44-45

Related texts: GENESIS 7:1-4; MATTHEW 15:1-20; MARK 7:1-23; ACTS 10; ROMANS 14

The Law: *The Festivals*

Observe the month of Abib and celebrate the Passover of the LORD your God, because in the month of Abib he brought you out of Egypt by night. Sacrifice as the Passover to the LORD your God an animal from your flock or herd at the place the LORD will choose as a dwelling for his Name.

For six days eat unleavened bread and on the seventh day hold an assembly to the LORD your God and do no work.

Count off seven weeks from the time you begin to put the sickle to the standing grain. Then celebrate the Feast of Weeks to the LORD your God by giving a freewill offering in proportion to the blessings the LORD your God has given you.

Celebrate the Feast of Tabernacles for seven days after you have gathered the produce of your threshing floor and your winepress. For seven days celebrate the Feast to the LORD your God at the place the LORD will choose. For the LORD your God will bless you in all your harvest and in all the work of your hands, and your joy will be complete.

Three times a year all your men must appear before the LORD your God at the place he will choose: at the Feast of Unleavened Bread, the Feast of Weeks and the Feast of Tabernacles. No man should appear before the LORD empty-handed: Each of you must bring a gift in proportion to the way the LORD your God has blessed you.

DEUTERONOMY 16:1-2, 8-10, 13, 15-17

THE ONE MINUTE BIBLE

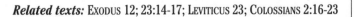

Related texts: EXODUS 12; 23:14-17; LEVITICUS 23; COLOSSIANS 2:16-23

Honor Your Mother

**THE ONE
MINUTE
BIBLE**

Honor your father and your mother, as the LORD your God has commanded you, so that you may live long and that it may go well with you in the land the LORD your God is giving you.

Then some Pharisees and teachers of the law came to Jesus from Jerusalem and asked, "Why do your disciples break the tradition of the elders? They don't wash their hands before they eat!"

Jesus replied, "And why do you break the command of God for the sake of your tradition? For God said, 'Honor your father and mother' and 'Anyone who curses his father or mother must be put to death.' But you say that if a man says to his father or mother, 'Whatever help you might otherwise have received from me is a gift devoted to God,' he is not to 'honor his father' with it. Thus you nullify the word of God for the sake of your tradition. You hypocrites! Isaiah was right when he prophesied about you:

"'These people honor me with their lips,
    but their hearts are far from me.
They worship me in vain;
    their teachings are but rules taught by men.'"

DEUTERONOMY 5:16; MATTHEW 15:1-9

Related texts: EXODUS 20:12; 21:15; LEVITICUS 20:9; EPHESIANS 6:1-2

The LORD Has a Mother's Compassion

Shout for joy, O heavens;
  rejoice, O earth;
  burst into song, O mountains!
For the LORD comforts his people
  and will have compassion on his afflicted ones.

But Zion said, "The LORD has forsaken me,
  the Lord has forgotten me."

"Can a mother forget the baby at her breast
  and have no compassion on the child she has borne?
Though she may forget,
  I will not forget you!
See, I have engraved you on the palms of my hands;
  your walls are ever before me.
Your sons hasten back,
  and those who laid you waste depart from you.
Lift up your eyes and look around;
  all your sons gather and come to you.
As surely as I live," declares the LORD,
  "you will wear them all as ornaments;
  you will put them on, like a bride.

"Though you were ruined and made desolate
  and your land laid waste,
now you will be too small for your people,
  and those who devoured you will be far away."

ISAIAH 49:13-19

Related texts: PSALMS 51:1-9; 77:1-8; 103:1-18; ISAIAH 66:12-14;
LAMENTATIONS 3:22-33; COLOSSIANS 3:12-14

A Happy Mother

**THE ONE
MINUTE
BIBLE**

Praise the LORD.

Praise, O servants of the LORD,
    praise the name of the LORD.
Let the name of the LORD be praised,
    both now and forevermore.
From the rising of the sun to the place where it sets,
    the name of the LORD is to be praised.

The LORD is exalted over all the nations,
    his glory above the heavens.
Who is like the LORD our God,
    the One who sits enthroned on high,
who stoops down to look
    on the heavens and the earth?

He raises the poor from the dust
    and lifts the needy from the ash heap;
he seats them with princes,
    with the princes of their people.
He settles the barren woman in her home
    as a happy mother of children.

Praise the LORD.

PSALM 113

Related texts: 1 SAMUEL 2:1-10; JOB 42:12-16; PSALM 127:3-5;
PROVERBS 17:6; ISAIAH 54:1-8; LUKE 1

A Mother's Teaching

Listen, my son, to your father's instruction
    and do not forsake your mother's teaching.
They will be a garland to grace your head
    and a chain to adorn your neck.

The sayings of King Lemuel—an oracle his mother taught him:

> "O my son, O son of my womb,
>   O son of my vows,
> do not spend your strength on women,
>   your vigor on those who ruin kings.
>
> "It is not for kings, O Lemuel—
>   not for kings to drink wine,
>   not for rulers to crave beer,
> lest they drink and forget what the law decrees,
>   and deprive all the oppressed of their rights.
> Give beer to those who are perishing,
>   wine to those who are in anguish;
> let them drink and forget their poverty
>   and remember their misery no more.
>
> "Speak up for those who cannot speak for
>   themselves,
>   for the rights of all who are destitute.
> Speak up and judge fairly;
>   defend the rights of the poor and needy."

PROVERBS 1:8-9; 31:1-9

Related texts: EXODUS 2:1-9; PROVERBS 6:20-24; 2 TIMOTHY 1:5; 3:14-17

THE ONE MINUTE BIBLE

The Noble Wife: Part 1

A wife of noble character is her husband's crown,
    but a disgraceful wife is like decay in his bones.

A wife of noble character who can find?
    She is worth far more than rubies.
Her husband has full confidence in her
    and lacks nothing of value.
She brings him good, not harm,
    all the days of her life.
She selects wool and flax
    and works with eager hands.
She is like the merchant ships,
    bringing her food from afar.
She gets up while it is still dark;
    she provides food for her family
    and portions for her servant girls.
She considers a field and buys it;
    out of her earnings she plants a vineyard.
She sets about her work vigorously;
    her arms are strong for her tasks.
She sees that her trading is profitable,
    and her lamp does not go out at night.
In her hand she holds the distaff
    and grasps the spindle with her fingers.
She opens her arms to the poor
    and extends her hands to the needy.

PROVERBS 12:4; 31:10-20

Related texts: GENESIS 24; ACTS 18:23-26; ROMANS 16:1-6

The Noble Wife: Part 2

**THE ONE
MINUTE
BIBLE**

A wife of noble character who can find?
　　She is worth far more than rubies.

When it snows, she has no fear for her household;
　　for all of them are clothed in scarlet.
She makes coverings for her bed;
　　she is clothed in fine linen and purple.
Her husband is respected at the city gate,
　　where he takes his seat among the elders of the land.
She makes linen garments and sells them,
　　and supplies the merchants with sashes.
She is clothed with strength and dignity;
　　she can laugh at the days to come.
She speaks with wisdom,
　　and faithful instruction is on her tongue.
She watches over the affairs of her household
　　and does not eat the bread of idleness.
Her children arise and call her blessed;
　　her husband also, and he praises her:
"Many women do noble things,
　　but you surpass them all."
Charm is deceptive, and beauty is fleeting;
　　but a woman who fears the LORD is to be praised.
Give her the reward she has earned,
　　and let her works bring her praise at the city gate.

He who finds a wife finds what is good
　　and receives favor from the LORD.

PROVERBS 31:10, 21-31; 18:22

Related texts: 1 SAMUEL 25:1-42; PROVERBS 19:14; LUKE 1:26-55;
EPHESIANS 5:21-24; 1 PETER 3:1-6

Your Maker Is Your Husband

**THE ONE
MINUTE
BIBLE**

"Sing, O barren woman,
you who never bore a child;
burst into song, shout for joy,
you who were never in labor;
because more are the children of the desolate woman
than of her who has a husband,"

says the LORD.

"Enlarge the place of your tent,
stretch your tent curtains wide,
do not hold back;
lengthen your cords,
strengthen your stakes.

"Do not be afraid; you will not suffer shame.
Do not fear disgrace; you will not be humiliated.
You will forget the shame of your youth
and remember no more the reproach of your
widowhood.
For your Maker is your husband—
the LORD Almighty is his name—
the Holy One of Israel is your Redeemer;
he is called the God of all the earth.
The LORD will call you back
as if you were a wife deserted and distressed in spirit—
a wife who married young,
only to be rejected," says your God.
"For a brief moment I abandoned you,
but with deep compassion I will bring you back.
In a surge of anger
I hid my face from you for a moment,
but with everlasting kindness
I will have compassion on you,"
says the LORD your Redeemer.

ISAIAH 54:1-2, 4-8

Related texts: PSALM 45; SONG OF SONGS 4; ISAIAH 62:1-7;
REVELATION 19:5-9; 21:1-4

The Law: *Women's Rights*

**THE ONE
MINUTE
BIBLE**

If a man sells his daughter as a servant, she is not to go free as menservants do. If she does not please the master who has selected her for himself, he must let her be redeemed. He has no right to sell her to foreigners, because he has broken faith with her. If he selects her for his son, he must grant her the rights of a daughter. If he marries another woman, he must not deprive the first one of her food, clothing and marital rights. If he does not provide her with these three things, she is to go free, without any payment of money.

Do not degrade your daughter by making her a prostitute, or the land will turn to prostitution and be filled with wickedness.

If brothers are living together and one of them dies without a son, his widow must not marry outside the family. Her husband's brother shall take her and marry her and fulfill the duty of a brother-in-law to her. The first son she bears shall carry on the name of the dead brother so that his name will not be blotted out from Israel.

EXODUS 21:7-11; LEVITICUS 19:29; DEUTERONOMY 25:5-6

Related texts: EXODUS 22:16,17; NUMBERS 27; 30; 36;
DEUTERONOMY 21:10-17; 22:13-30; 25:7-10; RUTH 3–4; 1 TIMOTHY 3:2, 12

The Law: *The Tabernacle*

**THE ONE
MINUTE
BIBLE**

Now the first covenant had regulations for worship and also an earthly sanctuary. A tabernacle was set up. In its first room were the lampstand, the table and the consecrated bread; this was called the Holy Place. Behind the second curtain was a room called the Most Holy Place, which had the golden altar of incense and the gold-covered ark of the covenant. This ark contained the gold jar of manna, Aaron's staff that had budded, and the stone tablets of the covenant. Above the ark were the cherubim of the Glory, overshadowing the atonement cover. But we cannot discuss these things in detail now.

When everything had been arranged like this, the priests entered regularly into the outer room to carry on their ministry. But only the high priest entered the inner room, and that only once a year, and never without blood, which he offered for himself and for the sins the people had committed in ignorance.

When Christ came as high priest of the good things that are already here, he went through the greater and more perfect tabernacle that is not man-made, that is to say, not a part of this creation. He did not enter by means of the blood of goats and calves; but he entered the Most Holy Place once for all by his own blood, having obtained eternal redemption.

HEBREWS 9:1-7, 11-12

Related texts: EXODUS 25–27; 35–40; MARK 15:37,38; HEBREWS 9:13-28; 10:19-23

The Law: *The Priesthood*

The L ORD said to Aaron, "You, your sons and your father's family are to bear the responsibility for offenses against the sanctuary, and you and your sons alone are to bear the responsibility for offenses against the priesthood. Bring your fellow Levites from your ancestral tribe to join you and assist you when you and your sons minister before the Tent of the Testimony.

"You are to be responsible for the care of the sanctuary and the altar, so that wrath will not fall on the Israelites again. I myself have selected your fellow Levites from among the Israelites as a gift to you, dedicated to the L ORD to do the work at the Tent of Meeting. But only you and your sons may serve as priests in connection with everything at the altar and inside the curtain. I am giving you the service of the priesthood as a gift. Anyone else who comes near the sanctuary must be put to death.

"Whatever is set aside from the holy offerings the Israelites present to the L ORD I give to you and your sons and daughters as your regular share. It is an everlasting covenant of salt before the L ORD for both you and your offspring."

The L ORD said to Aaron, "You will have no inheritance in their land, nor will you have any share among them; I am your share and your inheritance among the Israelites."

N UMBERS 18:1-2, 5-7, 19-20

THE ONE MINUTE BIBLE

Related texts: L EVITICUS 1–7; 21–22; N UMBERS 3; H EBREWS 7–9; 1 P ETER 2:4-10

The Law: *Driving Out the Nations*

THE ONE MINUTE BIBLE

When the LORD your God brings you into the land you are entering to possess and drives out before you many nations—the Hittites, Girgashites, Amorites, Canaanites, Perizzites, Hivites and Jebusites, seven nations larger and stronger than you—and when the LORD your God has delivered them over to you and you have defeated them, then you must destroy them totally. Make no treaty with them, and show them no mercy. Do not intermarry with them. Do not give your daughters to their sons or take their daughters for your sons, for they will turn your sons away from following me to serve other gods, and the LORD's anger will burn against you and will quickly destroy you.

This is what you are to do to them: Break down their altars, smash their sacred stones, cut down their Asherah poles and burn their idols in the fire. For you are a people holy to the LORD your God. The LORD your God has chosen you out of all the peoples on the face of the earth to be his people, his treasured possession.

The LORD did not set his affection on you and choose you because you were more numerous than other peoples, for you were the fewest of all peoples. But it was because the LORD loved you and kept the oath he swore to your forefathers that he brought you out with a mighty hand and redeemed you from the land of slavery, from the power of Pharaoh king of Egypt.

DEUTERONOMY 7:1-8

Related texts: DEUTERONOMY 8:18–9:5; JUDGES 2:10-23; 2 CORINTHIANS 6:14–7:1; COLOSSIANS 4:4-6; 1 PETER 2:1-12

The Law: *Not Too Difficult*

Now what I am commanding you today is not too difficult for you or beyond your reach. It is not up in heaven, so that you have to ask, "Who will ascend into heaven to get it and proclaim it to us so we may obey it?" Nor is it beyond the sea, so that you have to ask, "Who will cross the sea to get it and proclaim it to us so we may obey it?" No, the word is very near you; it is in your mouth and in your heart so you may obey it.

See, I set before you today life and prosperity, death and destruction. For I command you today to love the Lord your God, to walk in his ways, and to keep his commands, decrees and laws; then you will live and increase, and the Lord your God will bless you in the land you are entering to possess.

But if your heart turns away and you are not obedient, and if you are drawn away to bow down to other gods and worship them, I declare to you this day that you will certainly be destroyed. You will not live long in the land you are crossing the Jordan to enter and possess.

This day I call heaven and earth as witnesses against you that I have set before you life and death, blessings and curses. Now choose life, so that you and your children may live and that you may love the Lord your God, listen to his voice, and hold fast to him. For the Lord is your life, and he will give you many years in the land he swore to give to your fathers, Abraham, Isaac and Jacob.

DEUTERONOMY 30:11-20

Related texts: DEUTERONOMY 7:9-15; 10:12-13; MICAH 6:6-8;
JOHN 14:15; ROMANS 10:5-13; 1 JOHN 5:3

Sermon on the Mount: *The Beatitudes*

**THE ONE
MINUTE
BIBLE**

Now when Jesus saw the crowds, he went up on a mountainside and sat down. His disciples came to him, and he began to teach them, saying:

"Blessed are the poor in spirit,
for theirs is the kingdom of heaven.
Blessed are those who mourn,
for they will be comforted.
Blessed are the meek,
for they will inherit the earth.
Blessed are those who hunger and thirst for
righteousness,
for they will be filled.
Blessed are the merciful,
for they will be shown mercy.
Blessed are the pure in heart,
for they will see God.
Blessed are the peacemakers,
for they will be called sons of God.
Blessed are those who are persecuted because
of righteousness,
for theirs is the kingdom of heaven."

MATTHEW 5:1-10

Related texts: GENESIS 12:1-3; PSALMS 1; 84; LUKE 6:17-26; 11:27-28;
JOHN 20:24-29

Sermon on the Mount: *Salt and Light*

Blessed are you when people insult you, persecute you and falsely say all kinds of evil against you because of me. Rejoice and be glad, because great is your reward in heaven, for in the same way they persecuted the prophets who were before you.

You are the salt of the earth. But if the salt loses its saltiness, how can it be made salty again? It is no longer good for anything, except to be thrown out and trampled by men.

You are the light of the world. A city on a hill cannot be hidden. Neither do people light a lamp and put it under a bowl. Instead they put it on its stand, and it gives light to everyone in the house. In the same way, let your light shine before men, that they may see your good deeds and praise your Father in heaven.

For you were once darkness, but now you are light in the Lord. Live as children of light (for the fruit of the light consists in all goodness, righteousness and truth) and find out what pleases the Lord.

MATTHEW 5:11-16; EPHESIANS 5:8-10

THE ONE MINUTE BIBLE

Related texts: PROVERBS 13:9; MARK 9:50; LUKE 14:34-35; 1 PETER 4:12-19

**THE ONE
MINUTE
BIBLE**

Sermon on the Mount: *Fulfilling the Law*

Do not think that I have come to abolish the Law or the Prophets; I have not come to abolish them but to fulfill them. I tell you the truth, until heaven and earth disappear, not the smallest letter, not the least stroke of a pen, will by any means disappear from the Law until everything is accomplished.

Anyone who breaks one of the least of these commandments and teaches others to do the same will be called least in the kingdom of heaven, but whoever practices and teaches these commands will be called great in the kingdom of heaven. For I tell you that unless your righteousness surpasses that of the Pharisees and the teachers of the law, you will certainly not enter the kingdom of heaven.

Therefore, there is now no condemnation for those who are in Christ Jesus, because through Christ Jesus the law of the Spirit of life set me free from the law of sin and death. For what the law was powerless to do in that it was weakened by the sinful nature, God did by sending his own Son in the likeness of sinful man to be a sin offering. And so he condemned sin in sinful man, in order that the righteous requirements of the law might be fully met in us, who do not live according to the sinful nature but according to the Spirit.

MATTHEW 5:17-20; ROMANS 8:1-4

Related texts: PSALM 119:161-176; MATTHEW 22:34-40; ROMANS 3:21-31; 7-8

Sermon on the Mount: *Murder and Hate*

THE ONE
MINUTE
BIBLE

You have heard that it was said to the people long ago, "Do not murder, and anyone who murders will be subject to judgment." But I tell you that anyone who is angry with his brother will be subject to judgment. Again, anyone who says to his brother, "Raca," is answerable to the Sanhedrin. But anyone who says, "You fool!" will be in danger of the fire of hell.

Therefore, if you are offering your gift at the altar and there remember that your brother has something against you, leave your gift there in front of the altar. First go and be reconciled to your brother; then come and offer your gift.

Settle matters quickly with your adversary who is taking you to court. Do it while you are still with him on the way, or he may hand you over to the judge, and the judge may hand you over to the officer, and you may be thrown into prison. I tell you the truth, you will not get out until you have paid the last penny.

Anyone who claims to be in the light but hates his brother is still in the darkness. Whoever loves his brother lives in the light, and there is nothing in him to make him stumble. But whoever hates his brother is in the darkness and walks around in the darkness; he does not know where he is going, because the darkness has blinded him.

MATTHEW 5:21-26; 1 JOHN 2:9-11

Related texts: EXODUS 20:13; PROVERBS 8:12-13; MATTHEW 5:38-48; LUKE 6:22-36

Sermon on the Mount: *Adultery*

THE ONE MINUTE BIBLE

You have heard that it was said, "Do not commit adultery." But I tell you that anyone who looks at a woman lustfully has already committed adultery with her in his heart. If your right eye causes you to sin, gouge it out and throw it away. It is better for you to lose one part of your body than for your whole body to be thrown into hell. And if your right hand causes you to sin, cut it off and throw it away. It is better for you to lose one part of your body than for your whole body to go into hell.

It has been said, "Anyone who divorces his wife must give her a certificate of divorce." But I tell you that anyone who divorces his wife, except for marital unfaithfulness, causes her to become an adulteress, and anyone who marries the divorced woman commits adultery.

It is God's will that you should be sanctified: that you should avoid sexual immorality; that each of you should learn to control his own body in a way that is holy and honorable, not in passionate lust like the heathen, who do not know God; and that in this matter no one should wrong his brother or take advantage of him. The Lord will punish men for all such sins, as we have already told you and warned you. For God did not call us to be impure, but to live a holy life. Therefore, he who rejects this instruction does not reject man but God, who gives you his Holy Spirit.

MATTHEW 5:27-32; 1 THESSALONIANS 4:3-8

Related texts: DEUTERONOMY 24:1-4; PROVERBS 5; MALACHI 2:10-16; MATTHEW 19:3-12; 1 CORINTHIANS 7

Sermon on the Mount: *Love, Not Revenge*

THE ONE MINUTE BIBLE

You have heard that it was said, "Eye for eye, and tooth for tooth." But I tell you, Do not resist an evil person. If someone strikes you on the right cheek, turn to him the other also. And if someone wants to sue you and take your tunic, let him have your cloak as well. If someone forces you to go one mile, go with him two miles. Give to the one who asks you, and do not turn away from the one who wants to borrow from you.

You have heard that it was said, "Love your neighbor and hate your enemy." But I tell you: Love your enemies and pray for those who persecute you, that you may be sons of your Father in heaven. He causes his sun to rise on the evil and the good, and sends rain on the righteous and the unrighteous. If you love those who love you, what reward will you get? Are not even the tax collectors doing that? And if you greet only your brothers, what are you doing more than others? Do not even pagans do that? Be perfect, therefore, as your heavenly Father is perfect.

Dear friends, let us love one another, for love comes from God. Everyone who loves has been born of God and knows God. Whoever does not love does not know God, because God is love.

MATTHEW 5:38-48; 1 JOHN 4:7-8

Related texts: GENESIS 12:1-3; LEVITICUS 24:17-20; LUKE 6:27-37; ROMANS 12:14-18

Sermon on the Mount: *Treasure in Heaven*

**THE ONE
MINUTE
BIBLE**

Be careful not to do your "acts of righteousness" before men, to be seen by them. If you do, you will have no reward from your Father in heaven.

So when you give to the needy, do not announce it with trumpets, as the hypocrites do in the synagogues and on the streets, to be honored by men. I tell you the truth, they have received their reward in full. But when you give to the needy, do not let your left hand know what your right hand is doing, so that your giving may be in secret. Then your Father, who sees what is done in secret, will reward you.

Do not store up for yourselves treasures on earth, where moth and rust destroy, and where thieves break in and steal. But store up for yourselves treasures in heaven, where moth and rust do not destroy, and where thieves do not break in and steal. For where your treasure is, there your heart will be also.

The eye is the lamp of the body. If your eyes are good, your whole body will be full of light. But if your eyes are bad, your whole body will be full of darkness. If then the light within you is darkness, how great is that darkness!

No one can serve two masters. Either he will hate the one and love the other, or he will be devoted to the one and despise the other. You cannot serve both God and Money.

MATTHEW 6:1-4, 19-24

Related texts: PROVERBS 11:24-25; MARK 10:17-31; LUKE 6:38; 12:32-34; ACTS 20:32-35; 2 CORINTHIANS 9:6-15

Sermon on the Mount: *Prayer*

**THE ONE
MINUTE
BIBLE**

And when you pray, do not be like the hypocrites, for they love to pray standing in the synagogues and on the street corners to be seen by men. I tell you the truth, they have received their reward in full. But when you pray, go into your room, close the door and pray to your Father, who is unseen. Then your Father, who sees what is done in secret, will reward you. And when you pray, do not keep on babbling like pagans, for they think they will be heard because of their many words. Do not be like them, for your Father knows what you need before you ask him.

This, then, is how you should pray:

"Our Father in heaven,
hallowed be your name,
your kingdom come,
your will be done
    on earth as it is in heaven.
Give us today our daily bread.
Forgive us our debts,
    as we also have forgiven our debtors.
And lead us not into temptation,
but deliver us from the evil one."

For if you forgive men when they sin against you, your heavenly Father will also forgive you. But if you do not forgive men their sins, your Father will not forgive your sins.

MATTHEW 6:5-15

Related texts: PSALM 5; MARK 11:22-26; LUKE 11:1-13; 18:1-14;
JAMES 5:13-20

**THE ONE
MINUTE
BIBLE**

Sermon on the Mount: *Fasting*

When you fast, do not look somber as the hypocrites do, for they disfigure their faces to show men they are fasting. I tell you the truth, they have received their reward in full. But when you fast, put oil on your head and wash your face, so that it will not be obvious to men that you are fasting, but only to your Father, who is unseen; and your Father, who sees what is done in secret, will reward you.

Now John's disciples and the Pharisees were fasting. Some people came and asked Jesus, "How is it that John's disciples and the disciples of the Pharisees are fasting, but yours are not?"

Jesus answered, "How can the guests of the bridegroom fast while he is with them? They cannot, so long as they have him with them. But the time will come when the bridegroom will be taken from them, and on that day they will fast.

"No one sews a patch of unshrunk cloth on an old garment. If he does, the new piece will pull away from the old, making the tear worse. And no one pours new wine into old wineskins. If he does, the wine will burst the skins, and both the wine and the wineskins will be ruined. No, he pours new wine into new wineskins."

MATTHEW 6:16-18; MARK 2:18-22

Related texts: ESTHER 3–4; ISAIAH 58; JONAH 3; ZECHARIAH 7–8; ACTS 14:21-23

Sermon on the Mount: *Why Worry?*

THE ONE
MINUTE
BIBLE

Therefore I tell you, do not worry about your life, what you will eat or drink; or about your body, what you will wear. Is not life more important than food, and the body more important than clothes? Look at the birds of the air; they do not sow or reap or store away in barns, and yet your heavenly Father feeds them. Are you not much more valuable than they? Who of you by worrying can add a single hour to his life?

And why do you worry about clothes? See how the lilies of the field grow. They do not labor or spin. Yet I tell you that not even Solomon in all his splendor was dressed like one of these. If that is how God clothes the grass of the field, which is here today and tomorrow is thrown into the fire, will he not much more clothe you, O you of little faith?

So do not worry, saying, "What shall we eat?" or "What shall we drink?" or "What shall we wear?" For the pagans run after all these things, and your heavenly Father knows that you need them. But seek first his kingdom and his righteousness, and all these things will be given to you as well. Therefore do not worry about tomorrow, for tomorrow will worry about itself. Each day has enough trouble of its own.

MATTHEW 6:25-34

Related texts: PROVERBS 12:25; MARK 13:11; LUKE 12:11-34; PHILIPPIANS 4:6-7

**THE ONE
MINUTE
BIBLE**

Sermon on the Mount: *Judging and Asking*

Do not judge, or you too will be judged. For in the same way you judge others, you will be judged, and with the measure you use, it will be measured to you.

Why do you look at the speck of sawdust in your brother's eye and pay no attention to the plank in your own eye? How can you say to your brother, "Let me take the speck out of your eye," when all the time there is a plank in your own eye? You hypocrite, first take the plank out of your own eye, and then you will see clearly to remove the speck from your brother's eye.

Do not give dogs what is sacred; do not throw your pearls to pigs. If you do, they may trample them under their feet, and then turn and tear you to pieces.

Ask and it will be given to you; seek and you will find; knock and the door will be opened to you. For everyone who asks receives; he who seeks finds; and to him who knocks, the door will be opened.

Which of you, if his son asks for bread, will give him a stone? Or if he asks for a fish, will give him a snake? If you, then, though you are evil, know how to give good gifts to your children, how much more will your Father in heaven give good gifts to those who ask him! So in everything, do to others what you would have them do to you, for this sums up the Law and the Prophets.

MATTHEW 7:1-12

Related texts: ROMANS 14:1-13; JOHN 16:24; 1 CORINTHIANS 5; JAMES 4:1-3; 1 JOHN 3:21-22

Sermon on the Mount: *The Two Ways*

THE ONE MINUTE BIBLE

"Enter through the narrow gate. For wide is the gate and broad is the road that leads to destruction, and many enter through it. But small is the gate and narrow the road that leads to life, and only a few find it.

"Not everyone who says to me, 'Lord, Lord,' will enter the kingdom of heaven, but only he who does the will of my Father who is in heaven. Many will say to me on that day, 'Lord, Lord, did we not prophesy in your name, and in your name drive out demons and perform many miracles?' Then I will tell them plainly, 'I never knew you. Away from me, you evildoers!'

"Therefore everyone who hears these words of mine and puts them into practice is like a wise man who built his house on the rock. The rain came down, the streams rose, and the winds blew and beat against that house; yet it did not fall, because it had its foundation on the rock. But everyone who hears these words of mine and does not put them into practice is like a foolish man who built his house on sand. The rain came down, the streams rose, and the winds blew and beat against that house, and it fell with a great crash."

When Jesus had finished saying these things, the crowds were amazed at his teaching, because he taught as one who had authority, and not as their teachers of the law.

MATTHEW 7:13-14, 21-29

Related texts: PROVERBS 14:11-12; LUKE 13:22-30; JOHN 10:1-10; EPHESIANS 2:13-22

By the reading of Scripture I am so renewed that all nature seems renewed around me and with me. The whole world is charged with the glory of God and I feel fire and music under my feet.
Thomas Merton (1915-1968)
AMERICAN MONK

The Scripture...dispels the darkness and gives us a clear view of the true God.
John Calvin (1509-1564)
FRENCH THEOLOGIAN AND REFORMER

Give me a used Bible and I will, I think, be able to tell you about a man by the places that are edged with the dirt of seeking fingers.
John Steinbeck (1902-1968)
AMERICAN NOVELIST

The Golden Calf

**THE ONE
MINUTE
BIBLE**

When the people saw that Moses was so long in coming down from the mountain, they gathered around Aaron and said, "Come, make us gods who will go before us. As for this fellow Moses who brought us up out of Egypt, we don't know what has happened to him."

Aaron answered them, "Take off the gold earrings that your wives, your sons and your daughters are wearing, and bring them to me." So all the people took off their earrings and brought them to Aaron. He took what they handed him and made it into an idol cast in the shape of a calf, fashioning it with a tool. Then they said, "These are your gods, O Israel, who brought you up out of Egypt."

When Aaron saw this, he built an altar in front of the calf and announced, "Tomorrow there will be a festival to the LORD." So the next day the people rose early and sacrificed burnt offerings and presented fellowship offerings. Afterward they sat down to eat and drink and got up to indulge in revelry.

Then the LORD said to Moses, "Go down, because your people, whom you brought up out of Egypt, have become corrupt. They have been quick to turn away from what I commanded them and have made themselves an idol cast in the shape of a calf. They have bowed down to it and sacrificed to it and have said, 'These are your gods, O Israel, who brought you up out of Egypt.'

"I have seen these people," the LORD said to Moses, "and they are a stiff-necked people. Now leave me alone so that my anger may burn against them and that I may destroy them. Then I will make you into a great nation."

EXODUS 32:1-10

Related texts: DEUTERONOMY 9:7-15; NEHEMIAH 9:16-19;
PSALM 106:19-22; ACTS 7:37-41

Moses Pleads for the Israelites

**THE ONE
MINUTE
BIBLE**

But Moses sought the favor of the LORD his God. "O LORD," he said, "why should your anger burn against your people, whom you brought out of Egypt with great power and a mighty hand? Why should the Egyptians say, 'It was with evil intent that he brought them out, to kill them in the mountains and to wipe them off the face of the earth'? Turn from your fierce anger; relent and do not bring disaster on your people. Remember your servants Abraham, Isaac and Israel, to whom you swore by your own self: 'I will make your descendants as numerous as the stars in the sky and I will give your descendants all this land I promised them, and it will be their inheritance forever.'" Then the LORD relented and did not bring on his people the disaster he had threatened.

Moses turned and went down the mountain with the two tablets of the Testimony in his hands. They were inscribed on both sides, front and back. The tablets were the work of God; the writing was the writing of God, engraved on the tablets.

When Moses approached the camp and saw the calf and the dancing, his anger burned and he threw the tablets out of his hands, breaking them to pieces at the foot of the mountain. And he took the calf they had made and burned it in the fire; then he ground it to powder, scattered it on the water and made the Israelites drink it.

EXODUS 32:11-16, 19-20

Related texts: GENESIS 15:1-5; 22:15-18; 26:2-4; DEUTERONOMY 9:16-21; PSALM 106:23; JONAH 3; ACTS 7:40-42

Israel's History Is Our Warning

For I do not want you to be ignorant of the fact, brothers, that our forefathers were all under the cloud and that they all passed through the sea. They were all baptized into Moses in the cloud and in the sea. They all ate the same spiritual food and drank the same spiritual drink; for they drank from the spiritual rock that accompanied them, and that rock was Christ. Nevertheless, God was not pleased with most of them; their bodies were scattered over the desert.

Now these things occurred as examples to keep us from setting our hearts on evil things as they did. Do not be idolaters, as some of them were; as it is written: "The people sat down to eat and drink and got up to indulge in pagan revelry." We should not commit sexual immorality, as some of them did—and in one day twenty-three thousand of them died.

These things happened to them as examples and were written down as warnings for us, on whom the fulfillment of the ages has come. So, if you think you are standing firm, be careful that you don't fall! No temptation has seized you except what is common to man. And God is faithful; he will not let you be tempted beyond what you can bear. But when you are tempted, he will also provide a way out so that you can stand up under it.

1 CORINTHIANS 10:1-8, 11-13

THE ONE MINUTE BIBLE

Related texts: EXODUS 14; 17:1-7; 32; JOHN 6; HEBREWS 2:9-18; JAMES 1:12-15

God Forgives Those Who Repent

**THE ONE
MINUTE
BIBLE**

The LORD said to Moses, "Chisel out two stone tablets like the first ones, and I will write on them the words that were on the first tablets, which you broke."

So Moses chiseled out two stone tablets like the first ones and went up Mount Sinai early in the morning, as the LORD had commanded him; and he carried the two stone tablets in his hands. Then the LORD came down in the cloud and stood there with him and proclaimed his name, the LORD. And he passed in front of Moses, proclaiming, "The LORD, the LORD, the compassionate and gracious God, slow to anger, abounding in love and faithfulness, maintaining love to thousands, and forgiving wickedness, rebellion and sin. Yet he does not leave the guilty unpunished; he punishes the children and their children for the sin of the fathers to the third and fourth generation."

Moses bowed to the ground at once and worshiped. "O Lord, if I have found favor in your eyes," he said, "then let the Lord go with us. Although this is a stiff-necked people, forgive our wickedness and our sin, and take us as your inheritance."

Then the LORD said: "I am making a covenant with you. Before all your people I will do wonders never before done in any nation in all the world. The people you live among will see how awesome is the work that I, the LORD, will do for you."

EXODUS 34:1, 4-10

Related texts: PSALMS 86:15; 103:8; 145:8; JOHN 3:16-21; 1 JOHN 1:9

God Is Compassionate

Do not be like your fathers and brothers, who were unfaithful to the Lord, the God of their fathers, so that he made them an object of horror, as you see. Do not be stiff-necked, as your fathers were; submit to the Lord. Come to the sanctuary, which he has consecrated forever. Serve the Lord your God, so that his fierce anger will turn away from you. If you return to the Lord, then your brothers and your children will be shown compassion by their captors and will come back to this land, for the Lord your God is gracious and compassionate. He will not turn his face from you if you return to him.

The Lord is gracious and compassionate,
    slow to anger and rich in love.
The Lord is good to all;
    he has compassion on all he has made.

Praise be to the God and Father of our Lord Jesus Christ, the Father of compassion and the God of all comfort, who comforts us in all our troubles, so that we can comfort those in any trouble with the comfort we ourselves have received from God. For just as the sufferings of Christ flow over into our lives, so also through Christ our comfort overflows.

2 Chronicles 30:7-9; Psalm 145:8-9; 2 Corinthians 1:3-5

Related texts: Exodus 33:19; 2 Chronicles 30:7-9; Nehemiah 9:16-19; Psalm 103; Lamentations 3:19-23; Colossians 3:12-14

God Is Forgiving

**THE ONE
MINUTE
BIBLE**

Who is a God like you,
    who pardons sin and forgives the transgression
    of the remnant of his inheritance?
You do not stay angry forever
    but delight to show mercy.
You will again have compassion on us;
    you will tread our sins underfoot
    and hurl all our iniquities into the depths of the sea.
You will be true to Jacob,
    and show mercy to Abraham,
as you pledged on oath to our fathers
    in days long ago.

This is the message we have heard from him and declare to you: God is light; in him there is no darkness at all. If we claim to have fellowship with him yet walk in the darkness, we lie and do not live by the truth. But if we walk in the light, as he is in the light, we have fellowship with one another, and the blood of Jesus, his Son, purifies us from all sin.

If we claim to be without sin, we deceive ourselves and the truth is not in us. If we confess our sins, he is faithful and just and will forgive us our sins and purify us from all unrighteousness. If we claim we have not sinned, we make him out to be a liar and his word has no place in our lives.

MICAH 7:18-20; 1 JOHN 1:5-10

Related texts: NUMBERS 14:1-35; 1 KINGS 8:27-53; PSALM 32:1-5;
DANIEL 9:1-19; MATTHEW 6:14-15; 18:21-35

God Is Gracious

The LORD is gracious and righteous;
  our God is full of compassion.
The LORD protects the simplehearted;
  when I was in great need, he saved me.
Be at rest once more, O my soul,
  for the LORD has been good to you.

The Word became flesh and made his dwelling among us. We have seen his glory, the glory of the One and Only, who came from the Father, full of grace and truth.

From the fullness of his grace we have all received one blessing after another. For the law was given through Moses; grace and truth came through Jesus Christ.

But because of his great love for us, God, who is rich in mercy, made us alive with Christ even when we were dead in transgressions—it is by grace you have been saved. And God raised us up with Christ and seated us with him in the heavenly realms in Christ Jesus, in order that in the coming ages he might show the incomparable riches of his grace, expressed in his kindness to us in Christ Jesus. For it is by grace you have been saved, through faith—and this not from yourselves, it is the gift of God—not by works, so that no one can boast.

PSALM 116:5-7; JOHN 1:14, 16-17; EPHESIANS 2:4-9

Related texts: NUMBERS 6:24-26; PROVERBS 3:33-35; ROMANS 5:12-21

God Is Holy

**THE ONE
MINUTE
BIBLE**

I am the LORD who brought you up out of Egypt to be your God; therefore be holy, because I am holy.

In the year that King Uzziah died, I saw the Lord seated on a throne, high and exalted, and the train of his robe filled the temple. Above him were seraphs, each with six wings: With two wings they covered their faces, with two they covered their feet, and with two they were flying. And they were calling to one another:

"Holy, holy, holy is the LORD Almighty;
the whole earth is full of his glory."

For this is what the high and lofty One says—
he who lives forever, whose name is holy:
"I live in a high and holy place,
but also with him who is contrite and lowly in spirit,
to revive the spirit of the lowly
and to revive the heart of the contrite.
I will not accuse forever,
nor will I always be angry,
for then the spirit of man would grow faint before me—
the breath of man that I have created."

As obedient children, do not conform to the evil desires you had when you lived in ignorance. But just as he who called you is holy, so be holy in all you do; for it is written: "Be holy, because I am holy."

LEVITICUS 11:45; ISAIAH 6:1-3; 57:15-16; 1 PETER 1:14-16

Related texts: EXODUS 15:11; LEVITICUS 22:31-33; PSALM 99;

REVELATION 4; 15:2-4

God Is Merciful

I lift up my eyes to you,
   to you whose throne is in heaven.
As the eyes of slaves look to the hand of their master,
   as the eyes of a maid look to the hand of her
      mistress,
so our eyes look to the LORD our God,
   till he shows us his mercy.

Have mercy on us, O LORD, have mercy on us,
   for we have endured much contempt.
We have endured much ridicule from the proud,
   much contempt from the arrogant.

    As for you, you were dead in your transgressions
and sins, in which you used to live when you followed
the ways of this world and of the ruler of the kingdom of
the air, the spirit who is now at work in those who are
disobedient. All of us also lived among them at one
time, gratifying the cravings of our sinful nature and
following its desires and thoughts. Like the rest, we
were by nature objects of wrath. But because of his
great love for us, God, who is rich in mercy, made us
alive with Christ even when we were dead in
transgressions—it is by grace you have been saved.

PSALM 123:1-4; EPHESIANS 2:1-5

Related texts: EXODUS 33:19; DEUTERONOMY 4:31; NEHEMIAH 9:29-31;
MICAH 7:18-20; ROMANS 9:11-18

God Is All-Powerful

**THE ONE
MINUTE
BIBLE**

Then Job replied to the LORD:
"I know that you can do all things;
no plan of yours can be thwarted."

Proclaim the power of God,
whose majesty is over Israel,
whose power is in the skies.
You are awesome, O God, in your sanctuary;
the God of Israel gives power and strength
to his people.
Praise be to God!

Ah, Sovereign LORD, you have made the heavens
and the earth by your great power and outstretched arm.
Nothing is too hard for you. You show love to thousands
but bring the punishment for the fathers' sins into the
laps of their children after them. O great and powerful
God, whose name is the LORD Almighty, great are your
purposes and mighty are your deeds. Your eyes are open
to all the ways of men; you reward everyone according
to his conduct and as his deeds deserve.

You are worthy, our Lord and God,
to receive glory and honor and power,
for you created all things,
and by your will they were created
and have their being.

JOB 42:1-2; PSALM 68:34-35; JEREMIAH 32:17-19; REVELATION 4:11

Related texts: GENESIS 18:14; EXODUS 15:1-18; PSALM 29; MARK 4:35-41

God Is Everywhere

Where can I go from your Spirit?
    Where can I flee from your presence?
If I go up to the heavens, you are there;
    if I make my bed in the depths, you are there.
If I rise on the wings of the dawn,
    if I settle on the far side of the sea,
even there your hand will guide me,
    your right hand will hold me fast.

If I say, "Surely the darkness will hide me
    and the light become night around me,"
even the darkness will not be dark to you;
    the night will shine like the day,
    for darkness is as light to you.

"Am I only a God nearby,"
                        declares the LORD,
    "and not a God far away?
Can anyone hide in secret places
    so that I cannot see him?"
                        declares the LORD.
    "Do not I fill heaven and earth?"
                        declares the LORD.

Then Jesus came to them and said, "All authority
in heaven and on earth has been given to me. Therefore
go and make disciples of all nations, baptizing them in
the name of the Father and of the Son and of the Holy
Spirit, and teaching them to obey everything I have
commanded you. And surely I am with you always, to the
very end of the age."

PSALM 139:7-12; JEREMIAH 23:23-24; MATTHEW 28:18-20

Related texts: DEUTERONOMY 4:7; 1 KINGS 8:27; JOHN 1:45-49; 14:16-17

THE ONE MINUTE BIBLE

God Knows Everything

**THE ONE
MINUTE
BIBLE**

O LORD, you have searched me
    and you know me.
You know when I sit and when I rise;
    you perceive my thoughts from afar.
You discern my going out and my lying down;
    you are familiar with all my ways.
Before a word is on my tongue
    you know it completely, O LORD.

You hem me in—behind and before;
    you have laid your hand upon me.
Such knowledge is too wonderful for me,
    too lofty for me to attain.

Oh, the depth of the riches of the wisdom
        and knowledge of God!
    How unsearchable his judgments,
    and his paths beyond tracing out!
"Who has known the mind of the Lord?
    Or who has been his counselor?"
"Who has ever given to God,
    that God should repay him?"
For from him and through him and to him are all things.
    To him be the glory forever! Amen.

    For the word of God is living and active. Sharper
than any double-edged sword, it penetrates even to
dividing soul and spirit, joints and marrow; it judges
the thoughts and attitudes of the heart. Nothing in
all creation is hidden from God's sight. Everything is
uncovered and laid bare before the eyes of him to
whom we must give account.

PSALM 139:1-6; ROMANS 11:33-36; HEBREWS 4:12-13

Related texts: PSALM 94:1-11; PROVERBS 5:21; 2 CHRONICLES 16:9;
1 CORINTHIANS 1:18-25; JOHN 3:19-20

God Is One

Hear, O Israel: The LORD our God, the LORD is one.

The LORD will be king over the whole earth. On that day there will be one LORD, and his name the only name.

Is God the God of Jews only? Is he not the God of Gentiles too? Yes, of Gentiles too, since there is only one God, who will justify the circumcised by faith and the uncircumcised through that same faith.

For even if there are so-called gods, whether in heaven or on earth (as indeed there are many "gods" and many "lords"), yet for us there is but one God, the Father, from whom all things came and for whom we live; and there is but one Lord, Jesus Christ, through whom all things came and through whom we live.

There is one body and one Spirit—just as you were called to one hope when you were called—one Lord, one faith, one baptism; one God and Father of all, who is over all and through all and in all.

DEUTERONOMY 6:4; ZECHARIAH 14:9; ROMANS 3:29-30;
1 CORINTHIANS 8:5-6; EPHESIANS 4:4-6

**THE ONE
MINUTE
BIBLE**

Related texts: ISAIAH 44:6-8; MALACHI 2:10; MATTHEW 19:16-17;
23:1-10; MARK 12:28-34

God Is Righteous

**THE ONE
MINUTE
BIBLE**

Arise, O LORD, in your anger;
  rise up against the rage of my enemies.
  Awake, my God; decree justice.
Let the assembled peoples gather around you.
  Rule over them from on high;
  let the LORD judge the peoples.
Judge me, O LORD, according to my righteousness,
  according to my integrity, O Most High.
O righteous God,
  who searches minds and hearts,
bring to an end the violence of the wicked
  and make the righteous secure.
My shield is God Most High,
  who saves the upright in heart.
God is a righteous judge,
  a God who expresses his wrath every day.

"The days are coming," declares the LORD,
  "when I will raise up to David a righteous Branch,
a King who will reign wisely
  and do what is just and right in the land.
In his days Judah will be saved
  and Israel will live in safety.
This is the name by which he will be called:
  The LORD Our Righteousness."

  My dear children, I write this to you so that you will
not sin. But if anybody does sin, we have one who speaks
to the Father in our defense—Jesus Christ, the Righteous
One. He is the atoning sacrifice for our sins, and not only
for ours but also for the sins of the whole world.

PSALM 7:6-11; JEREMIAH 23:5-6; 1 JOHN 2:1-2

Related texts: EZRA 9; PSALMS 36:5-10; 71; DANIEL 9:1-19;
MATTHEW 6:28-33; ACTS 3:12-16

Our Heavenly Father

You are all sons of God through faith in Christ Jesus, for all of you who were baptized into Christ have clothed yourselves with Christ. There is neither Jew nor Greek, slave nor free, male nor female, for you are all one in Christ Jesus. If you belong to Christ, then you are Abraham's seed, and heirs according to the promise.

THE ONE MINUTE BIBLE

What I am saying is that as long as the heir is a child, he is no different from a slave, although he owns the whole estate. He is subject to guardians and trustees until the time set by his father. So also, when we were children, we were in slavery under the basic principles of the world. But when the time had fully come, God sent his Son, born of a woman, born under law, to redeem those under law, that we might receive the full rights of sons. Because you are sons, God sent the Spirit of his Son into our hearts, the Spirit who calls out, "*Abba,* Father." So you are no longer a slave, but a son; and since you are a son, God has made you also an heir.

How great is the love the Father has lavished on us, that we should be called children of God! And that is what we are! The reason the world does not know us is that it did not know him. Dear friends, now we are children of God, and what we will be has not yet been made known. But we know that when he appears, we shall be like him, for we shall see him as he is.

GALATIANS 3:26-29; 4:1-7; 1 JOHN 3:1-2

Related texts: DEUTERONOMY 32:6; PSALM 2; ISAIAH 9:1-7; JOHN 1:12-13; ROMANS 8; HEBREWS 12:1-14

Honor Your Father

**THE ONE
MINUTE
BIBLE**

Honor your father and your mother, so that you may
    live long in the land the LORD your God is giving you.

To have a fool for a son brings grief;
    there is no joy for the father of a fool.

My son, if your heart is wise,
    then my heart will be glad;
my inmost being will rejoice
    when your lips speak what is right.
Listen, my son, and be wise,
    and keep your heart on the right path.

    Let the word of Christ dwell in you richly as you
teach and admonish one another with all wisdom, and as
you sing psalms, hymns and spiritual songs with
gratitude in your hearts to God. And whatever you do,
whether in word or deed, do it all in the name of the Lord
Jesus, giving thanks to God the Father through him.
    Wives, submit to your husbands, as is fitting
in the Lord.
    Husbands, love your wives and do not be harsh
with them.
    Children, obey your parents in everything, for this
pleases the Lord.
    Fathers, do not embitter your children, or they will
become discouraged.

EXODUS 20:12; PROVERBS 17:21; 23:15-16, 19; COLOSSIANS 3:16-21

Related texts: EXODUS 21:15; LEVITICUS 19:3; PROVERBS 10:1; 23:22-25; EPHESIANS 6:1-3

A Father's Instruction

Listen, my sons, to a father's instruction;
pay attention and gain understanding.
I give you sound learning,
so do not forsake my teaching.
When I was a boy in my father's house,
still tender, and an only child of my mother,
he taught me and said,
"Lay hold of my words with all your heart;
keep my commands and you will live.
Get wisdom, get understanding;
do not forget my words or swerve from them.
Do not forsake wisdom, and she will protect you;
love her, and she will watch over you.
Wisdom is supreme; therefore get wisdom.
Though it cost all you have, get understanding.
Esteem her, and she will exalt you;
embrace her, and she will honor you.
She will set a garland of grace on your head
and present you with a crown of splendor."

Listen, my son, accept what I say,
and the years of your life will be many.
I guide you in the way of wisdom
and lead you along straight paths.
When you walk, your steps will not be hampered;
when you run, you will not stumble.

PROVERBS 4:1-12

**THE ONE
MINUTE
BIBLE**

Related texts: DEUTERONOMY 6:1-9; PROVERBS 1:8; 6:20-24; 31:1-9;
2 TIMOTHY 1:2-3

A Father's Discipline

**THE ONE
MINUTE
BIBLE**

In your struggle against sin, you have not yet resisted to the point of shedding your blood. And you have forgotten that word of encouragement that addresses you as sons:

"My son, do not make light of the Lord's discipline,
	and do not lose heart when he rebukes you,
because the Lord disciplines those he loves,
	and he punishes everyone he accepts as a son."

Endure hardship as discipline; God is treating you as sons. For what son is not disciplined by his father? If you are not disciplined (and everyone undergoes discipline), then you are illegitimate children and not true sons. Moreover, we have all had human fathers who disciplined us and we respected them for it. How much more should we submit to the Father of our spirits and live!

Our fathers disciplined us for a little while as they thought best; but God disciplines us for our good, that we may share in his holiness. No discipline seems pleasant at the time, but painful. Later on, however, it produces a harvest of righteousness and peace for those who have been trained by it.

HEBREWS 12:4-11

Related texts: DEUTERONOMY 8:5; 1 SAMUEL 2:12-36; PROVERBS 3:11-12; 15:5; REVELATION 3:14-20

A Faithful Husband

**THE ONE
MINUTE
BIBLE**

My son, pay attention to my wisdom,
    listen well to my words of insight,
that you may maintain discretion
    and your lips may preserve knowledge.
For the lips of an adulteress drip honey,
    and her speech is smoother than oil;
but in the end she is bitter as gall,
    sharp as a double-edged sword.

Drink water from your own cistern,
    running water from your own well.
Should your springs overflow in the streets,
    your streams of water in the public squares?
Let them be yours alone,
    never to be shared with strangers.
May your fountain be blessed,
    and may you rejoice in the wife of your youth.
A loving doe, a graceful deer—
    may her breasts satisfy you always,
    may you ever be captivated by her love.
Why be captivated, my son, by an adulteress?
    Why embrace the bosom of another man's wife?

For a man's ways are in full view of the LORD,
    and he examines all his paths.
The evil deeds of a wicked man ensnare him;
    the cords of his sin hold him fast.
He will die for lack of discipline,
    led astray by his own great folly.

PROVERBS 5:1-4, 15-23

Related texts: EXODUS 20:14; LEVITICUS 20:10; PROVERBS 2:16-22;
6:23-35; 7; EPHESIANS 5:1-3

**THE ONE
MINUTE
BIBLE**

Love Song to a Husband

Like an apple tree among the trees of the forest
    is my lover among the young men.
I delight to sit in his shade,
    and his fruit is sweet to my taste.
He has taken me to the banquet hall,
    and his banner over me is love.
Strengthen me with raisins,
    refresh me with apples,
    for I am faint with love.
His left arm is under my head,
    and his right arm embraces me.
Listen! My lover!
    Look! Here he comes,
leaping across the mountains,
    bounding over the hills.
My lover is like a gazelle or a young stag.
    Look! There he stands behind our wall,
gazing through the windows,
    peering through the lattice.
My lover spoke and said to me,
    "Arise, my darling,
    my beautiful one, and come with me.
See! The winter is past;
    the rains are over and gone.
Flowers appear on the earth;
    the season of singing has come,
the cooing of doves
    is heard in our land.
The fig tree forms its early fruit;
    the blossoming vines spread their fragrance.
Arise, come, my darling;
    my beautiful one, come with me."

SONG OF SONGS 2:3-6, 8-13

Related texts: PSALM 45; SONG OF SONGS 1–8; 2 CORINTHIANS 11:2-3;
1 PETER 3:1-6

Husbands, Love Your Wives

Husbands, love your wives, just as Christ loved the church and gave himself up for her to make her holy, cleansing her by the washing with water through the word, and to present her to himself as a radiant church, without stain or wrinkle or any other blemish, but holy and blameless. In this same way, husbands ought to love their wives as their own bodies.

He who loves his wife loves himself. After all, no one ever hated his own body, but he feeds and cares for it, just as Christ does the church—for we are members of his body. "For this reason a man will leave his father and mother and be united to his wife, and the two will become one flesh." This is a profound mystery—but I am talking about Christ and the church. However, each one of you also must love his wife as he loves himself, and the wife must respect her husband.

Husbands, in the same way be considerate as you live with your wives, and treat them with respect as the weaker partner and as heirs with you of the gracious gift of life, so that nothing will hinder your prayers.

EPHESIANS 5:25-33; 1 PETER 3:7

THE ONE MINUTE BIBLE

Related texts: GENESIS 2:18-25; HOSEA 3:1-3; MALACHI 2:13-16; COLOSSIANS 3:19; REVELATION 21:1-4

God's Daily Guidance for Israel

THE ONE
MINUTE
BIBLE

On the day the tabernacle, the Tent of the Testimony, was set up, the cloud covered it. From evening till morning the cloud above the tabernacle looked like fire. That is how it continued to be; the cloud covered it, and at night it looked like fire. Whenever the cloud lifted from above the Tent, the Israelites set out; wherever the cloud settled, the Israelites encamped.

At the LORD's command the Israelites set out, and at his command they encamped. As long as the cloud stayed over the tabernacle, they remained in camp. When the cloud remained over the tabernacle a long time, the Israelites obeyed the LORD's order and did not set out. Sometimes the cloud was over the tabernacle only a few days; at the LORD's command they would encamp, and then at his command they would set out. Sometimes the cloud stayed only from evening till morning, and when it lifted in the morning, they set out. Whether by day or by night, whenever the cloud lifted, they set out. Whether the cloud stayed over the tabernacle for two days or a month or a year, the Israelites would remain in camp and not set out; but when it lifted, they would set out.

At the LORD's command they encamped, and at the LORD's command they set out. They obeyed the LORD's order, in accordance with his command through Moses.

NUMBERS 9:15-23

Related texts: EXODUS 13:22, 33; 40:34-38; NUMBERS 14:11-14; 1 CORINTHIANS 10:1-2

Israel Puts God to the Test

THE ONE
MINUTE
BIBLE

Israel willfully put God to the test
   by demanding the food they craved.
They spoke against God, saying,
   "Can God spread a table in the desert?
When he struck the rock, water gushed out,
   and streams flowed abundantly.
But can he also give us food?
   Can he supply meat for his people?"
When the LORD heard them, he was very angry;
   his fire broke out against Jacob,
   and his wrath rose against Israel,
for they did not believe in God
   or trust in his deliverance.
Yet he gave a command to the skies above
   and opened the doors of the heavens;
he rained down manna for the people to eat,
   he gave them the grain of heaven.
Men ate the bread of angels;
   he sent them all the food they could eat.
He let loose the east wind from the heavens
   and led forth the south wind by his power.
He rained meat down on them like dust,
   flying birds like sand on the seashore.
He made them come down inside their camp,
   all around their tents.
They ate till they had more than enough,
   for he had given them what they craved.
But before they turned from the food they craved,
   even while it was still in their mouths,
God's anger rose against them;
   he put to death the sturdiest among them,
   cutting down the young men of Israel.
In spite of all this, they kept on sinning;
   in spite of his wonders, they did not believe.

PSALM 78:18-32

Related texts: NUMBERS 11; PSALM 106:1-15; LUKE 4:1-13; JAMES 4:1-4

Israel Rejects the Promised Land

**THE ONE
MINUTE
BIBLE**

The LORD said to Moses, "Send some men to explore the land of Canaan, which I am giving to the Israelites. From each ancestral tribe send one of its leaders."

They came back to Moses and Aaron and the whole Israelite community at Kadesh in the Desert of Paran. There they reported to them and to the whole assembly and showed them the fruit of the land. They gave Moses this account: "We went into the land to which you sent us, and it does flow with milk and honey! Here is its fruit. But the people who live there are powerful, and the cities are fortified and very large."

Then Caleb silenced the people before Moses and said, "We should go up and take possession of the land, for we can certainly do it."

But the men who had gone up with him said, "We can't attack those people; they are stronger than we are."

That night all the people of the community raised their voices and wept aloud. All the Israelites grumbled against Moses and Aaron, and the whole assembly said to them, "If only we had died in Egypt! Or in this desert! Why is the LORD bringing us to this land only to let us fall by the sword? Our wives and children will be taken as plunder. Wouldn't it be better for us to go back to Egypt?" And they said to each other, "We should choose a leader and go back to Egypt."

NUMBERS 13:1-2, 26-28a, 30-31; 14:1-4

Forty Years in the Desert

**THE ONE
MINUTE
BIBLE**

Then Moses and Aaron fell facedown in front of the whole Israelite assembly gathered there. Joshua son of Nun and Caleb son of Jephunneh, who were among those who had explored the land, tore their clothes and said to the entire Israelite assembly, "The land we passed through and explored is exceedingly good. If the LORD is pleased with us, he will lead us into that land, a land flowing with milk and honey, and will give it to us. Only do not rebel against the LORD. And do not be afraid of the people of the land, because we will swallow them up. Their protection is gone, but the LORD is with us. Do not be afraid of them."

The LORD said to Moses and Aaron: "How long will this wicked community grumble against me? I have heard the complaints of these grumbling Israelites. So tell them, 'As surely as I live, declares the LORD, I will do to you the very things I heard you say: In this desert your bodies will fall—every one of you twenty years old or more who was counted in the census and who has grumbled against me. Not one of you will enter the land I swore with uplifted hand to make your home, except Caleb son of Jephunneh and Joshua son of Nun. For forty years—one year for each of the forty days you explored the land—you will suffer for your sins and know what it is like to have me against you.'"

What, then, shall we say in response to this? If God is for us, who can be against us?

NUMBERS 14:5-9, 26-30, 34; ROMANS 8:31

Related texts: JOSHUA 5:1-6; JOHN 6:48-51; 1 CORINTHIANS 10:1-6; HEBREWS 3:7–4:7

Listen to God's Voice

THE ONE MINUTE BIBLE

So, as the Holy Spirit says:

> "Today, if you hear his voice,
>   do not harden your hearts
> as you did in the rebellion,
>   during the time of testing in the desert,
> where your fathers tested and tried me
>   and for forty years saw what I did.
> That is why I was angry with that generation,
>   and I said, 'Their hearts are always going astray,
>   and they have not known my ways.'
> So I declared on oath in my anger,
>   'They shall never enter my rest.'"

See to it, brothers, that none of you has a sinful, unbelieving heart that turns away from the living God. But encourage one another daily, as long as it is called Today, so that none of you may be hardened by sin's deceitfulness. We have come to share in Christ if we hold firmly till the end the confidence we had at first. As has just been said:

> "Today, if you hear his voice,
>   do not harden your hearts
> as you did in the rebellion."

Who were they who heard and rebelled? Were they not all those Moses led out of Egypt? And with whom was he angry for forty years? Was it not with those who sinned, whose bodies fell in the desert? And to whom did God swear that they would never enter his rest if not to those who disobeyed? So we see that they were not able to enter, because of their unbelief.

HEBREWS 3:7-19

Related texts: PSALM 95; MATTHEW 17:1-5; JOHN 14:15-24; ACTS 3:19-23; HEBREWS 4

God Crushes Rebellion

**THE ONE
MINUTE
BIBLE**

Korah son of Izhar, the son of Kohath, the son of Levi, and certain Reubenites—Dathan and Abiram, sons of Eliab, and On son of Peleth—became insolent and rose up against Moses. With them were 250 Israelite men, well-known community leaders who had been appointed members of the council. They came as a group to oppose Moses and Aaron and said to them, "You have gone too far! The whole community is holy, every one of them, and the LORD is with them. Why then do you set yourselves above the LORD's assembly?"

When Moses heard this, he fell facedown. Then he said to Korah and all his followers: "In the morning the LORD will show who belongs to him and who is holy, and he will have that person come near him. The man he chooses he will cause to come near him. You, Korah, and all your followers are to do this: Take censers and tomorrow put fire and incense in them before the LORD. The man the LORD chooses will be the one who is holy. You Levites have gone too far!"

When Korah had gathered all his followers in opposition to them at the entrance to the Tent of Meeting, the glory of the LORD appeared to the entire assembly.

And the earth opened its mouth and swallowed them, with their households and all Korah's men and all their possessions. They went down alive into the grave, with everything they owned; the earth closed over them, and they perished and were gone from the community.

NUMBERS 16:1-7, 19, 32-33

Related texts: PSALM 106:16-17; HEBREWS 10:26-31; 12:23-29; 2 PETER 1:16–2:22; JUDE 1:11

Moses Disobeys God

**THE ONE
MINUTE
BIBLE**

In the first month the whole Israelite community arrived at the Desert of Zin, and they stayed at Kadesh. There Miriam died and was buried.

Now there was no water for the community, and the people gathered in opposition to Moses and Aaron. They quarreled with Moses and said, "If only we had died when our brothers fell dead before the LORD! Why did you bring the LORD's community into this desert, that we and our livestock should die here? Why did you bring us up out of Egypt to this terrible place? It has no grain or figs, grapevines or pomegranates. And there is no water to drink!"

Moses and Aaron went from the assembly to the entrance to the Tent of Meeting and fell facedown, and the glory of the LORD appeared to them. The LORD said to Moses, "Take the staff, and you and your brother Aaron gather the assembly together. Speak to that rock before their eyes and it will pour out its water. You will bring water out of the rock for the community so they and their livestock can drink."

So Moses took the staff from the LORD's presence, just as he commanded him. He and Aaron gathered the assembly together in front of the rock and Moses said to them, "Listen, you rebels, must we bring you water out of this rock?" Then Moses raised his arm and struck the rock twice with his staff. Water gushed out, and the community and their livestock drank.

But the LORD said to Moses and Aaron, "Because you did not trust in me enough to honor me as holy in the sight of the Israelites, you will not bring this community into the land I give them."

NUMBERS 20:1-12

Related texts: EXODUS 7:19-21; 8:16-17; 17:1-6; DEUTERONOMY 4:20-22; ACTS 5:1-11

Look Up and Live

They traveled from Mount Hor along the route to the Red Sea, to go around Edom. But the people grew impatient on the way; they spoke against God and against Moses, and said, "Why have you brought us up out of Egypt to die in the desert? There is no bread! There is no water! And we detest this miserable food!"

Then the LORD sent venomous snakes among them; they bit the people and many Israelites died. The people came to Moses and said, "We sinned when we spoke against the LORD and against you. Pray that the LORD will take the snakes away from us." So Moses prayed for the people.

The LORD said to Moses, "Make a snake and put it up on a pole; anyone who is bitten can look at it and live." So Moses made a bronze snake and put it up on a pole. Then when anyone was bitten by a snake and looked at the bronze snake, he lived.

Just as Moses lifted up the snake in the desert, so the Son of Man must be lifted up, that everyone who believes in him may have eternal life.

For God so loved the world that he gave his one and only Son, that whoever believes in him shall not perish but have eternal life. For God did not send his Son into the world to condemn the world, but to save the world through him.

NUMBERS 21:4-9; JOHN 3:14-17

Related texts: EXODUS 16:6-12; NUMBERS 14:26-37; 2 KINGS 18:1-4; LAMENTATIONS 3:25-40; 1 CORINTHIANS 10:1-11

Balaam Hired to Curse Israel

**THE ONE
MINUTE
BIBLE**

Then the Israelites traveled to the plains of Moab and camped along the Jordan across from Jericho.

Now Balak son of Zippor saw all that Israel had done to the Amorites, and Moab was terrified because there were so many people. Indeed, Moab was filled with dread because of the Israelites.

So Balak son of Zippor, who was king of Moab at that time, sent messengers to summon Balaam son of Beor, who was at Pethor, near the River, in his native land. Balak said:

> "A people has come out of Egypt; they cover
> the face of the land and have settled next to me.
> Now come and put a curse on these people,
> because they are too powerful for me. Perhaps
> then I will be able to defeat them and drive them
> out of the country. For I know that those you bless
> are blessed, and those you curse are cursed."

No Ammonite or Moabite or any of his descendants may enter the assembly of the LORD, even down to the tenth generation. For they did not come to meet you with bread and water on your way when you came out of Egypt, and they hired Balaam son of Beor from Pethor in Aram Naharaim to pronounce a curse on you. However, the LORD your God would not listen to Balaam but turned the curse into a blessing for you, because the LORD your God loves you.

NUMBERS 22:1-3, 4b-6; DEUTERONOMY 23:3-5

Related texts: GENESIS 12:1-3; NUMBERS 22–24; JOSHUA 24:8-10;
2 PETER 2:15-16

*This Bible is for the government
of the people, by the people,
and for the people.*
John Wycliffe (1328-1384)
ENGLISH THEOLOGIAN
(Preface to translation of the Bible)

*The more this Bible enters
into our national life the
grander and purer and better
will that life become.*
David Josiah Brewer (1837-1910)
UNITED STATES SUPREME COURT JUSTICE

*It is impossible to rightly
govern the world without
God and the Bible.*
George Washington (1732-1799)
UNITED STATES PRESIDENT

Balaam Blesses Israel

When Balaam looked out and saw Israel encamped tribe by tribe, the Spirit of God came upon him and he uttered his oracle:

"The oracle of Balaam son of Beor,
    the oracle of one whose eye sees clearly,
the oracle of one who hears the words of God,
    who sees a vision from the Almighty,
    who falls prostrate, and whose eyes are opened:

"How beautiful are your tents, O Jacob,
    your dwelling places, O Israel!

"Like valleys they spread out,
    like gardens beside a river,
like aloes planted by the LORD,
    like cedars beside the waters.
Water will flow from their buckets;
    their seed will have abundant water.

"Their king will be greater than Agag;
    their kingdom will be exalted.

"God brought them out of Egypt;
    they have the strength of a wild ox.
They devour hostile nations
    and break their bones in pieces;
    with their arrows they pierce them.
Like a lion they crouch and lie down,
    like a lioness—who dares to rouse them?

"May those who bless you be blessed
    and those who curse you be cursed!"

NUMBERS 24:2-9

THE ONE MINUTE BIBLE

Related texts: GENESIS 12:1-3; 22:15-18; 27:26-29; DEUTERONOMY 23:3-5; JOSHUA 13:22; 24:8-10; REVELATION 2:12-14

Judgment for Immorality

**THE ONE
MINUTE
BIBLE**

While Israel was staying in Shittim, the men began to indulge in sexual immorality with Moabite women, who invited them to the sacrifices to their gods. The people ate and bowed down before these gods. So Israel joined in worshiping the Baal of Peor. And the LORD's anger burned against them.

The LORD said to Moses, "Take all the leaders of these people, kill them and expose them in broad daylight before the LORD, so that the LORD's fierce anger may turn away from Israel."

So Moses said to Israel's judges, "Each of you must put to death those of your men who have joined in worshiping the Baal of Peor."

Then an Israelite man brought to his family a Midianite woman right before the eyes of Moses and the whole assembly of Israel while they were weeping at the entrance to the Tent of Meeting. When Phinehas son of Eleazar, the son of Aaron, the priest, saw this, he left the assembly, took a spear in his hand and followed the Israelite into the tent. He drove the spear through both of them—through the Israelite and into the woman's body. Then the plague against the Israelites was stopped; but those who died in the plague numbered 24,000.

Flee from sexual immorality. All other sins a man commits are outside his body, but he who sins sexually sins against his own body. Do you not know that your body is a temple of the Holy Spirit, who is in you, whom you have received from God? You are not your own; you were bought at a price. Therefore honor God with your body.

NUMBERS 25:1-9; 1 CORINTHIANS 6:18-20

Related texts: DEUTERONOMY 4:1-4; JOSHUA 22:16-20; PSALM 106:28-31; HOSEA 9:10; 1 CORINTHIANS 10:1-8

Vengeance Against Midian

**THE ONE
MINUTE
BIBLE**

The LORD said to Moses, "Take vengeance on the Midianites for the Israelites. After that, you will be gathered to your people."

So Moses said to the people, "Arm some of your men to go to war against the Midianites and to carry out the LORD's vengeance on them. Send into battle a thousand men from each of the tribes of Israel." So twelve thousand men armed for battle, a thousand from each tribe, were supplied from the clans of Israel.

They fought against Midian, as the LORD commanded Moses, and killed every man. Among their victims were Evi, Rekem, Zur, Hur and Reba—the five kings of Midian. They also killed Balaam son of Beor with the sword. The Israelites captured the Midianite women and children and took all the Midianite herds, flocks and goods as plunder. They burned all the towns where the Midianites had settled, as well as all their camps.

Moses, Eleazar the priest and all the leaders of the community went to meet them outside the camp. Moses was angry with the officers of the army—the commanders of thousands and commanders of hundreds—who returned from the battle.

"Have you allowed all the women to live?" he asked them. "They were the ones who followed Balaam's advice and were the means of turning the Israelites away from the LORD in what happened at Peor, so that a plague struck the LORD's people."

NUMBERS 31:1-5, 7-10, 13-16

Related texts: NUMBERS 25; DEUTERONOMY 21:10-14; JOSHUA 13:16-22; JUDGES 6–8; ROMANS 12:16-21

Love the LORD Your God

These are the commands, decrees and laws the LORD your God directed me to teach you to observe in the land that you are crossing the Jordan to possess, so that you, your children and their children after them may fear the LORD your God as long as you live by keeping all his decrees and commands that I give you, and so that you may enjoy long life. Hear, O Israel, and be careful to obey so that it may go well with you and that you may increase greatly in a land flowing with milk and honey, just as the LORD, the God of your fathers, promised you.

Hear, O Israel: The LORD our God, the LORD is one. Love the LORD your God with all your heart and with all your soul and with all your strength. These commandments that I give you today are to be upon your hearts. Impress them on your children. Talk about them when you sit at home and when you walk along the road, when you lie down and when you get up. Tie them as symbols on your hands and bind them on your foreheads. Write them on the doorframes of your houses and on your gates.

Oh, how I love your law!
I meditate on it all day long.

DEUTERONOMY 6:1-9; PSALM 119:97

Related texts: DEUTERONOMY 10:12-16; 11:18-21; PSALMS 1; 119; PROVERBS 22:6; MARK 12:28-34; LUKE 10:25-28; 1 JOHN 5:1-4

Joshua Succeeds Moses

Then Moses went out and spoke these words to all Israel: "I am now a hundred and twenty years old and I am no longer able to lead you. The LORD has said to me, 'You shall not cross the Jordan.' The LORD your God himself will cross over ahead of you. He will destroy these nations before you, and you will take possession of their land.

"Joshua also will cross over ahead of you, as the LORD said. And the LORD will do to them what he did to Sihon and Og, the kings of the Amorites, whom he destroyed along with their land. The LORD will deliver them to you, and you must do to them all that I have commanded you. Be strong and courageous. Do not be afraid or terrified because of them, for the LORD your God goes with you; he will never leave you nor forsake you."

Then Moses summoned Joshua and said to him in the presence of all Israel, "Be strong and courageous, for you must go with this people into the land that the LORD swore to their forefathers to give them, and you must divide it among them as their inheritance. The LORD himself goes before you and will be with you; he will never leave you nor forsake you. Do not be afraid; do not be discouraged."

So Moses wrote down this law and gave it to the priests, the sons of Levi, who carried the ark of the covenant of the LORD, and to all the elders of Israel.

DEUTERONOMY 31:1-9

Related texts: NUMBERS 21:21-35; DEUTERONOMY 2:24–3:17; 1 KINGS 8:54-57; HEBREWS 13:5-6

Be Strong and Courageous

**THE ONE
MINUTE
BIBLE**

After the death of Moses the servant of the LORD, the LORD said to Joshua son of Nun, Moses' aide: "Moses my servant is dead. Now then, you and all these people, get ready to cross the Jordan River into the land I am about to give to them—to the Israelites. I will give you every place where you set your foot, as I promised Moses. Your territory will extend from the desert to Lebanon, and from the great river, the Euphrates—all the Hittite country—to the Great Sea on the west. No one will be able to stand up against you all the days of your life. As I was with Moses, so I will be with you; I will never leave you nor forsake you.

"Be strong and courageous, because you will lead these people to inherit the land I swore to their forefathers to give them. Be strong and very courageous. Be careful to obey all the law my servant Moses gave you; do not turn from it to the right or to the left, that you may be successful wherever you go. Do not let this Book of the Law depart from your mouth; meditate on it day and night, so that you may be careful to do everything written in it. Then you will be prosperous and successful. Have I not commanded you? Be strong and courageous. Do not be terrified; do not be discouraged, for the LORD your God will be with you wherever you go."

JOSHUA 1:1-9

Related texts: DEUTERONOMY 11:22-25; PSALMS 1; 19; 119;
1 CORINTHIANS 16:13-14; HEBREWS 3:1-6

Rahab Hides the Israelite Spies

Then Joshua son of Nun secretly sent two spies from Shittim. "Go, look over the land," he said, "especially Jericho." So they went and entered the house of a prostitute named Rahab and stayed there.

The king of Jericho was told, "Look! Some of the Israelites have come here tonight to spy out the land." So the king of Jericho sent this message to Rahab: "Bring out the men who came to you and entered your house, because they have come to spy out the whole land."

But the woman had taken the two men and hidden them. She said, "Yes, the men came to me, but I did not know where they had come from. At dusk, when it was time to close the city gate, the men left. I don't know which way they went. Go after them quickly. You may catch up with them." (But she had taken them up to the roof and hidden them under the stalks of flax she had laid out on the roof.)

When they left, they went into the hills and stayed there three days, until the pursuers had searched all along the road and returned without finding them. Then the two men started back. They went down out of the hills, forded the river and came to Joshua son of Nun and told him everything that had happened to them. They said to Joshua, "The LORD has surely given the whole land into our hands; all the people are melting in fear because of us."

JOSHUA 2:1-6, 22-24

THE ONE MINUTE BIBLE

Related texts: MATTHEW 1:1-6; HEBREWS 11:31; JAMES 2:25

The Israelites Conquer Jericho

**THE ONE
MINUTE
BIBLE**

Now Jericho was tightly shut up because of the Israelites. No one went out and no one came in.

Then the LORD said to Joshua, "See, I have delivered Jericho into your hands, along with its king and its fighting men. March around the city once with all the armed men. Do this for six days. Have seven priests carry trumpets of rams' horns in front of the ark. On the seventh day, march around the city seven times, with the priests blowing the trumpets. When you hear them sound a long blast on the trumpets, have all the people give a loud shout; then the wall of the city will collapse and the people will go up, every man straight in."

When the trumpets sounded, the people shouted, and at the sound of the trumpet, when the people gave a loud shout, the wall collapsed; so every man charged straight in, and they took the city. They devoted the city to the LORD and destroyed with the sword every living thing in it—men and women, young and old, cattle, sheep and donkeys.

But Joshua spared Rahab the prostitute, with her family and all who belonged to her, because she hid the men Joshua had sent as spies to Jericho—and she lives among the Israelites to this day.

JOSHUA 6:1-5, 20-21, 25

Related texts: NUMBERS 10:1-10; JUDGES 7:1-22; MATTHEW 1:1-6

Joshua Conquers the Land of Canaan

As the L<small>ORD</small> commanded his servant Moses, so Moses commanded Joshua, and Joshua did it; he left nothing undone of all that the L<small>ORD</small> commanded Moses.

So Joshua took this entire land: the hill country, all the Negev, the whole region of Goshen, the western foothills, the Arabah and the mountains of Israel with their foothills, from Mount Halak, which rises toward Seir, to Baal Gad in the Valley of Lebanon below Mount Hermon. He captured all their kings and struck them down, putting them to death. Joshua waged war against all these kings for a long time. Except for the Hivites living in Gibeon, not one city made a treaty of peace with the Israelites, who took them all in battle. For it was the L<small>ORD</small> himself who hardened their hearts to wage war against Israel, so that he might destroy them totally, exterminating them without mercy, as the L<small>ORD</small> had commanded Moses.

So Joshua took the entire land, just as the L<small>ORD</small> had directed Moses, and he gave it as an inheritance to Israel according to their tribal divisions.

Then the land had rest from war.

J<small>OSHUA</small> 11:15-20, 23

THE ONE MINUTE BIBLE

Related texts: D<small>EUTERONOMY</small> 7; 9:1-6; 18:9-14; 20:16-18; J<small>OSHUA</small> 7–10

Joshua's Farewell Address

**THE ONE
MINUTE
BIBLE**

[Joshua said,] "Now fear the LORD and serve him with all faithfulness. Throw away the gods your forefathers worshiped beyond the River and in Egypt, and serve the LORD. But if serving the LORD seems undesirable to you, then choose for yourselves this day whom you will serve, whether the gods your forefathers served beyond the River, or the gods of the Amorites, in whose land you are living. But as for me and my household, we will serve the LORD."

Then the people answered, "Far be it from us to forsake the LORD to serve other gods! It was the LORD our God himself who brought us and our fathers up out of Egypt, from that land of slavery, and performed those great signs before our eyes. He protected us on our entire journey and among all the nations through which we traveled. And the LORD drove out before us all the nations, including the Amorites, who lived in the land. We too will serve the LORD, because he is our God."

Joshua said to the people, "You are not able to serve the LORD. He is a holy God; he is a jealous God. He will not forgive your rebellion and your sins. If you forsake the LORD and serve foreign gods, he will turn and bring disaster on you and make an end of you, after he has been good to you."

But the people said to Joshua, "No! We will serve the LORD."

JOSHUA 24:14-21

Related texts: EXODUS 24:3-8; LEVITICUS 26; ROMANS 6; HEBREWS 3–4

The Days of the Judges

The people served the LORD throughout the lifetime of Joshua and of the elders who outlived him and who had seen all the great things the LORD had done for Israel.

After that whole generation had been gathered to their fathers, another generation grew up, who knew neither the LORD nor what he had done for Israel. Then the Israelites did evil in the eyes of the LORD and served the Baals.

In his anger against Israel the LORD handed them over to raiders who plundered them. He sold them to their enemies all around, whom they were no longer able to resist. Whenever Israel went out to fight, the hand of the LORD was against them to defeat them, just as he had sworn to them. They were in great distress.

Then the LORD raised up judges, who saved them out of the hands of these raiders. Whenever the LORD raised up a judge for them, he was with the judge and saved them out of the hands of their enemies as long as the judge lived; for the LORD had compassion on them as they groaned under those who oppressed and afflicted them. But when the judge died, the people returned to ways even more corrupt than those of their fathers, following other gods and serving and worshiping them. They refused to give up their evil practices and stubborn ways.

JUDGES 2:7, 10-11, 14-16, 18-19

Related texts: DEUTERONOMY 4:1-10; 11:18-25; JUDGES 2:19–3:31; PSALM 78:1-6; EPHESIANS 2:1-10

Deborah: Prophetess and Judge

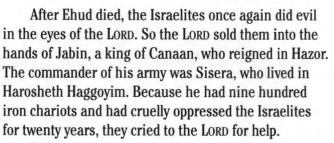

**THE ONE
MINUTE
BIBLE**

After Ehud died, the Israelites once again did evil in the eyes of the LORD. So the LORD sold them into the hands of Jabin, a king of Canaan, who reigned in Hazor. The commander of his army was Sisera, who lived in Harosheth Haggoyim. Because he had nine hundred iron chariots and had cruelly oppressed the Israelites for twenty years, they cried to the LORD for help.

Deborah, a prophetess, the wife of Lappidoth, was leading Israel at that time. She held court under the Palm of Deborah between Ramah and Bethel in the hill country of Ephraim, and the Israelites came to her to have their disputes decided. She sent for Barak son of Abinoam from Kedesh in Naphtali and said to him, "The LORD, the God of Israel, commands you: 'Go, take with you ten thousand men of Naphtali and Zebulun and lead the way to Mount Tabor. I will lure Sisera, the commander of Jabin's army, with his chariots and his troops to the Kishon River and give him into your hands.'"

Barak said to her, "If you go with me, I will go; but if you don't go with me, I won't go."

"Very well," Deborah said, "I will go with you. But because of the way you are going about this, the honor will not be yours, for the LORD will hand Sisera over to a woman."

JUDGES 4:1-9a

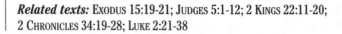

Related texts: EXODUS 15:19-21; JUDGES 5:1-12; 2 KINGS 22:11-20; 2 CHRONICLES 34:19-28; LUKE 2:21-38

Jael Kills the Canaanite General

**THE ONE
MINUTE
BIBLE**

Then Deborah said to Barak, "Go! This is the day the LORD has given Sisera into your hands. Has not the LORD gone ahead of you?" So Barak went down Mount Tabor, followed by ten thousand men. At Barak's advance, the LORD routed Sisera and all his chariots and army by the sword, and Sisera abandoned his chariot and fled on foot. But Barak pursued the chariots and army as far as Harosheth Haggoyim. All the troops of Sisera fell by the sword; not a man was left.

Sisera, however, fled on foot to the tent of Jael, the wife of Heber the Kenite, because there were friendly relations between Jabin king of Hazor and the clan of Heber the Kenite.

Jael went out to meet Sisera and said to him, "Come, my lord, come right in. Don't be afraid." So he entered her tent, and she put a covering over him.

"I'm thirsty," he said. "Please give me some water." She opened a skin of milk, gave him a drink, and covered him up.

"Stand in the doorway of the tent," he told her. "If someone comes by and asks you, 'Is anyone here?' say 'No.'"

But Jael, Heber's wife, picked up a tent peg and a hammer and went quietly to him while he lay fast asleep, exhausted. She drove the peg through his temple into the ground, and he died.

JUDGES 4:14-21

Related texts: JUDGES 3:12-30; 5:13-31; 1 SAMUEL 12:8-11; HEBREWS 11:32-34

The Birth of Samson the Strongman

**THE ONE
MINUTE
BIBLE**

Again the Israelites did evil in the eyes of the LORD so the LORD delivered them into the hands of the Philistines for forty years.

A certain man of Zorah, named Manoah, from the clan of the Danites, had a wife who was sterile and remained childless. The angel of the LORD appeared to her and said, "You are sterile and childless, but you are going to conceive and have a son. Now see to it that you drink no wine or other fermented drink and that you do not eat anything unclean, because you will conceive and give birth to a son. No razor may be used on his head, because the boy is to be a Nazirite, set apart to God from birth, and he will begin the deliverance of Israel from the hands of the Philistines."

The woman gave birth to a boy and named him Samson. He grew and the LORD blessed him, and the Spirit of the LORD began to stir him while he was in Mahaneh Dan, between Zorah and Eshtaol.

Samson led Israel for twenty years in the days of the Philistines.

JUDGES 13:1-5, 24-25; 15:20

Related texts: GENESIS 25:21-24; NUMBERS 6:1-21; JUDGES 14-15; LUKE 1

Samson and Delilah

THE ONE
MINUTE
BIBLE

One day Samson went to Gaza, where he saw a prostitute. He went in to spend the night with her. The people of Gaza were told, "Samson is here!" So they surrounded the place and lay in wait for him all night at the city gate. They made no move during the night, saying, "At dawn we'll kill him."

But Samson lay there only until the middle of the night. Then he got up and took hold of the doors of the city gate, together with the two posts, and tore them loose, bar and all. He lifted them to his shoulders and carried them to the top of the hill that faces Hebron.

Some time later, Samson fell in love with a woman in the Valley of Sorek whose name was Delilah. The rulers of the Philistines went to her and said, "See if you can lure him into showing you the secret of his great strength and how we can overpower him so we may tie him up and subdue him. Each one of us will give you eleven hundred shekels of silver."

So Delilah said to Samson, "Tell me the secret of your great strength and how you can be tied up and subdued."

Samson answered her, "If anyone ties me with seven fresh thongs that have not been dried, I'll become as weak as any other man."

Then the rulers of the Philistines brought her seven fresh thongs that had not been dried, and she tied him with them. With men hidden in the room, she called to him, "Samson, the Philistines are upon you!" But he snapped the thongs as easily as a piece of string snaps when it comes close to a flame. So the secret of his strength was not discovered.

JUDGES 16:1-9

Related texts: JUDGES 14–15; PROVERBS 5; 6:20–7:27; 31:1-3; 2 TIMOTHY 2:20-23

The Philistines Blind Samson

**THE ONE
MINUTE
BIBLE**

Then Delilah said to Samson, "How can you say, 'I love you,' when you won't confide in me? This is the third time you have made a fool of me and haven't told me the secret of your great strength." With such nagging she prodded him day after day until he was tired to death.

So he told her everything. "No razor has ever been used on my head," he said, "because I have been a Nazirite set apart to God since birth. If my head were shaved, my strength would leave me, and I would become as weak as any other man."

When Delilah saw that he had told her everything, she sent word to the rulers of the Philistines, "Come back once more; he has told me everything." So the rulers of the Philistines returned with the silver in their hands. Having put him to sleep on her lap, she called a man to shave off the seven braids of his hair, and so began to subdue him. And his strength left him.

Then she called, "Samson, the Philistines are upon you!"

He awoke from his sleep and thought, "I'll go out as before and shake myself free." But he did not know that the LORD had left him.

Then the Philistines seized him, gouged out his eyes and took him down to Gaza. Binding him with bronze shackles, they set him to grinding in the prison.

JUDGES 16:15-21

Related texts: NUMBERS 6:2-21; 30:1-2; PROVERBS 11:13; 20:19; ECCLESIASTES 5:4-6; LUKE 12:47-48

Samson's Revenge

Now the rulers of the Philistines assembled to offer a great sacrifice to Dagon their god and to celebrate, saying, "Our god has delivered Samson, our enemy, into our hands."

While they were in high spirits, they shouted, "Bring out Samson to entertain us." So they called Samson out of the prison, and he performed for them.

When they stood him among the pillars, Samson said to the servant who held his hand, "Put me where I can feel the pillars that support the temple, so that I may lean against them." Now the temple was crowded with men and women; all the rulers of the Philistines were there, and on the roof were about three thousand men and women watching Samson perform.

Then Samson prayed to the LORD, "O Sovereign LORD, remember me. O God, please strengthen me just once more, and let me with one blow get revenge on the Philistines for my two eyes." Then Samson reached toward the two central pillars on which the temple stood. Bracing himself against them, his right hand on the one and his left hand on the other, Samson said, "Let me die with the Philistines!" Then he pushed with all his might, and down came the temple on the rulers and all the people in it. Thus he killed many more when he died than while he lived.

JUDGES 16:23, 25-30

THE ONE MINUTE BIBLE

Related texts: PSALM 3; ISAIAH 1:24; JEREMIAH 5:7-9, 29; 9:9; HEBREWS 11:32-34

Naomi and Ruth: Love and Loyalty

**THE ONE
MINUTE
BIBLE**

In the days when the judges ruled, there was a famine in the land, and a man from Bethlehem in Judah, together with his wife and two sons, went to live for a while in the country of Moab. The man's name was Elimelech, his wife's name Naomi, and the names of his two sons were Mahlon and Kilion.

Now Elimelech, Naomi's husband, died, and she was left with her two sons. They married Moabite women, one named Orpah and the other Ruth. After they had lived there about ten years, both Mahlon and Kilion also died, and Naomi was left without her two sons and her husband.

Then Naomi said to her two daughters-in-law, "Go back, each of you, to your mother's home. May the LORD show kindness to you, as you have shown to your dead and to me. May the LORD grant that each of you will find rest in the home of another husband."

But Ruth replied, "Don't urge me to leave you or to turn back from you. Where you go I will go, and where you stay I will stay. Your people will be my people and your God my God. Where you die I will die, and there I will be buried. May the LORD deal with me, be it ever so severely, if anything but death separates you and me."

So Naomi returned from Moab accompanied by Ruth the Moabitess, her daughter-in-law, arriving in Bethlehem as the barley harvest was beginning.

RUTH 1:1-2a, 3-5, 8-9a, 16-17, 22

Related texts: 2 SAMUEL 3:14-16; PROVERBS 20:6; SONG OF SONGS 8:6-7; 1 CORINTHIANS 13

Ruth Meets Boaz

**THE ONE
MINUTE
BIBLE**

Now Naomi had a relative on her husband's side, from the clan of Elimelech, a man of standing, whose name was Boaz.

And Ruth the Moabitess said to Naomi, "Let me go to the fields and pick up the leftover grain behind anyone in whose eyes I find favor."

Naomi said to her, "Go ahead, my daughter." So she went out and began to glean in the fields behind the harvesters. As it turned out, she found herself working in a field belonging to Boaz, who was from the clan of Elimelech.

So Boaz said to Ruth, "My daughter, listen to me. Don't go and glean in another field and don't go away from here. Stay here with my servant girls."

At this, she bowed down with her face to the ground. She exclaimed, "Why have I found such favor in your eyes that you notice me—a foreigner?"

Boaz replied, "I've been told all about what you have done for your mother-in-law since the death of your husband—how you left your father and mother and your homeland and came to live with a people you did not know before. May the LORD repay you for what you have done. May you be richly rewarded by the LORD, the God of Israel, under whose wings you have come to take refuge."

RUTH 2:1-3, 8, 10-12

Related texts: LEVITICUS 25:25-27, 49-50; PSALM 91; JEREMIAH 32:6-14

Ruth Proposes Marriage to Boaz

**THE ONE
MINUTE
BIBLE**

One day Naomi Ruth's mother-in-law said to her, "My daughter, should I not try to find a home for you, where you will be well provided for? Is not Boaz, with whose servant girls you have been, a kinsman of ours? Tonight he will be winnowing barley on the threshing floor. Wash and perfume yourself, and put on your best clothes. Then go down to the threshing floor, but don't let him know you are there until he has finished eating and drinking. When he lies down, note the place where he is lying. Then go and uncover his feet and lie down. He will tell you what to do."

When Boaz had finished eating and drinking and was in good spirits, he went over to lie down at the far end of the grain pile. Ruth approached quietly, uncovered his feet and lay down. In the middle of the night something startled the man, and he turned and discovered a woman lying at his feet.

"Who are you?" he asked.

"I am your servant Ruth," she said. "Spread the corner of your garment over me, since you are a kinsman-redeemer."

"The LORD bless you, my daughter," he replied. "This kindness is greater than that which you showed earlier: You have not run after the younger men, whether rich or poor. And now, my daughter, don't be afraid. I will do for you all you ask. All my fellow townsmen know that you are a woman of noble character."

RUTH 3:1-4, 7-11

Related texts: GENESIS 38:8-10; DEUTERONOMY 25:5-10; HEBREWS 13:4

Ruth Marries Boaz

Then Boaz announced to the elders and all the people, "Today you are witnesses that I have bought from Naomi all the property of Elimelech, Kilion and Mahlon. I have also acquired Ruth the Moabitess, Mahlon's widow, as my wife, in order to maintain the name of the dead with his property, so that his name will not disappear from among his family or from the town records. Today you are witnesses!"

Then the elders and all those at the gate said, "We are witnesses. May the LORD make the woman who is coming into your home like Rachel and Leah, who together built up the house of Israel. May you have standing in Ephrathah and be famous in Bethlehem. Through the offspring the LORD gives you by this young woman, may your family be like that of Perez, whom Tamar bore to Judah."

So Boaz took Ruth and she became his wife. Then he went to her, and the LORD enabled her to conceive, and she gave birth to a son. The women said to Naomi: "Praise be to the LORD, who this day has not left you without a kinsman-redeemer. May he become famous throughout Israel! He will renew your life and sustain you in your old age. For your daughter-in-law, who loves you and who is better to you than seven sons, has given him birth."

Then Naomi took the child, laid him in her lap and cared for him.

RUTH 4:9-15

**THE ONE
MINUTE
BIBLE**

Related texts: GENESIS 29:31–30:4; 38; MICAH 5:2; MATTHEW 1:1-6

I Am: *The Bread of Life*

So the people asked Jesus, "What miraculous sign then will you give that we may see it and believe you? What will you do? Our forefathers ate the manna in the desert; as it is written: 'He gave them bread from heaven to eat.'"

Jesus said to them, "I tell you the truth, it is not Moses who has given you the bread from heaven, but it is my Father who gives you the true bread from heaven. For the bread of God is he who comes down from heaven and gives life to the world."

"Sir," they said, "from now on give us this bread."

Then Jesus declared, "I am the bread of life. He who comes to me will never go hungry, and he who believes in me will never be thirsty. But as I told you, you have seen me and still you do not believe. All that the Father gives me will come to me, and whoever comes to me I will never drive away. For I have come down from heaven not to do my will but to do the will of him who sent me. And this is the will of him who sent me, that I shall lose none of all that he has given me, but raise them up at the last day. For my Father's will is that everyone who looks to the Son and believes in him shall have eternal life, and I will raise him up at the last day."

JOHN 6:30-40

Related texts: DEUTERONOMY 8:2; PROVERBS 30:7-9; JOHN 6:25-59; 1 CORINTHIANS 10:16-17; REVELATION 2:17

I Am: *The Light of the World*

**THE ONE
MINUTE
BIBLE**

When Jesus spoke again to the people, he said, "I am the light of the world. Whoever follows me will never walk in darkness, but will have the light of life."

As he went along, he saw a man blind from birth. His disciples asked him, "Rabbi, who sinned, this man or his parents, that he was born blind?"

"Neither this man nor his parents sinned," said Jesus, "but this happened so that the work of God might be displayed in his life. As long as it is day, we must do the work of him who sent me. Night is coming, when no one can work. While I am in the world, I am the light of the world."

Having said this, he spit on the ground, made some mud with the saliva, and put it on the man's eyes. "Go," he told him, "wash in the Pool of Siloam" (this word means Sent). So the man went and washed, and came home seeing.

In him was life, and that life was the light of men. The light shines in the darkness, but the darkness has not understood it.

JOHN 8:12; 9:1-7; 1:4-5

Related texts: PSALM 27:1; JOHN 1:1-14; 3:19-22; 12:44-46; 1 JOHN 1:1-7; REVELATION 21:2-27

**THE ONE
MINUTE
BIBLE**

I Am: *The Gate for the Sheep*

[Jesus said,] "I tell you the truth, the man who does not enter the sheep pen by the gate, but climbs in by some other way, is a thief and a robber. The man who enters by the gate is the shepherd of his sheep. The watchman opens the gate for him, and the sheep listen to his voice. He calls his own sheep by name and leads them out. When he has brought out all his own, he goes on ahead of them, and his sheep follow him because they know his voice. But they will never follow a stranger; in fact, they will run away from him because they do not recognize a stranger's voice." Jesus used this figure of speech, but they did not understand what he was telling them.

Therefore Jesus said again, "I tell you the truth, I am the gate for the sheep. All who ever came before me were thieves and robbers, but the sheep did not listen to them. I am the gate; whoever enters through me will be saved. He will come in and go out, and find pasture. The thief comes only to steal and kill and destroy; I have come that they may have life, and have it to the full."

JOHN 10:1-10

Related texts: PSALM 118:17-21; MATTHEW 7:13-14; 25:1-13; LUKE 13:23-29; JOHN 14

I Am: *The Good Shepherd*

**THE ONE
MINUTE
BIBLE**

[Jesus said,] "I am the good shepherd. The good shepherd lays down his life for the sheep. The hired hand is not the shepherd who owns the sheep. So when he sees the wolf coming, he abandons the sheep and runs away. Then the wolf attacks the flock and scatters it. The man runs away because he is a hired hand and cares nothing for the sheep.

"I am the good shepherd; I know my sheep and my sheep know me— just as the Father knows me and I know the Father—and I lay down my life for the sheep. I have other sheep that are not of this sheep pen. I must bring them also. They too will listen to my voice, and there shall be one flock and one shepherd. The reason my Father loves me is that I lay down my life—only to take it up again. No one takes it from me, but I lay it down of my own accord. I have authority to lay it down and authority to take it up again. This command I received from my Father."

Jesus himself bore our sins in his body on the tree, so that we might die to sins and live for righteousness; by his wounds you have been healed. For you were like sheep going astray, but now you have returned to the Shepherd and Overseer of your souls.

JOHN 10:11-18; 1 PETER 2:24-25

Related texts: PSALM 23; ISAIAH 40:10-11; ZECHARIAH 11:4-17; MATTHEW 25:31-46; LUKE 15:3-7; HEBREWS 13:20-21

I Am: *The Resurrection and the Life*

**THE ONE
MINUTE
BIBLE**

Now a man named Lazarus was sick. He was from Bethany, the village of Mary and her sister Martha.

When he heard this, Jesus said, "This sickness will not end in death. No, it is for God's glory so that God's Son may be glorified through it."

On his arrival, Jesus found that Lazarus had already been in the tomb for four days.

"Lord," Martha said to Jesus, "if you had been here, my brother would not have died. But I know that even now God will give you whatever you ask."

Jesus said to her, "Your brother will rise again."

Martha answered, "I know he will rise again in the resurrection at the last day."

Jesus said to her, "I am the resurrection and the life. He who believes in me will live, even though he dies; and whoever lives and believes in me will never die. Do you believe this?"

"Yes, Lord," she told him, "I believe that you are the Christ, the Son of God, who was to come into the world."

When he had said this, Jesus called in a loud voice, "Lazarus, come out!" The dead man came out, his hands and feet wrapped with strips of linen, and a cloth around his face.

Jesus said to them, "Take off the grave clothes and let him go."

JOHN 11:1, 4, 17, 21-27, 43-44

Related texts: DEUTERONOMY 32:39; JOHN 5:19-26; ROMANS 5–6; 2 TIMOTHY 1:8-10; 1 JOHN 1:1-3

I Am: *The Way and the Truth and the Life*

THE ONE MINUTE BIBLE

[Jesus said,] "Do not let your hearts be troubled. Trust in God; trust also in me. In my Father's house are many rooms; if it were not so, I would have told you. I am going there to prepare a place for you. And if I go and prepare a place for you, I will come back and take you to be with me that you also may be where I am. You know the way to the place where I am going."

Thomas said to him, "Lord, we don't know where you are going, so how can we know the way?"

Jesus answered, "I am the way and the truth and the life. No one comes to the Father except through me. If you really knew me, you would know my Father as well. From now on, you do know him and have seen him."

Philip said, "Lord, show us the Father and that will be enough for us."

Jesus answered: "Don't you know me, Philip, even after I have been among you such a long time? Anyone who has seen me has seen the Father."

JOHN 14:1-9

Related texts: PSALM 96; JOHN 1:1-18; 3:13-16; ACTS 4:12; HEBREWS 10:19-22

I Am: *The True Vine*

**THE ONE
MINUTE
BIBLE**

[Jesus said,] "I am the true vine, and my Father is the gardener. He cuts off every branch in me that bears no fruit, while every branch that does bear fruit he prunes so that it will be even more fruitful. You are already clean because of the word I have spoken to you. Remain in me, and I will remain in you. No branch can bear fruit by itself; it must remain in the vine. Neither can you bear fruit unless you remain in me.

"I am the vine; you are the branches. If a man remains in me and I in him, he will bear much fruit; apart from me you can do nothing. If anyone does not remain in me, he is like a branch that is thrown away and withers; such branches are picked up, thrown into the fire and burned. If you remain in me and my words remain in you, ask whatever you wish, and it will be given you. This is to my Father's glory, that you bear much fruit, showing yourselves to be my disciples.

"As the Father has loved me, so have I loved you. Now remain in my love. If you obey my commands, you will remain in my love, just as I have obeyed my Father's commands and remain in his love. I have told you this so that my joy may be in you and that your joy may be complete."

JOHN 15:1-11

Related texts: PSALM 80:8-19; ISAIAH 5:1-7; 27:2-6; LUKE 6:43-45; GALATIANS 5:22-23; COLOSSIANS 1:3-12

Hannah Prays for a Son

**THE ONE
MINUTE
BIBLE**

There was a certain man from Ramathaim, a
Zuphite from the hill country of Ephraim, whose name
was Elkanah son of Jeroham, the son of Elihu, the son
of Tohu, the son of Zuph, an Ephraimite. He had two
wives; one was called Hannah and the other Peninnah.
Peninnah had children, but Hannah had none.

Year after year this man went up from his town to
worship and sacrifice to the LORD Almighty at Shiloh,
where Hophni and Phinehas, the two sons of Eli, were
priests of the LORD. Whenever the day came for Elkanah
to sacrifice, he would give portions of the meat to his
wife Peninnah and to all her sons and daughters. But to
Hannah he gave a double portion because he loved her,
and the LORD had closed her womb. And because the
LORD had closed her womb, her rival kept provoking her
in order to irritate her.

In bitterness of soul Hannah wept much and prayed
to the LORD. And she made a vow, saying, "O LORD
Almighty, if you will only look upon your servant's
misery and remember me, and not forget your servant
but give her a son, then I will give him to the LORD for
all the days of his life, and no razor will ever be used on
his head."

1 SAMUEL 1:1-6, 10-11

Related texts: GENESIS 11:29-30; 25:21; 29:31; PSALM 113:9;
ISAIAH 54:1; LUKE 1:4-22; 23:28-30; HEBREWS 11:11

**THE ONE
MINUTE
BIBLE**

July 30

Samuel: Hannah's Firstborn

Early the next morning they arose and worshiped before the Lord and then went back to their home at Ramah. Elkanah lay with Hannah his wife, and the Lord remembered her. So in the course of time Hannah conceived and gave birth to a son. She named him Samuel, saying, "Because I asked the Lord for him."

When the man Elkanah went up with all his family to offer the annual sacrifice to the Lord and to fulfill his vow, Hannah did not go. She said to her husband, "After the boy is weaned, I will take him and present him before the Lord, and he will live there always."

After he was weaned, she took the boy with her, young as he was, along with a three-year-old bull, an ephah of flour and a skin of wine, and brought him to the house of the Lord at Shiloh. When they had slaughtered the bull, they brought the boy to Eli, and she said to him, "As surely as you live, my lord, I am the woman who stood here beside you praying to the Lord. I prayed for this child, and the Lord has granted me what I asked of him. So now I give him to the Lord. For his whole life he will be given over to the Lord." And he worshiped the Lord there.

1 Samuel 1:19-22, 24-28

Related texts: Genesis 8:1; 19:29; 30:22; Exodus 2:24; Luke 1:23-45; Acts 10:25-31; Revelation 16:19; 18:5

Samuel: *Prophet and Judge*

Eli's sons were wicked men; they had no regard for the LORD.

But Samuel was ministering before the LORD—a boy wearing a linen ephod. Each year his mother made him a little robe and took it to him when she went up with her husband to offer the annual sacrifice. Eli would bless Elkanah and his wife, saying, "May the LORD give you children by this woman to take the place of the one she prayed for and gave to the LORD." Then they would go home. And the LORD was gracious to Hannah; she conceived and gave birth to three sons and two daughters. Meanwhile, the boy Samuel grew up in the presence of the LORD.

The LORD was with Samuel as he grew up, and he let none of his words fall to the ground. And all Israel from Dan to Beersheba recognized that Samuel was attested as a prophet of the LORD. The LORD continued to appear at Shiloh, and there he revealed himself to Samuel through his word.

Samuel continued as judge over Israel all the days of his life. From year to year he went on a circuit from Bethel to Gilgal to Mizpah, judging Israel in all those places. But he always went back to Ramah, where his home was, and there he also judged Israel. And he built an altar there to the LORD.

1 SAMUEL 2:12, 18-21; 3:19-21; 7:15-17

RELATED TEXTS: GENESIS 4:25-26; DEUTERONOMY 18:15-19; JOSHUA 21:45; LUKE 1:13-17

Sin will keep you from this Book.
This Book will keep you from sin.
Dwight L. Moody (1837-1899)
AMERICAN EVANGELIST

The Bible is the greatest benefit which
the human race has ever experienced.
A single line in the Bible has consoled
me more than all the books I ever
read besides.
Immanuel Kant (1724-1804)
GERMAN PHILOSOPHER

The Bible is the one Book to which
any thoughtful man may go with
any honest question of life or destiny
and find the answer of God by
honest searching.
John Ruskin (1819-1900)
ENGLISH AUTHOR, REFORMER

Israel Asks for a King

When Samuel grew old, he appointed his sons as judges for Israel. But his sons did not walk in his ways. They turned aside after dishonest gain and accepted bribes and perverted justice.

So all the elders of Israel gathered together and came to Samuel at Ramah. They said to him, "You are old, and your sons do not walk in your ways; now appoint a king to lead us, such as all the other nations have."

But when they said, "Give us a king to lead us," this displeased Samuel; so he prayed to the LORD. And the LORD told him: "Listen to all that the people are saying to you; it is not you they have rejected, but they have rejected me as their king. As they have done from the day I brought them up out of Egypt until this day, forsaking me and serving other gods, so they are doing to you. Now listen to them; but warn them solemnly and let them know what the king who will reign over them will do."

Samuel told all the words of the LORD to the people who were asking him for a king.

But the people refused to listen to Samuel. "No!" they said. "We want a king over us. Then we will be like all the other nations, with a king to lead us and to go out before us and fight our battles."

When Samuel heard all that the people said, he repeated it before the LORD. The LORD answered, "Listen to them and give them a king."

1 SAMUEL 8:1, 3-10, 19-22a

THE ONE MINUTE BIBLE

Related texts: DEUTERONOMY 17:14-20; 1 SAMUEL 8:11-18; ISAIAH 9:6; JEREMIAH 10:1-10; 1 TIMOTHY 1:17

Saul: The First King of Israel

**THE ONE
MINUTE
BIBLE**

Samuel summoned the people of Israel to the Lord at Mizpah and said to them, "This is what the Lord, the God of Israel, says: 'I brought Israel up out of Egypt, and I delivered you from the power of Egypt and all the kingdoms that oppressed you.' But you have now rejected your God, who saves you out of all your calamities and distresses. And you have said, 'No, set a king over us.' So now present yourselves before the Lord by your tribes and clans."

When Samuel brought all the tribes of Israel near, the tribe of Benjamin was chosen. Then he brought forward the tribe of Benjamin, clan by clan, and Matri's clan was chosen. Finally Saul son of Kish was chosen. But when they looked for him, he was not to be found. So they inquired further of the Lord, "Has the man come here yet?"

And the Lord said, "Yes, he has hidden himself among the baggage."

They ran and brought him out, and as he stood among the people he was a head taller than any of the others. Samuel said to all the people, "Do you see the man the Lord has chosen? There is no one like him among all the people."

Then the people shouted, "Long live the king!"

Samuel explained to the people the regulations of the kingship. He wrote them down on a scroll and deposited it before the Lord. Then Samuel dismissed the people, each to his own home.

1 Samuel 10:17-25

Related texts: Deuteronomy 17:14-20; 1 Samuel 9:1–10:16; 11–14; John 12:12-15

The LORD Rejects Saul as King

**THE ONE
MINUTE
BIBLE**

Samuel said to Saul, "I am the one the LORD sent to anoint you king over his people Israel; so listen now to the message from the LORD. This is what the LORD Almighty says: 'I will punish the Amalekites for what they did to Israel when they waylaid them as they came up from Egypt. Now go, attack the Amalekites and totally destroy everything that belongs to them.'"

Then Saul attacked the Amalekites all the way from Havilah to Shur, to the east of Egypt. But Saul and the army spared Agag and the best of the sheep and cattle, the fat calves and lambs—everything that was good. These they were unwilling to destroy completely, but everything that was despised and weak they totally destroyed.

Then the word of the LORD came to Samuel: "I am grieved that I have made Saul king, because he has turned away from me and has not carried out my instructions."

When Samuel reached him, Saul said, "The LORD bless you! I have carried out the LORD's instructions."

But Samuel replied:

"Does the LORD delight in burnt offerings and
        sacrifices
    as much as in obeying the voice of the LORD?
To obey is better than sacrifice,
    and to heed is better than the fat of rams.
For rebellion is like the sin of divination,
    and arrogance like the evil of idolatry.
Because you have rejected the word of the LORD,
    he has rejected you as king."

1 SAMUEL 15:1-3a, 7, 9-11a, 13, 22-23

Related texts: EXODUS 17:8-16; DEUTERONOMY 25:17-19; MICAH 6:6-8;
LUKE 16:10-13

Samuel Anoints David as King

**THE ONE
MINUTE
BIBLE**

The Lord said to Samuel, "How long will you mourn for Saul, since I have rejected him as king over Israel? Fill your horn with oil and be on your way; I am sending you to Jesse of Bethlehem. I have chosen one of his sons to be king."

When they arrived, Samuel saw Eliab and thought, "Surely the Lord's anointed stands here before the Lord."

But the Lord said to Samuel, "Do not consider his appearance or his height, for I have rejected him. The Lord does not look at the things man looks at. Man looks at the outward appearance, but the Lord looks at the heart."

Jesse had seven of his sons pass before Samuel, but Samuel said to him, "The Lord has not chosen these." So he asked Jesse, "Are these all the sons you have?"

"There is still the youngest," Jesse answered, "but he is tending the sheep."

Samuel said, "Send for him; we will not sit down until he arrives."

So he sent and had him brought in. He was ruddy, with a fine appearance and handsome features.

Then the Lord said, "Rise and anoint him; he is the one."

So Samuel took the horn of oil and anointed him in the presence of his brothers, and from that day on the Spirit of the Lord came upon David in power.

1 Samuel 16:1, 6-7, 10-13a

Related texts: Psalm 78:70-72; Matthew 5:8; 12:33-35; Luke 6:43-45; Acts 13:21-23

Goliath Challenges the Armies of Israel

THE ONE
MINUTE
BIBLE

Now the Philistines gathered their forces for war and assembled at Socoh in Judah. They pitched camp at Ephes Dammim, between Socoh and Azekah. Saul and the Israelites assembled and camped in the Valley of Elah and drew up their battle line to meet the Philistines. The Philistines occupied one hill and the Israelites another, with the valley between them.

A champion named Goliath, who was from Gath, came out of the Philistine camp. He was over nine feet tall. He had a bronze helmet on his head and wore a coat of scale armor of bronze weighing five thousand shekels; on his legs he wore bronze greaves, and a bronze javelin was slung on his back. His spear shaft was like a weaver's rod, and its iron point weighed six hundred shekels. His shield bearer went ahead of him.

Goliath stood and shouted to the ranks of Israel, "Why do you come out and line up for battle? Am I not a Philistine, and are you not the servants of Saul? Choose a man and have him come down to me. If he is able to fight and kill me, we will become your subjects; but if I overcome him and kill him, you will become our subjects and serve us." Then the Philistine said, "This day I defy the ranks of Israel! Give me a man and let us fight each other." On hearing the Philistine's words, Saul and all the Israelites were dismayed and terrified.

1 SAMUEL 17:1-11

Related texts: NUMBERS 13:26-33; DEUTERONOMY 11:22-25; PSALM 15; PROVERBS 14:27; 15:33; 29:25

David Accepts Goliath's Challenge

**THE ONE
MINUTE
BIBLE**

David said to Saul, "Let no one lose heart on account of this Philistine; your servant will go and fight him."

Saul replied, "You are not able to go out against this Philistine and fight him; you are only a boy, and he has been a fighting man from his youth."

But David said to Saul, "Your servant has been keeping his father's sheep. When a lion or a bear came and carried off a sheep from the flock, I went after it, struck it and rescued the sheep from its mouth. When it turned on me, I seized it by its hair, struck it and killed it. Your servant has killed both the lion and the bear; this uncircumcised Philistine will be like one of them, because he has defied the armies of the living God. The LORD who delivered me from the paw of the lion and the paw of the bear will deliver me from the hand of this Philistine."

Saul said to David, "Go, and the LORD be with you."

Then he took his staff in his hand, chose five smooth stones from the stream, put them in the pouch of his shepherd's bag and, with his sling in his hand, approached the Philistine.

1 SAMUEL 17:32-37, 40

Related texts: PSALMS 31:11-18; 97:10; 144; EPHESIANS 6:10-18;
1 TIMOTHY 4:12

David Kills Goliath

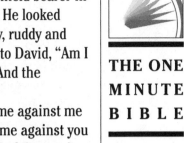

**THE ONE
MINUTE
BIBLE**

Meanwhile, the Philistine, with his shield bearer in front of him, kept coming closer to David. He looked David over and saw that he was only a boy, ruddy and handsome, and he despised him. He said to David, "Am I a dog, that you come at me with sticks?" And the Philistine cursed David by his gods.

David said to the Philistine, "You come against me with sword and spear and javelin, but I come against you in the name of the LORD Almighty, the God of the armies of Israel, whom you have defied. This day the LORD will hand you over to me, and I'll strike you down and cut off your head. Today I will give the carcasses of the Philistine army to the birds of the air and the beasts of the earth, and the whole world will know that there is a God in Israel. All those gathered here will know that it is not by sword or spear that the LORD saves; for the battle is the LORD's, and he will give all of you into our hands."

As the Philistine moved closer to attack him, David ran quickly toward the battle line to meet him. Reaching into his bag and taking out a stone, he slung it and struck the Philistine on the forehead. The stone sank into his forehead, and he fell facedown on the ground.

So David triumphed over the Philistine with a sling and a stone; without a sword in his hand he struck down the Philistine and killed him.

1 SAMUEL 17:41-43, 45-50

Related texts: 2 SAMUEL 21:15-22; PSALM 27; HEBREWS 11:32-34

Saul Becomes Jealous of David

THE ONE MINUTE BIBLE

After David had finished talking with Saul, Jonathan became one in spirit with David, and he loved him as himself. From that day Saul kept David with him and did not let him return to his father's house. And Jonathan made a covenant with David because he loved him as himself. Jonathan took off the robe he was wearing and gave it to David, along with his tunic, and even his sword, his bow and his belt.

Whatever Saul sent him to do, David did it so successfully that Saul gave him a high rank in the army. This pleased all the people, and Saul's officers as well.

When the men were returning home after David had killed the Philistine, the women came out from all the towns of Israel to meet King Saul with singing and dancing, with joyful songs and with tambourines and lutes. As they danced, they sang:

> "Saul has slain his thousands,
> and David his tens of thousands."

Saul was very angry; this refrain galled him. "They have credited David with tens of thousands," he thought, "but me with only thousands. What more can he get but the kingdom?" And from that time on Saul kept a jealous eye on David.

1 SAMUEL 18:1-9

Related texts: PROVERBS 27:4; ACTS 5:12-19; 7:9-10; ROMANS 13:12-14; 2 CORINTHIANS 11:2; GALATIANS 5:19-20

Saul Tries to Kill David

Saul told his son Jonathan and all the attendants to kill David. But Jonathan was very fond of David and warned him, "My father Saul is looking for a chance to kill you. Be on your guard tomorrow morning; go into hiding and stay there. I will go out and stand with my father in the field where you are. I'll speak to him about you and will tell you what I find out."

Jonathan spoke well of David to Saul his father and said to him, "Let not the king do wrong to his servant David; he has not wronged you, and what he has done has benefited you greatly. He took his life in his hands when he killed the Philistine. The LORD won a great victory for all Israel, and you saw it and were glad. Why then would you do wrong to an innocent man like David by killing him for no reason?"

Saul listened to Jonathan and took this oath: "As surely as the LORD lives, David will not be put to death."

So Jonathan called David and told him the whole conversation. He brought him to Saul, and David was with Saul as before.

But an evil spirit from the LORD came upon Saul as he was sitting in his house with his spear in his hand. While David was playing the harp, Saul tried to pin him to the wall with his spear, but David eluded him as Saul drove the spear into the wall. That night David made good his escape.

1 SAMUEL 19:1-7, 9-10

Related texts: 1 SAMUEL 19–30; PSALMS 52; 54; 57; 59; JAMES 1:13-15

The Death of Saul and His Sons

**THE ONE
MINUTE
BIBLE**

Now the Philistines fought against Israel; the Israelites fled before them, and many fell slain on Mount Gilboa. The Philistines pressed hard after Saul and his sons, and they killed his sons Jonathan, Abinadab and Malki-Shua. The fighting grew fierce around Saul, and when the archers overtook him, they wounded him.

Saul said to his armor-bearer, "Draw your sword and run me through, or these uncircumcised fellows will come and abuse me."

But his armor-bearer was terrified and would not do it; so Saul took his own sword and fell on it. When the armor-bearer saw that Saul was dead, he too fell on his sword and died. So Saul and his three sons died, and all his house died together.

When all the Israelites in the valley saw that the army had fled and that Saul and his sons had died, they abandoned their towns and fled. And the Philistines came and occupied them.

Saul died because he was unfaithful to the LORD; he did not keep the word of the LORD and even consulted a medium for guidance, and did not inquire of the LORD. So the LORD put him to death and turned the kingdom over to David son of Jesse.

1 CHRONICLES 10:1-7, 13-14

Related texts: 1 SAMUEL 28; 30–31; 2 SAMUEL 1; 16:15–17:23; MATTHEW 27:1-5; ACTS 16:22-28

The LORD Makes a Covenant With David

After the king was settled in his palace and the LORD had given him rest from all his enemies around him, he said to Nathan the prophet, "Here I am, living in a palace of cedar, while the ark of God remains in a tent."

Nathan replied to the king, "Whatever you have in mind, go ahead and do it, for the LORD is with you."

That night the word of the LORD came to Nathan, saying:

"Now then, tell my servant David, 'This is what the LORD Almighty says: I took you from the pasture and from following the flock to be ruler over my people Israel. I have been with you wherever you have gone, and I have cut off all your enemies from before you. Now I will make your name great, like the names of the greatest men of the earth.

"'The LORD declares to you that the LORD himself will establish a house for you: When your days are over and you rest with your fathers, I will raise up your offspring to succeed you, who will come from your own body, and I will establish his kingdom. He is the one who will build a house for my Name, and I will establish the throne of his kingdom forever. I will be his father, and he will be my son. When he does wrong, I will punish him with the rod of men, with floggings inflicted by men. But my love will never be taken away from him, as I took it away from Saul, whom I removed from before you. Your house and your kingdom will endure forever before me; your throne will be established forever.'"

2 SAMUEL 7:1-4, 8-9, 11b-16

Related texts: 1 CHRONICLES 17; PSALMS 2; 89; JEREMIAH 33:14-26; ROMANS 1:1-4

The LORD Is My Shepherd

**THE ONE
MINUTE
BIBLE**

A psalm of David

The LORD is my shepherd, I shall not be in want.
    He makes me lie down in green pastures,
he leads me beside quiet waters,
    he restores my soul.
He guides me in paths of righteousness
    for his name's sake.
Even though I walk
    through the valley of the shadow of death,
I will fear no evil,
    for you are with me;
your rod and your staff,
    they comfort me.

You prepare a table before me
    in the presence of my enemies.
You anoint my head with oil;
    my cup overflows.
Surely goodness and love will follow me
    all the days of my life,
and I will dwell in the house of the LORD
    forever.

[Jesus said,] "I am the good shepherd. The good
shepherd lays down his life for the sheep."

PSALM 23:1-6; JOHN 10:11

Related texts: ISAIAH 40:10-11; MICAH 5:2-5; HEBREWS 13:20-21;
1 PETER 2:21-25; REVELATION 7:15-17

David Commits Adultery with Bathsheba

In the spring, at the time when kings go off to war, David sent Joab out with the king's men and the whole Israelite army. They destroyed the Ammonites and besieged Rabbah. But David remained in Jerusalem.

One evening David got up from his bed and walked around on the roof of the palace. From the roof he saw a woman bathing. The woman was very beautiful, and David sent someone to find out about her. The man said, "Isn't this Bathsheba, the daughter of Eliam and the wife of Uriah the Hittite?" Then David sent messengers to get her. She came to him, and he slept with her. (She had purified herself from her uncleanness.) Then she went back home. The woman conceived and sent word to David, saying, "I am pregnant."

So David sent this word to Joab: "Send me Uriah the Hittite." And Joab sent him to David. When Uriah came to him, David asked him how Joab was, how the soldiers were and how the war was going. Then David said to Uriah, "Go down to your house and wash your feet." So Uriah left the palace, and a gift from the king was sent after him. But Uriah slept at the entrance to the palace with all his master's servants and did not go down to his house.

2 SAMUEL 11:1-9

THE ONE MINUTE BIBLE

Related texts: DEUTERONOMY 5:18; JOB 31:1; PSALM 119:9-16; PROVERBS 5–6; 1 CORINTHIANS 6:9-11

David Arranges Uriah's Death

**THE ONE
MINUTE
BIBLE**

In the morning David wrote a letter to Joab and sent it with Uriah. In it he wrote, "Put Uriah in the front line where the fighting is fiercest. Then withdraw from him so he will be struck down and die."

So while Joab had the city under siege, he put Uriah at a place where he knew the strongest defenders were. When the men of the city came out and fought against Joab, some of the men in David's army fell; moreover, Uriah the Hittite died.

When Uriah's wife heard that her husband was dead, she mourned for him. After the time of mourning was over, David had her brought to his house, and she became his wife and bore him a son. But the thing David had done displeased the LORD.

Then David said to Nathan, "I have sinned against the LORD."

Nathan replied, "The LORD has taken away your sin. You are not going to die. But because by doing this you have made the enemies of the LORD show utter contempt, the son born to you will die."

For the wages of sin is death, but the gift of God is eternal life in Christ Jesus our Lord.

2 SAMUEL 11:14-17, 26-27; 12:13-14; ROMANS 6:23

Related texts: NUMBERS 32:23; 2 SAMUEL 12:15-25; PROVERBS 26:27; MATTHEW 1:1-6; HEBREWS 13:4

David's Prayer of Repentance

**THE ONE
MINUTE
BIBLE**

For the director of music. A psalm of David.
When the prophet Nathan came to him after David
had committed adultery with Bathsheba.

Have mercy on me, O God,
    according to your unfailing love;
according to your great compassion
    blot out my transgressions.
Wash away all my iniquity
    and cleanse me from my sin.
For I know my transgressions,
    and my sin is always before me.
Against you, you only, have I sinned
    and done what is evil in your sight,
so that you are proved right when you speak
    and justified when you judge.
Surely I was sinful at birth,
    sinful from the time my mother conceived me.
Surely you desire truth in the inner parts;
    you teach me wisdom in the inmost place.
Cleanse me with hyssop, and I will be clean;
    wash me, and I will be whiter than snow.
Let me hear joy and gladness;
    let the bones you have crushed rejoice.
Hide your face from my sins
    and blot out all my iniquity.
Create in me a pure heart, O God,
    and renew a steadfast spirit within me.
Do not cast me from your presence
    or take your Holy Spirit from me.
Restore to me the joy of your salvation
    and grant me a willing spirit, to sustain me.
Then I will teach transgressors your ways,
    and sinners will turn back to you.

PSALM 51:1-13

Related texts: 2 SAMUEL 12; PSALM 32; ISAIAH 40:28-31; HABAKKUK 3:2;
TITUS 3:3-7

**THE ONE
MINUTE
BIBLE**

David Appoints Solomon as King

When the time drew near for David to die, he gave a charge to Solomon his son.

"I am about to go the way of all the earth," he said. "So be strong, show yourself a man, and observe what the LORD your God requires: Walk in his ways, and keep his decrees and commands, his laws and requirements, as written in the Law of Moses, so that you may prosper in all you do and wherever you go, and that the LORD may keep his promise to me: 'If your descendants watch how they live, and if they walk faithfully before me with all their heart and soul, you will never fail to have a man on the throne of Israel.'"

So Solomon sat on the throne of the LORD as king in place of his father David. He prospered and all Israel obeyed him. All the officers and mighty men, as well as all of King David's sons, pledged their submission to King Solomon.

The LORD highly exalted Solomon in the sight of all Israel and bestowed on him royal splendor such as no king over Israel ever had before.

Trust in the LORD with all your heart
    and lean not on your own understanding;
in all your ways acknowledge him,
    and he will make your paths straight.

1 KINGS 2:1-4; 1 CHRONICLES 29:23-25; PROVERBS 3:5-6

Related texts: 2 SAMUEL 7; 1 KINGS 1; 1 CHRONICLES 17; 23–29; MATTHEW 1:1-6; LUKE 12:22-31

Solomon Asks for Wisdom

At Gibeon the LORD appeared to Solomon during the night in a dream, and God said, "Ask for whatever you want me to give you."

[Solomon answered,] "Now, O LORD my God, you have made your servant king in place of my father David. But I am only a little child and do not know how to carry out my duties. Your servant is here among the people you have chosen, a great people, too numerous to count or number. So give your servant a discerning heart to govern your people and to distinguish between right and wrong. For who is able to govern this great people of yours?"

The Lord was pleased that Solomon had asked for this. So God said to him, "Since you have asked for this and not for long life or wealth for yourself, nor have asked for the death of your enemies but for discernment in administering justice, I will do what you have asked. I will give you a wise and discerning heart, so that there will never have been anyone like you, nor will there ever be. Moreover, I will give you what you have not asked for—both riches and honor—so that in your lifetime you will have no equal among kings. And if you walk in my ways and obey my statutes and commands as David your father did, I will give you a long life."

1 KINGS 3:5, 7-14

THE ONE MINUTE BIBLE

Related texts: 1 KINGS 3:16-28; 2 CHRONICLES 1:1-13; PROVERBS 1–4; 8:10-21; JAMES 1:5-8

The Wisdom of Solomon

**THE ONE
MINUTE
BIBLE**

The people of Judah and Israel were as numerous as the sand on the seashore; they ate, they drank and they were happy. And Solomon ruled over all the kingdoms from the River to the land of the Philistines, as far as the border of Egypt. These countries brought tribute and were Solomon's subjects all his life.

God gave Solomon wisdom and very great insight, and a breadth of understanding as measureless as the sand on the seashore. Solomon's wisdom was greater than the wisdom of all the men of the East, and greater than all the wisdom of Egypt. He was wiser than any other man, including Ethan the Ezrahite—wiser than Heman, Calcol and Darda, the sons of Mahol. And his fame spread to all the surrounding nations. He spoke three thousand proverbs and his songs numbered a thousand and five. He described plant life, from the cedar of Lebanon to the hyssop that grows out of walls. He also taught about animals and birds, reptiles and fish. Men of all nations came to listen to Solomon's wisdom, sent by all the kings of the world, who had heard of his wisdom.

1 KINGS 4:20-21, 29-34

Related texts: 1 KINGS 10:1-13; PSALM 72; PROVERBS 13:10; 16:16; 23:23; MATTHEW 12:38-42

The Proverbs of Solomon

**THE ONE
MINUTE
BIBLE**

The proverbs of Solomon son of David, king of Israel:

for attaining wisdom and discipline;
for understanding words of insight;
for acquiring a disciplined and prudent life,
doing what is right and just and fair;
for giving prudence to the simple,
knowledge and discretion to the young—
let the wise listen and add to their learning,
and let the discerning get guidance—
for understanding proverbs and parables,
the sayings and riddles of the wise.

The fear of the LORD is the beginning of
knowledge,
but fools despise wisdom and discipline.

As the crowds increased, Jesus said, "This is a wicked generation. It asks for a miraculous sign, but none will be given it except the sign of Jonah. For as Jonah was a sign to the Ninevites, so also will the Son of Man be to this generation. The Queen of the South will rise at the judgment with the men of this generation and condemn them; for she came from the ends of the earth to listen to Solomon's wisdom, and now one greater than Solomon is here."

PROVERBS 1:1-7; LUKE 11:29-31

Related texts: 2 CHRONICLES 9:1-12; PROVERBS 10:1; 25:1;
SONG OF SONGS 1–8; JONAH 3; 1 CORINTHIANS 12:1-11

Parables of Jesus: *The Sower*

**THE ONE
MINUTE
BIBLE**

While a large crowd was gathering and people were coming to Jesus from town after town, he told this parable: "A farmer went out to sow his seed. As he was scattering the seed, some fell along the path; it was trampled on, and the birds of the air ate it up. Some fell on rock, and when it came up, the plants withered because they had no moisture. Other seed fell among thorns, which grew up with it and choked the plants. Still other seed fell on good soil. It came up and yielded a crop, a hundred times more than was sown."

When he said this, he called out, "He who has ears to hear, let him hear."

His disciples asked him what this parable meant. He said, "The knowledge of the secrets of the kingdom of God has been given to you, but to others I speak in parables, so that,

"'though seeing, they may not see;
though hearing, they may not understand.'"

LUKE 8:4-10

Related texts: PSALM 126; PROVERBS 11:18-21; HOSEA 10:12-13; MATTHEW 13:1-17; MARK 4:1-12

Parables of Jesus: *The Sower Explained*

THE ONE MINUTE BIBLE

"This is the meaning of the parable: The seed is the word of God. Those along the path are the ones who hear, and then the devil comes and takes away the word from their hearts, so that they may not believe and be saved. Those on the rock are the ones who receive the word with joy when they hear it, but they have no root. They believe for a while, but in the time of testing they fall away. The seed that fell among thorns stands for those who hear, but as they go on their way they are choked by life's worries, riches and pleasures, and they do not mature. But the seed on good soil stands for those with a noble and good heart, who hear the word, retain it, and by persevering produce a crop.

"No one lights a lamp and hides it in a jar or puts it under a bed. Instead, he puts it on a stand, so that those who come in can see the light. For there is nothing hidden that will not be disclosed, and nothing concealed that will not be known or brought out into the open. Therefore consider carefully how you listen. Whoever has will be given more; whoever does not have, even what he thinks he has will be taken from him."

LUKE 8:11-18

Related texts: PROVERBS 11:30; MATTHEW 13:18-23; MARK 4:13-25; JOHN 15:1-17; GALATIANS 6:7-10

Parables of Jesus: *The Kingdom*

**THE ONE
MINUTE
BIBLE**

Jesus told them another parable: "The kingdom of heaven is like a mustard seed, which a man took and planted in his field. Though it is the smallest of all your seeds, yet when it grows, it is the largest of garden plants and becomes a tree, so that the birds of the air come and perch in its branches."

He told them still another parable: "The kingdom of heaven is like yeast that a woman took and mixed into a large amount of flour until it worked all through the dough.

"The kingdom of heaven is like treasure hidden in a field. When a man found it, he hid it again, and then in his joy went and sold all he had and bought that field.

"Again, the kingdom of heaven is like a merchant looking for fine pearls. When he found one of great value, he went away and sold everything he had and bought it.

"Once again, the kingdom of heaven is like a net that was let down into the lake and caught all kinds of fish. When it was full, the fishermen pulled it up on the shore. Then they sat down and collected the good fish in baskets, but threw the bad away. This is how it will be at the end of the age. The angels will come and separate the wicked from the righteous and throw them into the fiery furnace, where there will be weeping and gnashing of teeth."

MATTHEW 13:31-33, 44-50

Related texts: PSALM 45:6; MARK 1:1-15; 4:30-32; LUKE 13:18-19

Parables of Jesus: *Lost and Found*

Now the tax collectors and "sinners" were all gathering around to hear him. But the Pharisees and the teachers of the law muttered, "This man welcomes sinners and eats with them."

Then Jesus told them this parable: "Suppose one of you has a hundred sheep and loses one of them. Does he not leave the ninety-nine in the open country and go after the lost sheep until he finds it? And when he finds it, he joyfully puts it on his shoulders and goes home. Then he calls his friends and neighbors together and says, 'Rejoice with me; I have found my lost sheep.' I tell you that in the same way there will be more rejoicing in heaven over one sinner who repents than over ninety-nine righteous persons who do not need to repent.

"Or suppose a woman has ten silver coins and loses one. Does she not light a lamp, sweep the house and search carefully until she finds it? And when she finds it, she calls her friends and neighbors together and says, 'Rejoice with me; I have found my lost coin.' In the same way, I tell you, there is rejoicing in the presence of the angels of God over one sinner who repents."

LUKE 15:1-10

Related texts: PSALM 119:169-176; MATTHEW 18:12-14;
LUKE 9:22-26; 19:1-10

Parables of Jesus: *The Prodigal Son, Part 1*

**THE ONE
MINUTE
BIBLE**

Jesus continued: "There was a man who had two sons. The younger one said to his father, 'Father, give me my share of the estate.' So he divided his property between them.

"Not long after that, the younger son got together all he had, set off for a distant country and there squandered his wealth in wild living. After he had spent everything, there was a severe famine in that whole country, and he began to be in need. So he went and hired himself out to a citizen of that country, who sent him to his fields to feed pigs. He longed to fill his stomach with the pods that the pigs were eating, but no one gave him anything.

"When he came to his senses, he said, 'How many of my father's hired men have food to spare, and here I am starving to death! I will set out and go back to my father and say to him: Father, I have sinned against heaven and against you. I am no longer worthy to be called your son; make me like one of your hired men.' So he got up and went to his father.

"But while he was still a long way off, his father saw him and was filled with compassion for him; he ran to his son, threw his arms around him and kissed him.

"The son said to him, 'Father, I have sinned against heaven and against you. I am no longer worthy to be called your son.'"

LUKE 15:11-21

Related texts: 2 CHRONICLES 7:13-14; PROVERBS 17:6, 21; HOSEA 6:1-3; ACTS 3:19-20

Parables of Jesus: *The Prodigal Son, Part 2*

**THE ONE
MINUTE
BIBLE**

"But the father said to his servants, 'Quick! Bring the best robe and put it on him. Put a ring on his finger and sandals on his feet. Bring the fattened calf and kill it. Let's have a feast and celebrate. For this son of mine was dead and is alive again; he was lost and is found.' So they began to celebrate.

"Meanwhile, the older son was in the field. When he came near the house, he heard music and dancing. So he called one of the servants and asked him what was going on. 'Your brother has come,' he replied, 'and your father has killed the fattened calf because he has him back safe and sound.'

"The older brother became angry and refused to go in. So his father went out and pleaded with him. But he answered his father, 'Look! All these years I've been slaving for you and never disobeyed your orders. Yet you never gave me even a young goat so I could celebrate with my friends. But when this son of yours who has squandered your property with prostitutes comes home, you kill the fattened calf for him!'

"'My son,' the father said, 'you are always with me, and everything I have is yours. But we had to celebrate and be glad, because this brother of yours was dead and is alive again; he was lost and is found.'"

LUKE 15:22-32

Related texts: ISAIAH 55:6-7; MATTHEW 18:12-14; COLOSSIANS 1:1-14;
1 PETER 2:24-25

Solomon Builds the Temple

**THE ONE
MINUTE
BIBLE**

When Hiram king of Tyre heard that Solomon had been anointed king to succeed his father David, he sent his envoys to Solomon, because he had always been on friendly terms with David. Solomon sent back this message to Hiram:

"You know that because of the wars waged against my father David from all sides, he could not build a temple for the Name of the LORD his God until the LORD put his enemies under his feet. But now the LORD my God has given me rest on every side, and there is no adversary or disaster. I intend, therefore, to build a temple for the Name of the LORD my God, as the LORD told my father David, when he said, 'Your son whom I will put on the throne in your place will build the temple for my Name.'

"So give orders that cedars of Lebanon be cut for me. My men will work with yours, and I will pay you for your men whatever wages you set. You know that we have no one so skilled in felling timber as the Sidonians."

When Hiram heard Solomon's message, he was greatly pleased and said, "Praise be to the LORD today, for he has given David a wise son to rule over this great nation."

1 KINGS 5:1-7

Related texts: 1 KINGS 5–9; 2 CHRONICLES 2–8; PSALM 127; MATTHEW 12:1-6; JOHN 2:13-21; EPHESIANS 2:11-22

The Wisdom of the Teacher

I, the Teacher, was king over Israel in Jerusalem. I devoted myself to study and to explore by wisdom all that is done under heaven. What a heavy burden God has laid on men! I have seen all the things that are done under the sun; all of them are meaningless, a chasing after the wind.

THE ONE MINUTE BIBLE

There is a time for everything,
and a season for every activity under heaven:

a time to be born and a time to die,
a time to plant and a time to uproot,
a time to kill and a time to heal,
a time to tear down and a time to build,
a time to weep and a time to laugh,
a time to mourn and a time to dance,
a time to scatter stones and a time to gather them,
a time to embrace and a time to refrain,
a time to search and a time to give up,
a time to keep and a time to throw away,
a time to tear and a time to mend,
a time to be silent and a time to speak,
a time to love and a time to hate,
a time for war and a time for peace.

ECCLESIASTES 1:12-14; 3:1-8

Related texts: ECCLESIASTES 1:1-11; GALATIANS 4:4-5; 6:8-9; 1 TIMOTHY 2:3-6; 1 PETER 5:5-6

The Teacher's Proverbs and Conclusion

**THE ONE
MINUTE
BIBLE**

Two are better than one,
>   because they have a good return for their work:
If one falls down,
>   his friend can help him up.
But pity the man who falls
>   and has no one to help him up!
Also, if two lie down together, they will keep warm.
>   But how can one keep warm alone?
Though one may be overpowered,
>   two can defend themselves.
A cord of three strands is not quickly broken.

Not only was the Teacher wise, but also he imparted knowledge to the people. He pondered and searched out and set in order many proverbs. The Teacher searched to find just the right words, and what he wrote was upright and true.

The words of the wise are like goads, their collected sayings like firmly embedded nails—given by one Shepherd. Be warned, my son, of anything in addition to them.

Of making many books there is no end, and much study wearies the body.

Now all has been heard;
>   here is the conclusion of the matter:
Fear God and keep his commandments,
>   for this is the whole [duty] of man.
For God will bring every deed into judgment,
>   including every hidden thing,
>   whether it is good or evil.

ECCLESIASTES 4:9-12; 12:9-14

Related texts: 1 SAMUEL 20:24-42; PSALM 37; PROVERBS 17:17; 27:6, 10;
260 | 1 CORINTHIANS 4:5; REVELATION 20:11-15

The Sins of Solomon

King Solomon, however, loved many foreign women besides Pharaoh's daughter—Moabites, Ammonites, Edomites, Sidonians and Hittites. They were from nations about which the LORD had told the Israelites, "You must not intermarry with them, because they will surely turn your hearts after their gods." Nevertheless, Solomon held fast to them in love. As Solomon grew old, his wives turned his heart after other gods, and his heart was not fully devoted to the LORD his God, as the heart of David his father had been.

The LORD became angry with Solomon because his heart had turned away from the LORD, the God of Israel, who had appeared to him twice. Although he had forbidden Solomon to follow other gods, Solomon did not keep the LORD's command.

So the LORD said to Solomon, "Since this is your attitude and you have not kept my covenant and my decrees, which I commanded you, I will most certainly tear the kingdom away from you and give it to one of your subordinates. Nevertheless, for the sake of David your father, I will not do it during your lifetime. I will tear it out of the hand of your son. Yet I will not tear the whole kingdom from him, but will give him one tribe for the sake of David my servant and for the sake of Jerusalem, which I have chosen."

1 KINGS 11:1-2, 4, 9-13

Related texts: DEUTERONOMY 7; EZRA 9–10; NEHEMIAH 13:23-27; 1 CORINTHIANS 7:39; 2 CORINTHIANS 6:14-16

The Kingdom Divides

**THE ONE
MINUTE
BIBLE**

Solomon reigned in Jerusalem over all Israel forty years. Then he rested with his fathers and was buried in the city of David his father. And Rehoboam his son succeeded him as king.

Rehoboam went to Shechem, for all the Israelites had gone there to make him king. So they sent for Jeroboam, and he and the whole assembly of Israel went to Rehoboam and said to him: "Your father put a heavy yoke on us, but now lighten the harsh labor and the heavy yoke he put on us, and we will serve you."

Rehoboam answered, "Go away for three days and then come back to me." So the people went away.

The king answered the people harshly. Rejecting the advice given him by the elders, he followed the advice of the young men and said, "My father made your yoke heavy; I will make it even heavier. My father scourged you with whips; I will scourge you with scorpions."

When all Israel saw that the king refused to listen to them, they answered the king:

> "What share do we have in David,
>   what part in Jesse's son?
> To your tents, O Israel!
>   Look after your own house, O David!"

So the Israelites went home.

When all the Israelites heard that Jeroboam had returned, they sent and called him to the assembly and made him king over all Israel. Only the tribe of Judah remained loyal to the house of David.

1 KINGS 11:42-43; 12:1, 3-5, 13-14, 16, 20

Related texts: 1 KINGS 11:26-40; 2 CHRONICLES 9:29–10:19; PROVERBS 15:1

The Sins of Jeroboam

**THE ONE
MINUTE
BIBLE**

Then Jeroboam fortified Shechem in the hill country of Ephraim and lived there. From there he went out and built up Peniel.

Jeroboam thought to himself, "The kingdom will now likely revert to the house of David. If these people go up to offer sacrifices at the temple of the LORD in Jerusalem, they will again give their allegiance to their lord, Rehoboam king of Judah. They will kill me and return to King Rehoboam."

After seeking advice, the king made two golden calves. He said to the people, "It is too much for you to go up to Jerusalem. Here are your gods, O Israel, who brought you up out of Egypt." One he set up in Bethel, and the other in Dan. And this thing became a sin; the people went even as far as Dan to worship the one there.

Jeroboam built shrines on high places and appointed priests from all sorts of people, even though they were not Levites.

This was the sin of the house of Jeroboam that led to its downfall and to its destruction from the face of the earth.

1 KINGS 12:25-31; 13:34

Related texts: EXODUS 32; 2 KINGS 10:16-31; 23:1-15;
2 CHRONICLES 11:14-16; ACTS 17:15-31; 1 CORINTHIANS 6:9-10

*When you read God's word, you must
constantly be saying to yourself,
"It is talking to me, and about me."*
Soren Kierkegaard (1813-1855)
DANISH PHILOSOPHER

*I must confess to you that the majesty
of the Scriptures astonishes me...
if it had been the invention of men,
the inventors would be greater than
the greatest heroes.*
Jean Jacques Rousseau (1712-1778)
FRENCH PHILOSOPHER

*After more than sixty years of almost
daily reading of the Bible, I never
fail to find it always new and marvellously
in tune with the changing needs of every day.*
Cecil B. DeMille (1881-1959)
AMERICAN MOVIE PRODUCER

Elijah Confronts King Ahab

**THE ONE
MINUTE
BIBLE**

In the thirty-eighth year of Asa king of Judah, Ahab son of Omri became king of Israel, and he reigned in Samaria over Israel twenty-two years. Ahab son of Omri did more evil in the eyes of the LORD than any of those before him. He not only considered it trivial to commit the sins of Jeroboam son of Nebat, but he also married Jezebel daughter of Ethbaal king of the Sidonians, and began to serve Baal and worship him. He set up an altar for Baal in the temple of Baal that he built in Samaria. Ahab also made an Asherah pole and did more to provoke the LORD, the God of Israel, to anger than did all the kings of Israel before him.

Now Elijah the Tishbite, from Tishbe in Gilead, said to Ahab, "As the LORD, the God of Israel, lives, whom I serve, there will be neither dew nor rain in the next few years except at my word."

Then the word of the LORD came to Elijah: "Leave here, turn eastward and hide in the Kerith Ravine, east of the Jordan. You will drink from the brook, and I have ordered the ravens to feed you there."

So he did what the LORD had told him. He went to the Kerith Ravine, east of the Jordan, and stayed there. The ravens brought him bread and meat in the morning and bread and meat in the evening, and he drank from the brook.

When I shut up the heavens so that there is no rain, or command locusts to devour the land or send a plague among my people, if my people, who are called by my name, will humble themselves and pray and seek my face and turn from their wicked ways, then will I hear from heaven and will forgive their sin and will heal their land.

1 KINGS 16:29-33; 17:1-6; 2 CHRONICLES 7:13-14

Related texts: DEUTERONOMY 11:16-17; MARK 6:14-15; LUKE 1:11-17; 9:7-8; JAMES 5:17-18

Elijah Challenges the Prophets of Baal

**THE ONE
MINUTE
BIBLE**

After a long time, in the third year, the word of the LORD came to Elijah: "Go and present yourself to Ahab, and I will send rain on the land."

When Ahab saw Elijah, he said to him, "Is that you, you troubler of Israel?"

"I have not made trouble for Israel," Elijah replied. "But you and your father's family have. You have abandoned the LORD's commands and have followed the Baals. Now summon the people from all over Israel to meet me on Mount Carmel. And bring the four hundred and fifty prophets of Baal and the four hundred prophets of Asherah, who eat at Jezebel's table."

So Ahab sent word throughout all Israel and assembled the prophets on Mount Carmel. Elijah went before the people and said, "How long will you waver between two opinions? If the LORD is God, follow him; but if Baal is God, follow him."

But the people said nothing.

Then Elijah said to them, "I am the only one of the LORD's prophets left, but Baal has four hundred and fifty prophets. Get two bulls for us. Let them choose one for themselves, and let them cut it into pieces and put it on the wood but not set fire to it. I will prepare the other bull and put it on the wood but not set fire to it. Then you call on the name of your god, and I will call on the name of the LORD. The god who answers by fire—he is God."

Then all the people said, "What you say is good."

1 KINGS 18:1, 17-24

Related texts: DEUTERONOMY 12:28-31; 32:36-39; MARK 8:27-29; LUKE 9:28-36; JAMES 5:14-18

The LORD Defeats Baal

Elijah said to the prophets of Baal, "Choose one of the bulls and prepare it first, since there are so many of you. Call on the name of your god, but do not light the fire." So they took the bull given them and prepared it.

Then they called on the name of Baal from morning till noon. "O Baal, answer us!" they shouted. But there was no response; no one answered. And they danced around the altar they had made.

Midday passed, and they continued their frantic prophesying until the time for the evening sacrifice. But there was no response, no one answered, no one paid attention.

At the time of sacrifice, the prophet Elijah stepped forward and prayed: "O LORD, God of Abraham, Isaac and Israel, let it be known today that you are God in Israel and that I am your servant and have done all these things at your command. Answer me, O LORD, answer me, so these people will know that you, O LORD, are God, and that you are turning their hearts back again."

Then the fire of the LORD fell and burned up the sacrifice, the wood, the stones and the soil, and also licked up the water in the trench.

When all the people saw this, they fell prostrate and cried, "The LORD—he is God! The LORD—he is God!"

Then Elijah commanded them, "Seize the prophets of Baal. Don't let anyone get away!" They seized them, and Elijah had them brought down to the Kishon Valley and slaughtered there.

1 KINGS 18:25-26, 29, 36-40

THE ONE MINUTE BIBLE

Related texts: DEUTERONOMY 13; 17:2-5; 18:18-22; 1 KINGS 21-22; 2 KINGS 9:30-10:28; PHILIPPIANS 2:5-11

Jonah Disobeys the LORD

**THE ONE
MINUTE
BIBLE**

The word of the LORD came to Jonah son of Amittai: "Go to the great city of Nineveh and preach against it, because its wickedness has come up before me."

But Jonah ran away from the LORD and headed for Tarshish. He went down to Joppa, where he found a ship bound for that port. After paying the fare, he went aboard and sailed for Tarshish to flee from the LORD.

Then the LORD sent a great wind on the sea, and such a violent storm arose that the ship threatened to break up. All the sailors were afraid and each cried out to his own god.

Then the sailors said to each other, "Come, let us cast lots to find out who is responsible for this calamity." They cast lots and the lot fell on Jonah.

The sea was getting rougher and rougher. So they asked him, "What should we do to you to make the sea calm down for us?"

"Pick me up and throw me into the sea," he replied, "and it will become calm. I know that it is my fault that this great storm has come upon you."

Then they took Jonah and threw him overboard, and the raging sea grew calm. At this the men greatly feared the LORD, and they offered a sacrifice to the LORD and made vows to him.

But the LORD provided a great fish to swallow Jonah, and Jonah was inside the fish three days and three nights.

JONAH 1:1-5a, 7, 11-12, 15-17

Related texts: 2 KINGS 14:25; MATTHEW 12:38-41; 16:1-4; LUKE 11:29-32

Jonah Prays from the Belly of a Fish

From inside the fish Jonah prayed to the LORD his God.
He said:

> "In my distress I called to the LORD,
>   and he answered me.
> From the depths of the grave I called for help,
>   and you listened to my cry.
> You hurled me into the deep,
>   into the very heart of the seas,
>   and the currents swirled about me;
> all your waves and breakers
>   swept over me.
> I said, 'I have been banished
>   from your sight;
> yet I will look again
>   toward your holy temple.'
> The engulfing waters threatened me,
>   the deep surrounded me;
>   seaweed was wrapped around my head.
> To the roots of the mountains I sank down;
>   the earth beneath barred me in forever.
> But you brought my life up from the pit,
>   O LORD my God.
> "When my life was ebbing away,
>   I remembered you, LORD,
> and my prayer rose to you,
>   to your holy temple.
> "Those who cling to worthless idols
>   forfeit the grace that could be theirs.
> But I, with a song of thanksgiving,
>   will sacrifice to you.
> What I have vowed I will make good.
>   Salvation comes from the LORD."

And the LORD commanded the fish, and it vomited Jonah
onto dry land.

JONAH 2

**THE ONE
MINUTE
BIBLE**

Related texts: 2 KINGS 17:13-15; PSALMS 42; 69; ISAIAH 44:9-20;
ACTS 27

271

The LORD Relents from Sending Disaster

**THE ONE
MINUTE
BIBLE**

Then the word of the LORD came to Jonah a second time: "Go to the great city of Nineveh and proclaim to it the message I give you."

Jonah obeyed the word of the LORD and went to Nineveh. Now Nineveh was a very important city—a visit required three days. On the first day, Jonah started into the city. He proclaimed: "Forty more days and Nineveh will be overturned." The Ninevites believed God. They declared a fast, and all of them, from the greatest to the least, put on sackcloth.

When the news reached the king of Nineveh, he rose from his throne, took off his royal robes, covered himself with sackcloth and sat down in the dust. Then he issued a proclamation in Nineveh:

"By the decree of the king and his nobles:

Do not let any man or beast, herd or flock, taste anything; do not let them eat or drink. But let man and beast be covered with sackcloth. Let everyone call urgently on God. Let them give up their evil ways and their violence. Who knows? God may yet relent and with compassion turn from his fierce anger so that we will not perish."

When God saw what they did and how they turned from their evil ways, he had compassion and did not bring upon them the destruction he had threatened.

JONAH 3

Related texts: EXODUS 32:1-14; JEREMIAH 18:1-11; JOEL 2:12-14;
LUKE 11:29-32

Joel Calls Israel to Repent

"Even now," declares the LORD,
   "return to me with all your heart,
   with fasting and weeping and mourning."
Rend your heart
   and not your garments.
Return to the LORD your God,
   for he is gracious and compassionate,
slow to anger and abounding in love,
   and he relents from sending calamity.
Who knows? He may turn and have pity
   and leave behind a blessing—
grain offerings and drink offerings
   for the LORD your God.
Blow the trumpet in Zion,
   declare a holy fast,
   call a sacred assembly.
Gather the people,
   consecrate the assembly;
bring together the elders,
   gather the children,
   those nursing at the breast.
Let the bridegroom leave his room
   and the bride her chamber.
Let the priests, who minister before the LORD,
   weep between the temple porch and the altar.
Let them say, "Spare your people, O LORD.
   Do not make your inheritance an object of scorn,
   a byword among the nations.
Why should they say among the peoples,
   'Where is their God?'"
Then the LORD will be jealous for his land
   and take pity on his people.

JOEL 2:12-18

**THE ONE
MINUTE
BIBLE**

Related texts: EXODUS 34:1-7; DEUTERONOMY 10:16; JONAH 3;
JAMES 4:6-8

Amos: Judgment and Hope

**THE ONE
MINUTE
BIBLE**

"Surely the eyes of the Sovereign L ord
are on the sinful kingdom.
I will destroy it
from the face of the earth—
yet I will not totally destroy
the house of Jacob,"

declares the L ord.

"All the sinners among my people
will die by the sword,
all those who say,
'Disaster will not overtake or meet us.'

"In that day I will restore
David's fallen tent.
I will repair its broken places,
restore its ruins,
and build it as it used to be,
so that they may possess the remnant of Edom
and all the nations that bear my name,"
declares the L ord, who will do these things.

"The days are coming," declares the L ord,

"when the reaper will be overtaken by the plowman
and the planter by the one treading grapes.
New wine will drip from the mountains
and flow from all the hills.
I will bring back my exiled people Israel;
they will rebuild the ruined cities and live in them.
They will plant vineyards and drink their wine;
they will make gardens and eat their fruit.
I will plant Israel in their own land,
never again to be uprooted
from the land I have given them,"

says the L ord your God.

A mos 9:8, 10-15

Related texts: 2 S amuel 7; I saiah 55; A cts 15:1-21; R omans 9–11

Hosea: The LORD's Anger and Compassion

**THE ONE
MINUTE
BIBLE**

"When Israel was a child, I loved him,
    and out of Egypt I called my son.
But the more I called Israel,
    the further they went from me.
They sacrificed to the Baals
    and they burned incense to images.
It was I who taught Ephraim to walk,
    taking them by the arms;
but they did not realize
    it was I who healed them.
I led them with cords of human kindness,
    with ties of love;
I lifted the yoke from their neck
    and bent down to feed them.
"Will they not return to Egypt
    and will not Assyria rule over them
    because they refuse to repent?
"How can I give you up, Ephraim?
    How can I hand you over, Israel?
How can I treat you like Admah?
    How can I make you like Zeboiim?
My heart is changed within me;
    all my compassion is aroused.
I will not carry out my fierce anger,
    nor will I turn and devastate Ephraim.
For I am God, and not man—
    the Holy One among you.
    I will not come in wrath.
They will follow the LORD;
    he will roar like a lion.
When he roars,
    his children will come trembling from the west.
They will come trembling
    like birds from Egypt,
    like doves from Assyria.
I will settle them in their homes,"
    declares the LORD.

HOSEA 11:1-5, 8-11

Related texts: GENESIS 19:1-29; DEUTERONOMY 29:18-23;
ZECHARIAH 10:6-12; 2 PETER 3:8-15

Isaiah Sees the Lord

**THE ONE
MINUTE
BIBLE**

In the year that King Uzziah died, I saw the Lord seated on a throne, high and exalted, and the train of his robe filled the temple. Above him were seraphs, each with six wings: With two wings they covered their faces, with two they covered their feet, and with two they were flying. And they were calling to one another:

"Holy, holy, holy is the LORD Almighty;
the whole earth is full of his glory."

At the sound of their voices the doorposts and thresholds shook and the temple was filled with smoke.

"Woe to me!" I cried. "I am ruined! For I am a man of unclean lips, and I live among a people of unclean lips, and my eyes have seen the King, the LORD Almighty."

Then one of the seraphs flew to me with a live coal in his hand, which he had taken with tongs from the altar. With it he touched my mouth and said, "See, this has touched your lips; your guilt is taken away and your sin atoned for."

Then I heard the voice of the Lord saying, "Whom shall I send? And who will go for us?"

And I said, "Here am I. Send me!"

He said, "Go and tell this people:

"'Be ever hearing, but never understanding;
be ever seeing, but never perceiving.'
Make the heart of this people calloused;
make their ears dull
and close their eyes.
Otherwise they might see with their eyes,
hear with their ears,
understand with their hearts,
and turn and be healed."

ISAIAH 6:1-10

Related texts: EXODUS 3:1-6; 33:15-23; JOB 19:25-27; MATTHEW 5:8; 13:10-17; JOHN 12:37-41; REVELATION 4

Micah: The Sins of Israel

The word of the LORD that came to Micah of
Moresheth during the reigns of Jotham, Ahaz and
Hezekiah, kings of Judah—the vision he saw
concerning Samaria and Jerusalem.

Hear, O peoples, all of you,
  listen, O earth and all who are in it,
that the Sovereign LORD may witness against you,
  the Lord from his holy temple.
Look! The LORD is coming from his dwelling place;
  he comes down and treads the high places of
    the earth.
The mountains melt beneath him
  and the valleys split apart,
like wax before the fire,
  like water rushing down a slope.
All this is because of Jacob's transgression,
  because of the sins of the house of Israel.
What is Jacob's transgression?
  Is it not Samaria?
What is Judah's high place?
  Is it not Jerusalem?
"Therefore I will make Samaria a heap of rubble,
  a place for planting vineyards.
I will pour her stones into the valley
  and lay bare her foundations.
All her idols will be broken to pieces;
  all her temple gifts will be burned with fire;
  I will destroy all her images.
Since she gathered her gifts from the wages of
    prostitutes,
  as the wages of prostitutes they will again
    be used."

MICAH 1:1-7

**THE ONE
MINUTE
BIBLE**

Related texts: DEUTERONOMY 5:6-10; JUDGES 10:11-16;
PSALMS 68:1-3; 97; JEREMIAH 26; ACTS 1:1-8

Israel Goes into Exile

**THE ONE
MINUTE
BIBLE**

In the ninth year of Hoshea, the king of Assyria captured Samaria and deported the Israelites to Assyria. He settled them in Halah, in Gozan on the Habor River and in the towns of the Medes.

All this took place because the Israelites had sinned against the LORD their God, who had brought them up out of Egypt from under the power of Pharaoh king of Egypt. They worshiped other gods and followed the practices of the nations the LORD had driven out before them, as well as the practices that the kings of Israel had introduced. The Israelites secretly did things against the LORD their God that were not right. From watchtower to fortified city they built themselves high places in all their towns. They set up sacred stones and Asherah poles on every high hill and under every spreading tree. At every high place they burned incense, as the nations whom the LORD had driven out before them had done. They did wicked things that provoked the LORD to anger.

They worshiped idols, though the LORD had said, "You shall not do this." The LORD warned Israel and Judah through all his prophets and seers: "Turn from your evil ways. Observe my commands and decrees, in accordance with the entire Law that I commanded your fathers to obey and that I delivered to you through my servants the prophets."

But they would not listen and were as stiff-necked as their fathers, who did not trust in the LORD their God.

2 KINGS 17:6-14

Related texts: DEUTERONOMY 28:14-68; 2 KINGS 15:16-20; ACTS 7:51-53

Good King Hezekiah

In the third year of Hoshea son of Elah king of Israel, Hezekiah son of Ahaz king of Judah began to reign. He was twenty-five years old when he became king, and he reigned in Jerusalem twenty-nine years. His mother's name was Abijah daughter of Zechariah. He did what was right in the eyes of the LORD, just as his father David had done. He removed the high places, smashed the sacred stones and cut down the Asherah poles. He broke into pieces the bronze snake Moses had made, for up to that time the Israelites had been burning incense to it. (It was called Nehushtan.)

Hezekiah trusted in the LORD, the God of Israel. There was no one like him among all the kings of Judah, either before him or after him. He held fast to the LORD and did not cease to follow him; he kept the commands the LORD had given Moses. And the LORD was with him; he was successful in whatever he undertook. He rebelled against the king of Assyria and did not serve him. From watchtower to fortified city, he defeated the Philistines, as far as Gaza and its territory.

In King Hezekiah's fourth year, which was the seventh year of Hoshea son of Elah king of Israel, Shalmaneser king of Assyria marched against Samaria and laid siege to it. At the end of three years the Assyrians took it. So Samaria was captured in Hezekiah's sixth year, which was the ninth year of Hoshea king of Israel.

2 KINGS 18:1-10

THE ONE MINUTE BIBLE

Related texts: NUMBERS 21:1-9; DEUTERONOMY 28:1-14; 2 CHRONICLES 29–31; PROVERBS 25:1; MATTHEW 1:1-10

The LORD Delivers Judah from Assyria

**THE ONE
MINUTE
BIBLE**

In the fourteenth year of King Hezekiah's reign, Sennacherib king of Assyria attacked all the fortified cities of Judah and captured them.

And Hezekiah prayed to the LORD: "O LORD, God of Israel, enthroned between the cherubim, you alone are God over all the kingdoms of the earth. You have made heaven and earth. Give ear, O LORD, and hear; open your eyes, O LORD, and see; listen to the words Sennacherib has sent to insult the living God.

"It is true, O LORD, that the Assyrian kings have laid waste these nations and their lands. They have thrown their gods into the fire and destroyed them, for they were not gods but only wood and stone, fashioned by men's hands. Now, O LORD our God, deliver us from his hand, so that all kingdoms on earth may know that you alone, O LORD, are God."

Then Isaiah son of Amoz sent a message to Hezekiah: "This is what the LORD, the God of Israel, says: I have heard your prayer concerning Sennacherib king of Assyria."

That night the angel of the LORD went out and put to death a hundred and eighty-five thousand men in the Assyrian camp. When the people got up the next morning—there were all the dead bodies! So Sennacherib king of Assyria broke camp and withdrew. He returned to Nineveh and stayed there.

2 KINGS 18:13; 19:15-20, 35-36

Related texts: 2 KINGS 19–20; 2 CHRONICLES 32; ISAIAH 36–39; ACTS 12

Nahum: God's Vengeance on Assyria

The LORD is a jealous and avenging God;
the LORD takes vengeance and is filled with wrath.
The LORD takes vengeance on his foes
and maintains his wrath against his enemies.
The LORD is slow to anger and great in power;
the LORD will not leave the guilty unpunished.
His way is in the whirlwind and the storm,
and clouds are the dust of his feet.
Who can withstand his indignation?
Who can endure his fierce anger?
His wrath is poured out like fire;
the rocks are shattered before him.
The LORD is good,
a refuge in times of trouble.
He cares for those who trust in him,
but with an overwhelming flood
he will make an end of [Nineveh];
he will pursue his foes into darkness.
Whatever they plot against the LORD
he will bring to an end;
trouble will not come a second time.

O king of Assyria, your shepherds slumber;
your nobles lie down to rest.
Your people are scattered on the mountains
with no one to gather them.
Nothing can heal your wound;
your injury is fatal.
Everyone who hears the news about you
claps his hands at your fall,
for who has not felt
your endless cruelty?

NAHUM 1:2-3, 6-9; 3:18-19

THE ONE MINUTE BIBLE

Related texts: EXODUS 34:1-7; JONAH; JOHN 3:31-36; ROMANS 1:18-19; EPHESIANS 5:5-6

281

Zephaniah: Jerusalem's Correction

**THE ONE
MINUTE
BIBLE**

Woe to the city of oppressors,
    rebellious and defiled!
She obeys no one,
    she accepts no correction.
She does not trust in the LORD,
    she does not draw near to her God.
Her officials are roaring lions,
    her rulers are evening wolves,
    who leave nothing for the morning.
Her prophets are arrogant;
    they are treacherous men.
Her priests profane the sanctuary
    and do violence to the law.
The LORD within her is righteous;
    he does no wrong.
Morning by morning he dispenses his justice,
    and every new day he does not fail,
    yet the unrighteous know no shame.
Sing, O Daughter of Zion;
    shout aloud, O Israel!
Be glad and rejoice with all your heart,
    O Daughter of Jerusalem!
The LORD has taken away your punishment,
    he has turned back your enemy.
The LORD, the King of Israel, is with you;
    never again will you fear any harm.
On that day they will say to Jerusalem,
    "Do not fear, O Zion;
    do not let your hands hang limp.
The LORD your God is with you,
    he is mighty to save.
He will take great delight in you,
    he will quiet you with his love,
    he will rejoice over you with singing."

ZEPHANIAH 3:1-5, 14-17

Related texts: PSALM 25; 34:1-5; ISAIAH 40; ROMANS 10:9-11

The Call of Jeremiah: Part 1

The words of Jeremiah son of Hilkiah, one of the priests at Anathoth in the territory of Benjamin. The word of the LORD came to him in the thirteenth year of the reign of Josiah son of Amon king of Judah, and through the reign of Jehoiakim son of Josiah king of Judah, down to the fifth month of the eleventh year of Zedekiah son of Josiah king of Judah, when the people of Jerusalem went into exile.

THE ONE MINUTE BIBLE

The word of the LORD came to me, saying,

"Before I formed you in the womb I knew you,
before you were born I set you apart;
I appointed you as a prophet to the nations."

"Ah, Sovereign LORD," I said, "I do not know how to speak; I am only a child."

But the LORD said to me, "Do not say, 'I am only a child.' You must go to everyone I send you to and say whatever I command you. Do not be afraid of them, for I am with you and will rescue you," declares the LORD.

Then the LORD reached out his hand and touched my mouth and said to me, "Now, I have put my words in your mouth. See, today I appoint you over nations and kingdoms to uproot and tear down, to destroy and overthrow, to build and to plant."

JEREMIAH 1:1-10

Related texts: PSALM 136; ISAIAH 6; LUKE 1:13-16; 1 TIMOTHY 4:12

The Call of Jeremiah: Part 2

**THE ONE
MINUTE
BIBLE**

The word of the Lord came to me again: "What do you see?"

"I see a boiling pot, tilting away from the north," I answered.

The Lord said to me, "From the north disaster will be poured out on all who live in the land. I am about to summon all the peoples of the northern kingdoms," declares the Lord.

"Their kings will come and set up their thrones
    in the entrance of the gates of Jerusalem;
they will come against all her surrounding walls
    and against all the towns of Judah.
I will pronounce my judgments on my people
    because of their wickedness in forsaking me,
in burning incense to other gods
    and in worshiping what their hands have made.

"Get yourself ready! Stand up and say to them whatever I command you. Do not be terrified by them, or I will terrify you before them. Today I have made you a fortified city, an iron pillar and a bronze wall to stand against the whole land—against the kings of Judah, its officials, its priests and the people of the land. They will fight against you but will not overcome you, for I am with you and will rescue you," declares the Lord.

JEREMIAH 1:13-19

Related texts: DEUTERONOMY 28; JOSHUA 1; EZEKIEL 11; 24; 33:1-20; 1 JOHN 5:3-4

Jeremiah Is Saved by Micah's Prophecy

Early in the reign of Jehoiakim son of Josiah king of Judah, this word came from the LORD: "Say to them, 'This is what the LORD says: If you do not listen to me and follow my law, which I have set before you, and if you do not listen to the words of my servants the prophets, whom I have sent to you again and again (though you have not listened), then I will make this house like Shiloh and this city an object of cursing among all the nations of the earth.'"

But as soon as Jeremiah finished telling all the people everything the LORD had commanded him to say, the priests, the prophets and all the people seized him and said, "You must die! Why do you prophesy in the LORD's name that this house will be like Shiloh and this city will be desolate and deserted?" And all the people crowded around Jeremiah in the house of the LORD.

Some of the elders of the land stepped forward and said to the entire assembly of people, "Micah of Moresheth prophesied in the days of Hezekiah king of Judah. He told all the people of Judah, 'This is what the LORD Almighty says:

"'Zion will be plowed like a field,
    Jerusalem will become a heap of rubble,
    the temple hill a mound overgrown
        with thickets.'

"Did Hezekiah king of Judah or anyone else in Judah put him to death? Did not Hezekiah fear the LORD and seek his favor? And did not the LORD relent, so that he did not bring the disaster he pronounced against them? We are about to bring a terrible disaster on ourselves!"

JEREMIAH 26:1, 4-6, 8-9, 17-19

THE ONE MINUTE BIBLE

Related texts: JEREMIAH 18:1-11; 19:1–20:2; 38:1-13; LAMENTATIONS 3:52-57; MICAH 3:9-12; MATTHEW 16:13-14

Judah Goes into Exile

**THE ONE
MINUTE
BIBLE**

Zedekiah was twenty-one years old when he became king, and he reigned in Jerusalem eleven years. He did evil in the eyes of the LORD his God and did not humble himself before Jeremiah the prophet, who spoke the word of the LORD.

The LORD, the God of their fathers, sent word to them through his messengers again and again, because he had pity on his people and on his dwelling place. But they mocked God's messengers, despised his words and scoffed at his prophets until the wrath of the LORD was aroused against his people and there was no remedy. He brought up against them the king of the Babylonians, who killed their young men with the sword in the sanctuary, and spared neither young man nor young woman, old man or aged.

God handed all of them over to Nebuchadnezzar. He carried to Babylon all the articles from the temple of God, both large and small, and the treasures of the LORD's temple and the treasures of the king and his officials. They set fire to God's temple and broke down the wall of Jerusalem; they burned all the palaces and destroyed everything of value there.

He carried into exile to Babylon the remnant, who escaped from the sword, and they became servants to him and his sons until the kingdom of Persia came to power. The land enjoyed its sabbath rests; all the time of its desolation it rested, until the seventy years were completed in fulfillment of the word of the LORD spoken by Jeremiah.

2 CHRONICLES 36:11-12, 15-21

Related texts: LEVITICUS 26:1-43; 2 KINGS 20:12-18; 25; ISAIAH 39; JEREMIAH 25; 38; 52; MATTHEW 1:1-17

Lament over Fallen Jerusalem

**THE ONE
MINUTE
BIBLE**

How deserted lies the city,
    once so full of people!
How like a widow is she,
    who once was great among the nations!
She who was queen among the provinces
    has now become a slave.
Bitterly she weeps at night,
    tears are upon her cheeks.
Among all her lovers
    there is none to comfort her.
All her friends have betrayed her;
    they have become her enemies.

So I say, "My splendor is gone
    and all that I had hoped from the LORD."
I remember my affliction and my wandering,
    the bitterness and the gall.
I well remember them,
    and my soul is downcast within me.
Yet this I call to mind
    and therefore I have hope:
Because of the LORD's great love we are not consumed,
    for his compassions never fail.
They are new every morning;
    great is your faithfulness.
I say to myself, "The LORD is my portion;
    therefore I will wait for him."
The LORD is good to those whose hope is in him,
    to the one who seeks him;
it is good to wait quietly
    for the salvation of the LORD.

LAMENTATIONS 1:1-2; 3:18-26

Related texts: PSALM 137; EZEKIEL 19; 24; MATTHEW 23:33-39

The LORD Promises Vengeance on Babylon

THE ONE MINUTE BIBLE

"See, he is puffed up;
    his desires are not upright—
    but the righteous will live by his faith—
indeed, wine betrays him;
    he is arrogant and never at rest.
Because he is as greedy as the grave
    and like death is never satisfied,
he gathers to himself all the nations
    and takes captive all the peoples.

"Will not all of them taunt him with ridicule and scorn, saying,

    "'Woe to him who piles up stolen goods
        and makes himself wealthy by extortion!
        How long must this go on?'"

I heard and my heart pounded,
    my lips quivered at the sound;
decay crept into my bones,
    and my legs trembled.
Yet I will wait patiently for the day of calamity
    to come on the nation invading us.
Though the fig tree does not bud
    and there are no grapes on the vines,
though the olive crop fails
    and the fields produce no food,
though there are no sheep in the pen
    and no cattle in the stalls,
yet I will rejoice in the LORD,
    I will be joyful in God my Savior.

The Sovereign LORD is my strength;
    he makes my feet like the feet of a deer,
    he enables me to go on the heights.

HABAKKUK 2:4-6; 3:16-19a

Related texts: GENESIS 9:5-6; 12:1-3; ROMANS 1:16-17; GALATIANS 3:8-14; HEBREWS 10:32-39

*Obadiah: The Day of the L*ORD

"In that day," declares the LORD,
   "will I not destroy the wise men of Edom,
   men of understanding in the mountains of Esau?
Because of the violence against your brother Jacob,
   you will be covered with shame;
   you will be destroyed forever.
On the day you stood aloof
   while strangers carried off his wealth
and foreigners entered his gates
   and cast lots for Jerusalem,
   you were like one of them.
You should not look down on your brother
   in the day of his misfortune,
nor rejoice over the people of Judah
   in the day of their destruction,
nor boast so much
   in the day of their trouble.

"The day of the LORD is near
   for all nations.
As you have done, it will be done to you;
   your deeds will return upon your own head.
Just as you drank on my holy hill,
   so all the nations will drink continually;
they will drink and drink
   and be as if they had never been.
But on Mount Zion will be deliverance;
   it will be holy,
and the house of Jacob
   will possess its inheritance."

OBADIAH 1:8, 10-12, 15-17

THE ONE
MINUTE
BIBLE

Related texts: ISAIAH 13; JOEL 3; 2 PETER 3

Ezekiel Sees the Restoration of Israel

**THE ONE
MINUTE
BIBLE**

The hand of the LORD was upon me, and he brought me out by the Spirit of the LORD and set me in the middle of a valley; it was full of bones.

Then he said to me, "Prophesy to these bones and say to them, 'Dry bones, hear the word of the LORD! This is what the Sovereign LORD says to these bones: I will make breath enter you, and you will come to life. I will attach tendons to you and make flesh come upon you and cover you with skin; I will put breath in you, and you will come to life. Then you will know that I am the LORD.'"

So I prophesied as I was commanded. And as I was prophesying, there was a noise, a rattling sound, and the bones came together, bone to bone.

Then he said to me, "Prophesy to the breath; prophesy, son of man, and say to it, 'This is what the Sovereign LORD says: Come from the four winds, O breath, and breathe into these slain, that they may live.'" So I prophesied as he commanded me, and breath entered them; they came to life and stood up on their feet—a vast army.

Then he said to me: "Son of man, these bones are the whole house of Israel. They say, 'Our bones are dried up and our hope is gone; we are cut off.' Therefore prophesy and say to them: 'This is what the Sovereign LORD says: O my people, I am going to open your graves and bring you up from them; I will bring you back to the land of Israel. I will put my Spirit in you and you will live, and I will settle you in your own land. Then you will know that I the LORD have spoken, and I have done it, declares the LORD.'"

EZEKIEL 37:1, 4-7, 9-12, 14

Related texts: DEUTERONOMY 30:1-10; PSALM 80; ISAIAH 40; EZEKIEL 36; ACTS 17:24-25; 2 THESSALONIANS 2:7-8

The Writing on the Wall

King Belshazzar gave a great banquet for a thousand of his nobles and drank wine with them. While Belshazzar was drinking his wine, he gave orders to bring in the gold and silver goblets that Nebuchadnezzar his father had taken from the temple in Jerusalem, so that the king and his nobles, his wives and his concubines might drink from them. As they drank the wine, they praised the gods of gold and silver, of bronze, iron, wood and stone.

Suddenly the fingers of a human hand appeared and wrote on the plaster of the wall, near the lampstand in the royal palace. The king watched the hand as it wrote. His face turned pale and he was so frightened that his knees knocked together and his legs gave way.

The queen, hearing the voices of the king and his nobles, came into the banquet hall. "O king, live forever!" she said. "Don't be alarmed! Don't look so pale! There is a man in your kingdom who has the spirit of the holy gods in him. In the time of your father he was found to have insight and intelligence and wisdom like that of the gods. King Nebuchadnezzar your father—your father the king, I say—appointed him chief of the magicians, enchanters, astrologers and diviners. This man Daniel, whom the king called Belteshazzar, was found to have a keen mind and knowledge and understanding, and also the ability to interpret dreams, explain riddles and solve difficult problems. Call for Daniel, and he will tell you what the writing means."

DANIEL 5:1-2, 4-6, 10-12

Related texts: GENESIS 41; DANIEL 1–4; JOEL 2:28-32; ACTS 2:1-21

Daniel Interprets the Writing

**THE ONE
MINUTE
BIBLE**

So Daniel was brought before the king, and the king said to him, "Are you Daniel, one of the exiles my father the king brought from Judah? Now I have heard that you are able to give interpretations and to solve difficult problems. If you can read this writing and tell me what it means, you will be clothed in purple and have a gold chain placed around your neck, and you will be made the third highest ruler in the kingdom."

Then Daniel answered the king, "You may keep your gifts for yourself and give your rewards to someone else. Nevertheless, I will read the writing for the king and tell him what it means.

"You praised the gods of silver and gold, of bronze, iron, wood and stone, which cannot see or hear or understand. But you did not honor the God who holds in his hand your life and all your ways. Therefore he sent the hand that wrote the inscription.

"This is the inscription that was written:

MENE, MENE, TEKEL, PARSIN

"This is what these words mean:

Mene: God has numbered the days of your reign
and brought it to an end.
Tekel: You have been weighed on the scales and
found wanting.
Peres: Your kingdom is divided and given to the
Medes and Persians."

That very night Belshazzar, king of the Babylonians, was slain, and Darius the Mede took over the kingdom, at the age of sixty-two.

DANIEL 5:13, 16-17, 23b-28, 30-31

Related texts: ISAIAH 47; DANIEL 4; MATTHEW 24:14-22;
1 CORINTHIANS 12

Cyrus Sends Israel Home

In the first year of Cyrus king of Persia, in order to fulfill the word of the LORD spoken by Jeremiah, the LORD moved the heart of Cyrus king of Persia to make a proclamation throughout his realm and to put it in writing:

"This is what Cyrus king of Persia says:

"'The LORD, the God of heaven, has given me all the kingdoms of the earth and he has appointed me to build a temple for him at Jerusalem in Judah. Anyone of his people among you—may his God be with him, and let him go up to Jerusalem in Judah and build the temple of the LORD, the God of Israel, the God who is in Jerusalem. And the people of any place where survivors may now be living are to provide him with silver and gold, with goods and livestock, and with freewill offerings for the temple of God in Jerusalem.'"

Then the family heads of Judah and Benjamin, and the priests and Levites—everyone whose heart God had moved—prepared to go up and build the house of the LORD in Jerusalem. All their neighbors assisted them with articles of silver and gold, with goods and livestock, and with valuable gifts, in addition to all the freewill offerings. Moreover, King Cyrus brought out the articles belonging to the temple of the LORD, which Nebuchadnezzar had carried away from Jerusalem and had placed in the temple of his god.

EZRA 1:1-7

**THE ONE
MINUTE
BIBLE**

Related texts: 2 CHRONICLES 36:22-23; JEREMIAH 25:11-12; 29:10-14

Haggai: Rebuild the Temple!

**THE ONE
MINUTE
BIBLE**

This is what the LORD Almighty says: "These people say, 'The time has not yet come for the LORD's house to be built.'"

Then the word of the LORD came through the prophet Haggai: "Is it a time for you yourselves to be living in your paneled houses, while this house remains a ruin?"

Now this is what the LORD Almighty says: "Give careful thought to your ways. You have planted much, but have harvested little. You eat, but never have enough. You drink, but never have your fill. You put on clothes, but are not warm. You earn wages, only to put them in a purse with holes in it."

This is what the LORD Almighty says: "Give careful thought to your ways. Go up into the mountains and bring down timber and build the house, so that I may take pleasure in it and be honored," says the LORD. "You expected much, but see, it turned out to be little. What you brought home, I blew away. Why?" declares the LORD Almighty. "Because of my house, which remains a ruin, while each of you is busy with his own house. Therefore, because of you the heavens have withheld their dew and the earth its crops. I called for a drought on the fields and the mountains, on the grain, the new wine, the oil and whatever the ground produces, on men and cattle, and on the labor of your hands."

Then Zerubbabel son of Shealtiel, Joshua son of Jehozadak, the high priest, and the whole remnant of the people obeyed the voice of the LORD their God and the message of the prophet Haggai, because the LORD their God had sent him. And the people feared the LORD.

HAGGAI 1:2-12

Related texts: HAGGAI 2; ZECHARIAH 1–6; 1 CORINTHIANS 3:9-17;
2 CORINTHIANS 6:14-16; EPHESIANS 2:11-22

Zechariah Encourages the Exiles

**THE ONE
MINUTE
BIBLE**

On the twenty-fourth day of the eleventh month, the month of Shebat, in the second year of Darius, the word of the LORD came to the prophet Zechariah son of Berekiah, the son of Iddo.

During the night I had a vision—and there before me was a man riding a red horse! He was standing among the myrtle trees in a ravine. Behind him were red, brown and white horses.

And they reported to the angel of the LORD, who was standing among the myrtle trees, "We have gone throughout the earth and found the whole world at rest and in peace."

Then the angel of the LORD said, "LORD Almighty, how long will you withhold mercy from Jerusalem and from the towns of Judah, which you have been angry with these seventy years?" So the LORD spoke kind and comforting words to the angel who talked with me.

Then the angel who was speaking to me said, "Proclaim this word: This is what the LORD Almighty says: 'I am very jealous for Jerusalem and Zion, but I am very angry with the nations that feel secure. I was only a little angry, but they added to the calamity.'

"Therefore, this is what the LORD says: 'I will return to Jerusalem with mercy, and there my house will be rebuilt. And the measuring line will be stretched out over Jerusalem,' declares the LORD Almighty.

"Proclaim further: This is what the LORD Almighty says: 'My towns will again overflow with prosperity, and the LORD will again comfort Zion and choose Jerusalem.'"

ZECHARIAH 1:7-8, 11-17

Related texts: ISAIAH 40:1-2; ZECHARIAH 1–6; 1 CORINTHIANS 14:3; 2 CORINTHIANS 1:3-7

The Exiles Rebuild the Temple

**THE ONE
MINUTE
BIBLE**

When the enemies of Judah and Benjamin heard that the exiles were building a temple for the LORD, the God of Israel, they came to Zerubbabel and to the heads of the families and said, "Let us help you build because, like you, we seek your God and have been sacrificing to him since the time of Esarhaddon king of Assyria, who brought us here."

But Zerubbabel, Jeshua and the rest of the heads of the families of Israel answered, "You have no part with us in building a temple to our God. We alone will build it for the LORD, the God of Israel, as King Cyrus, the king of Persia, commanded us."

Then the peoples around them set out to discourage the people of Judah and make them afraid to go on building. They hired counselors to work against them and frustrate their plans during the entire reign of Cyrus king of Persia and down to the reign of Darius king of Persia.

Then, because of the decree King Darius had sent, Tattenai, governor of Trans-Euphrates, and Shethar-Bozenai and their associates carried it out with diligence. So the elders of the Jews continued to build and prosper under the preaching of Haggai the prophet and Zechariah, a descendant of Iddo. They finished building the temple according to the command of the God of Israel and the decrees of Cyrus, Darius and Artaxerxes, kings of Persia. The temple was completed on the third day of the month Adar, in the sixth year of the reign of King Darius.

EZRA 4:1-5; 6:13-15

Related texts: EZRA 3–6; EZEKIEL 40–48; HAGGAI 1–2; JOHN 2:13-21

*The Bible is always...with me. Indeed,
I am not apt to dip pen in ink without
first looking into the Book of Books.*
Hayyim Nahman Bialik (1873-1934)
HEBREW POET

*This book...is the best gift God has
given to man.... But for it we could
not know right from wrong.*
Abraham Lincoln (1809-1865)
UNITED STATES PRESIDENT

*The Bible, that great medicine chest
of humanity. This is called with cause
the Holy Scripture. He who lost his God
may find Him again in this book, and
he who has never known Him will
inhale here the breath of God's word.*
Heinrich Heine (1797-1856)
GERMAN POET

Nehemiah Prays for the Exiles

**THE ONE
MINUTE
BIBLE**

The words of Nehemiah son of Hacaliah:

In the month of Kislev in the twentieth year, while I was in the citadel of Susa, Hanani, one of my brothers, came from Judah with some other men, and I questioned them about the Jewish remnant that survived the exile, and also about Jerusalem.

They said to me, "Those who survived the exile and are back in the province are in great trouble and disgrace. The wall of Jerusalem is broken down, and its gates have been burned with fire."

When I heard these things, I sat down and wept. For some days I mourned and fasted and prayed before the God of heaven. Then I said:

"O LORD, God of heaven, the great and awesome God, who keeps his covenant of love with those who love him and obey his commands, let your ear be attentive and your eyes open to hear the prayer your servant is praying before you day and night for your servants, the people of Israel. I confess the sins we Israelites, including myself and my father's house, have committed against you. We have acted very wickedly toward you. We have not obeyed the commands, decrees and laws you gave your servant Moses.

"Remember the instruction you gave your servant Moses, saying, 'If you are unfaithful, I will scatter you among the nations, but if you return to me and obey my commands, then even if your exiled people are at the farthest horizon, I will gather them from there and bring them to the place I have chosen as a dwelling for my Name.'"

NEHEMIAH 1:1-9

Related texts: LEVITICUS 26:14-46; DEUTERONOMY 7:6-15; 28:15-68; DANIEL 9:1-19; JAMES 5:13-16

The Exiles Rebuild Jerusalem's Wall

**THE ONE
MINUTE
BIBLE**

So we rebuilt the wall till all of it reached half its height, for the people worked with all their heart.

But when Sanballat, Tobiah, the Arabs, the Ammonites and the men of Ashdod heard that the repairs to Jerusalem's walls had gone ahead and that the gaps were being closed, they were very angry. They all plotted together to come and fight against Jerusalem and stir up trouble against it. But we prayed to our God and posted a guard day and night to meet this threat.

From that day on, half of my men did the work, while the other half were equipped with spears, shields, bows and armor. The officers posted themselves behind all the people of Judah who were building the wall. Those who carried materials did their work with one hand and held a weapon in the other, and each of the builders wore his sword at his side as he worked.

So the wall was completed on the twenty-fifth of Elul, in fifty-two days. When all our enemies heard about this, all the surrounding nations were afraid and lost their self-confidence, because they realized that this work had been done with the help of our God.

Nehemiah 4:6-9, 16-18a; 6:15-16

Related texts: Nehemiah 2–6; Psalms 27; 51:18-19; 127:1; John 16:33; 1 John 4:4

Pray for the Peace of Jerusalem

A song of ascents. Of David.

I rejoiced with those who said to me,
    "Let us go to the house of the LORD."
Our feet are standing
    in your gates, O Jerusalem.

Jerusalem is built like a city
    that is closely compacted together.
That is where the tribes go up,
    the tribes of the LORD,
to praise the name of the LORD
    according to the statute given to Israel.
There the thrones for judgment stand,
    the thrones of the house of David.

Pray for the peace of Jerusalem:
    "May those who love you be secure.
May there be peace within your walls
    and security within your citadels."
For the sake of my brothers and friends,
    I will say, "Peace be within you."
For the sake of the house of the LORD our God,
    I will seek your prosperity.

PSALM 122

Related texts: PSALM 85; ZECHARIAH 9:9-17; LUKE 13:34-35;
EPHESIANS 2:11-22

Ezra Reads the Law to the Exiles

**THE ONE
MINUTE
BIBLE**

So on the first day of the seventh month Ezra the priest brought the Law before the assembly, which was made up of men and women and all who were able to understand. He read it aloud from daybreak till noon as he faced the square before the Water Gate in the presence of the men, women and others who could understand. And all the people listened attentively to the Book of the Law.

Ezra opened the book. All the people could see him because he was standing above them; and as he opened it, the people all stood up. Ezra praised the LORD, the great God; and all the people lifted their hands and responded, "Amen! Amen!" Then they bowed down and worshiped the LORD with their faces to the ground.

The Levites ... instructed the people in the Law while the people were standing there. They read from the Book of the Law of God, making it clear and giving the meaning so that the people could understand what was being read.

Then Nehemiah the governor, Ezra the priest and scribe, and the Levites who were instructing the people said to them all, "This day is sacred to the LORD your God. Do not mourn or weep." For all the people had been weeping as they listened to the words of the Law.

Nehemiah said, "Go and enjoy choice food and sweet drinks, and send some to those who have nothing prepared. This day is sacred to our Lord. Do not grieve, for the joy of the LORD is your strength."

NEHEMIAH 8:2-3, 5-10

Related texts: DEUTERONOMY 16:13-15; EZRA 6:19-22; ISAIAH 58; MATTHEW 13:18-23; ACTS 17:10-11

Persia Needs a New Queen

**THE ONE
MINUTE
BIBLE**

This is what happened during the time of Xerxes, the Xerxes who ruled over 127 provinces stretching from India to Cush: At that time King Xerxes reigned from his royal throne in the citadel of Susa, and in the third year of his reign he gave a banquet for all his nobles and officials.

On the seventh day, when King Xerxes was in high spirits from wine, he commanded the seven eunuchs who served him ... to bring before him Queen Vashti, wearing her royal crown, in order to display her beauty to the people and nobles, for she was lovely to look at. But when the attendants delivered the king's command, Queen Vashti refused to come. Then the king became furious and burned with anger.

Then Memucan replied in the presence of the king and the nobles, "Queen Vashti has done wrong, not only against the king but also against all the nobles and the peoples of all the provinces of King Xerxes.

"Therefore, if it pleases the king, let him issue a royal decree and let it be written in the laws of Persia and Media, which cannot be repealed, that Vashti is never again to enter the presence of King Xerxes. Also let the king give her royal position to someone else who is better than she. Then when the king's edict is proclaimed throughout all his vast realm, all the women will respect their husbands, from the least to the greatest."

ESTHER 1:1-3a, 10-12, 16, 19-20

Related texts: EZRA 4:1-6; PROVERBS 31:1-9; DANIEL 9:1-2;
1 CORINTHIANS 6:9-10

Esther Becomes Queen of Persia

THE ONE MINUTE BIBLE

Now there was in the citadel of Susa a Jew of the tribe of Benjamin, named Mordecai son of Jair, the son of Shimei, the son of Kish, who had been carried into exile from Jerusalem by Nebuchadnezzar king of Babylon, among those taken captive with Jehoiachin king of Judah. Mordecai had a cousin named Hadassah, whom he had brought up because she had neither father nor mother. This girl, who was also known as Esther, was lovely in form and features, and Mordecai had taken her as his own daughter when her father and mother died.

When the king's order and edict had been proclaimed, many girls were brought to the citadel of Susa and put under the care of Hegai. Esther also was taken to the king's palace and entrusted to Hegai, who had charge of the harem. The girl pleased him and won his favor. Immediately he provided her with her beauty treatments and special food. He assigned to her seven maids selected from the king's palace and moved her and her maids into the best place in the harem.

Esther had not revealed her nationality and family background, because Mordecai had forbidden her to do so.

Now the king was attracted to Esther more than to any of the other women, and she won his favor and approval more than any of the other virgins. So he set a royal crown on her head and made her queen instead of Vashti.

ESTHER 2:5-10, 17

Related texts: GENESIS 39; 41; NEHEMIAH 1:1-11; 1 PETER 3:1-6

Haman Plots to Kill the Jews

THE ONE MINUTE BIBLE

After these events, King Xerxes honored Haman son of Hammedatha, the Agagite, elevating him and giving him a seat of honor higher than that of all the other nobles. All the royal officials at the king's gate knelt down and paid honor to Haman, for the king had commanded this concerning him. But Mordecai would not kneel down or pay him honor.

When Haman saw that Mordecai would not kneel down or pay him honor, he was enraged. Yet having learned who Mordecai's people were, he scorned the idea of killing only Mordecai. Instead Haman looked for a way to destroy all Mordecai's people, the Jews, throughout the whole kingdom of Xerxes.

Then Haman said to King Xerxes, "There is a certain people dispersed and scattered among the peoples in all the provinces of your kingdom whose customs are different from those of all other people and who do not obey the king's laws; it is not in the king's best interest to tolerate them. If it pleases the king, let a decree be issued to destroy them, and I will put ten thousand talents of silver into the royal treasury for the men who carry out this business."

So the king took his signet ring from his finger and gave it to Haman son of Hammedatha, the Agagite, the enemy of the Jews. "Keep the money," the king said to Haman, "and do with the people as you please."

ESTHER 3:1-2, 5-6, 8-11

Related texts: GENESIS 12:1-3; DEUTERONOMY 30:1-7; ESTHER 4–6; PSALM 44:1-8; DANIEL 3; 6; ROMANS 9–11

Haman's Downfall

**THE ONE
MINUTE
BIBLE**

So the king and Haman went to dine with Queen Esther, and as they were drinking wine on that second day, the king again asked, "Queen Esther, what is your petition? It will be given you. What is your request? Even up to half the kingdom, it will be granted."

Then Queen Esther answered, "If I have found favor with you, O king, and if it pleases your majesty, grant me my life—this is my petition. And spare my people—this is my request. For I and my people have been sold for destruction and slaughter and annihilation. If we had merely been sold as male and female slaves, I would have kept quiet, because no such distress would justify disturbing the king."

King Xerxes asked Queen Esther, "Who is he? Where is the man who has dared to do such a thing?"

Esther said, "The adversary and enemy is this vile Haman."

Then Harbona, one of the eunuchs attending the king, said, "A gallows seventy-five feet high stands by Haman's house. He had it made for Mordecai, who spoke up to help the king."

The king said, "Hang him on it!" So they hanged Haman on the gallows he had prepared for Mordecai. Then the king's fury subsided.

ESTHER 7:1-6a, 9-10

Related texts: DEUTERONOMY 23:3-5; ESTHER 8–10; JOEL 3:1-8; OBADIAH 15; REVELATION 19:11–20:10

Malachi: Messenger of the Covenant

**THE ONE
MINUTE
BIBLE**

"See, I will send my messenger, who will prepare
the way before me. Then suddenly the Lord you are
seeking will come to his temple; the messenger of the
covenant, whom you desire, will come," says the LORD
Almighty.

But who can endure the day of his coming? Who
can stand when he appears? For he will be like a
refiner's fire or a launderer's soap. He will sit as a
refiner and purifier of silver; he will purify the Levites
and refine them like gold and silver. Then the LORD will
have men who will bring offerings in righteousness, and
the offerings of Judah and Jerusalem will be acceptable
to the LORD, as in days gone by, as in former years.

"Surely the day is coming; it will burn like a
furnace. All the arrogant and every evildoer will be
stubble, and that day that is coming will set them on
fire," says the LORD Almighty. "Not a root or a branch will
be left to them. But for you who revere my name, the
sun of righteousness will rise with healing in its wings.
And you will go out and leap like calves released from
the stall. Then you will trample down the wicked; they
will be ashes under the soles of your feet on the day
when I do these things," says the LORD Almighty.

"See, I will send you the prophet Elijah before that
great and dreadful day of the LORD comes. He will turn
the hearts of the fathers to their children, and the
hearts of the children to their fathers; or else I will come
and strike the land with a curse."

MALACHI 3:1-4; 4:1-3, 5-6

Related texts: ISAIAH 60; LUKE 1:1-17; MATTHEW 3:1-12; 17:10-13

The Promise of Jesus' Coming

**THE ONE
MINUTE
BIBLE**

And now the LORD says—
    he who formed me in the womb to be his servant
to bring Jacob back to him
    and gather Israel to himself,
for I am honored in the eyes of the LORD
    and my God has been my strength—
he says:
"It is too small a thing for you to be my servant
    to restore the tribes of Jacob
    and bring back those of Israel I have kept.
I will also make you a light for the Gentiles,
    that you may bring my salvation to the ends
        of the earth."

"But you, Bethlehem Ephrathah,
    though you are small among the clans of Judah,
out of you will come for me
    one who will be ruler over Israel,
whose origins are from of old,
    from ancient times."

Therefore Israel will be abandoned
    until the time when she who is in labor gives birth
and the rest of his brothers return
    to join the Israelites.
He will stand and shepherd his flock
    in the strength of the LORD,
    in the majesty of the name of the LORD his God.
And they will live securely, for then his greatness
    will reach to the ends of the earth.
    And he will be their peace.

ISAIAH 49:5-6; MICAH 5:2-5a

Related texts: GENESIS 35:14-19; RUTH 4:10-17; 1 SAMUEL 17:12;
MATTHEW 2:1-6

Jesus: Son of God, Son of Man

**THE ONE
MINUTE
BIBLE**

In my vision at night I looked, and there before me was one like a son of man, coming with the clouds of heaven. He approached the Ancient of Days and was led into his presence. He was given authority, glory and sovereign power; all peoples, nations and men of every language worshiped him. His dominion is an everlasting dominion that will not pass away, and his kingdom is one that will never be destroyed.

In the past God spoke to our forefathers through the prophets at many times and in various ways, but in these last days he has spoken to us by his Son, whom he appointed heir of all things, and through whom he made the universe. The Son is the radiance of God's glory and the exact representation of his being, sustaining all things by his powerful word. After he had provided purification for sins, he sat down at the right hand of the Majesty in heaven. So he became as much superior to the angels as the name he has inherited is superior to theirs.

For to which of the angels did God ever say,

"You are my Son;
today I have become your Father"?

Or again,

"I will be his Father,
and he will be my Son"?

DANIEL 7:13-14; HEBREWS 1:1-5

Related texts: 2 SAMUEL 7:14; 1 CHRONICLES 17:13; PSALM 2:7;
MATTHEW 23:63-64; MARK 14:61-62; LUKE 22:67-70; JOHN 1:32-34

Jesus Christ Is Born

**THE ONE
MINUTE
BIBLE**

This is how the birth of Jesus Christ came about: His mother Mary was pledged to be married to Joseph, but before they came together, she was found to be with child through the Holy Spirit. Because Joseph her husband was a righteous man and did not want to expose her to public disgrace, he had in mind to divorce her quietly.

But after he had considered this, an angel of the Lord appeared to him in a dream and said, "Joseph son of David, do not be afraid to take Mary home as your wife, because what is conceived in her is from the Holy Spirit. She will give birth to a son, and you are to give him the name Jesus, because he will save his people from their sins."

All this took place to fulfill what the Lord had said through the prophet: "The virgin will be with child and will give birth to a son, and they will call him Immanuel"—which means, "God with us."

When Joseph woke up, he did what the angel of the Lord had commanded him and took Mary home as his wife. But he had no union with her until she gave birth to a son. And he gave him the name Jesus.

MATTHEW 1:18-25

Related texts: ISAIAH 7:14; MATTHEW 2; LUKE 1–2; JOHN 4:1-42

The Boy Jesus in the Temple

Every year his parents went to Jerusalem for the Feast of the Passover. When he was twelve years old, they went up to the Feast, according to the custom. After the Feast was over, while his parents were returning home, the boy Jesus stayed behind in Jerusalem, but they were unaware of it. Thinking he was in their company, they traveled on for a day. Then they began looking for him among their relatives and friends. When they did not find him, they went back to Jerusalem to look for him.

After three days they found him in the temple courts, sitting among the teachers, listening to them and asking them questions. Everyone who heard him was amazed at his understanding and his answers. When his parents saw him, they were astonished. His mother said to him, "Son, why have you treated us like this? Your father and I have been anxiously searching for you."

"Why were you searching for me?" he asked. "Didn't you know I had to be in my Father's house?" But they did not understand what he was saying to them.

Then he went down to Nazareth with them and was obedient to them. But his mother treasured all these things in her heart. And Jesus grew in wisdom and stature, and in favor with God and men.

LUKE 2:41-52

**THE ONE
MINUTE
BIBLE**

Related texts: 1 SAMUEL 2:21, 26; PSALMS 26:8; 27:4; 65; MATTHEW 2:13-23; JOHN 2:13-17; 2 CORINTHIANS 4:18–5:4

Jesus Is Baptized

**THE ONE
MINUTE
BIBLE**

The beginning of the gospel about Jesus Christ, the Son of God.

It is written in Isaiah the prophet:

"I will send my messenger ahead of you,
who will prepare your way"—
"a voice of one calling in the desert,
'Prepare the way for the Lord,
make straight paths for him.'"

And so John came, baptizing in the desert region and preaching a baptism of repentance for the forgiveness of sins. The whole Judean countryside and all the people of Jerusalem went out to him. Confessing their sins, they were baptized by him in the Jordan River. John wore clothing made of camel's hair, with a leather belt around his waist, and he ate locusts and wild honey. And this was his message: "After me will come one more powerful than I, the thongs of whose sandals I am not worthy to stoop down and untie. I baptize you with water, but he will baptize you with the Holy Spirit."

At that time Jesus came from Nazareth in Galilee and was baptized by John in the Jordan. As Jesus was coming up out of the water, he saw heaven being torn open and the Spirit descending on him like a dove. And a voice came from heaven: "You are my Son, whom I love; with you I am well pleased."

MARK 1:1-11

Related texts: ISAIAH 40:3; MALACHI 3:1; MATTHEW 3; LUKE 3; JOHN 1:19-34

Jesus Is Tempted by the Devil

**THE ONE
MINUTE
BIBLE**

Then Jesus was led by the Spirit into the desert to be tempted by the devil. After fasting forty days and forty nights, he was hungry. The tempter came to him and said, "If you are the Son of God, tell these stones to become bread."

Jesus answered, "It is written: 'Man does not live on bread alone, but on every word that comes from the mouth of God.'"

Then the devil took him to the holy city and had him stand on the highest point of the temple. "If you are the Son of God," he said, "throw yourself down. For it is written:

"'He will command his angels concerning you,
    and they will lift you up in their hands,
so that you will not strike your foot against
      a stone.'"

Jesus answered him, "It is also written: 'Do not put the Lord your God to the test.'"

Again, the devil took him to a very high mountain and showed him all the kingdoms of the world and their splendor. "All this I will give you," he said, "if you will bow down and worship me."

Jesus said to him, "Away from me, Satan! For it is written: 'Worship the Lord your God, and serve him only.'"

Then the devil left him, and angels came and attended him.

MATTHEW 4:1-11

Related texts: DEUTERONOMY 6:13, 16; 8:3; PSALM 91:11-12;
MARK 1:12-13; LUKE 4:1-13

Jesus' First Miracle

**THE ONE
MINUTE
BIBLE**

On the third day a wedding took place at Cana in Galilee. Jesus' mother was there, and Jesus and his disciples had also been invited to the wedding. When the wine was gone, Jesus' mother said to him, "They have no more wine."

"Dear woman, why do you involve me?" Jesus replied. "My time has not yet come."

His mother said to the servants, "Do whatever he tells you."

Jesus said to the servants, "Fill the jars with water"; so they filled them to the brim.

Then he told them, "Now draw some out and take it to the master of the banquet."

They did so, and the master of the banquet tasted the water that had been turned into wine. He did not realize where it had come from, though the servants who had drawn the water knew. Then he called the bridegroom aside and said, "Everyone brings out the choice wine first and then the cheaper wine after the guests have had too much to drink; but you have saved the best till now."

This, the first of his miraculous signs, Jesus performed at Cana in Galilee. He thus revealed his glory, and his disciples put their faith in him.

Jesus did many other things as well. If every one of them were written down, I suppose that even the whole world would not have room for the books that would be written.

JOHN 2:1-5, 7-11; 21:25

Related texts: ISAIAH 55; JOEL 3:16-18; AMOS 9:11-15; JOHN 20:30-31

You Must Be Born Again

Now there was a man of the Pharisees named Nicodemus, a member of the Jewish ruling council. He came to Jesus at night and said, "Rabbi, we know you are a teacher who has come from God. For no one could perform the miraculous signs you are doing if God were not with him."

In reply Jesus declared, "I tell you the truth, no one can see the kingdom of God unless he is born again."

"How can a man be born when he is old?" Nicodemus asked. "Surely he cannot enter a second time into his mother's womb to be born!"

Jesus answered, "I tell you the truth, no one can enter the kingdom of God unless he is born of water and the Spirit."

"How can this be?" Nicodemus asked.

"You are Israel's teacher," said Jesus, "and do you not understand these things? I have spoken to you of earthly things and you do not believe; how then will you believe if I speak of heavenly things? No one has ever gone into heaven except the one who came from heaven—the Son of Man. Just as Moses lifted up the snake in the desert, so the Son of Man must be lifted up, that everyone who believes in him may have eternal life.

"For God so loved the world that he gave his one and only Son, that whoever believes in him shall not perish but have eternal life."

JOHN 3:1-5, 9-10, 12-16

**THE ONE
MINUTE
BIBLE**

Related texts: NUMBERS 21:1-9; JOHN 1:1-13; 1 PETER 1; 1 JOHN 2:28-29; 3:1-10; 4:7-8; 5

Jesus Calls His First Disciples

**THE ONE
MINUTE
BIBLE**

One day as Jesus was standing by the Lake of Gennesaret, with the people crowding around him and listening to the word of God, he saw at the water's edge two boats, left there by the fishermen, who were washing their nets. He got into one of the boats, the one belonging to Simon, and asked him to put out a little from shore. Then he sat down and taught the people from the boat.

When he had finished speaking, he said to Simon, "Put out into deep water, and let down the nets for a catch."

Simon answered, "Master, we've worked hard all night and haven't caught anything. But because you say so, I will let down the nets."

When they had done so, they caught such a large number of fish that their nets began to break. So they signaled their partners in the other boat to come and help them, and they came and filled both boats so full that they began to sink.

When Simon Peter saw this, he fell at Jesus' knees and said, "Go away from me, Lord; I am a sinful man!" For he and all his companions were astonished at the catch of fish they had taken, and so were James and John, the sons of Zebedee, Simon's partners.

Then Jesus said to Simon, "Don't be afraid; from now on you will catch men." So they pulled their boats up on shore, left everything and followed him.

LUKE 5:1-11

Related texts: PSALM 51:1-13; MATTHEW 4:18-22; MARK 1:16-20; JOHN 1:35-51

Healing Illness; Forgiving Sin

**THE ONE
MINUTE
BIBLE**

One day as Jesus was teaching, Pharisees and teachers of the law, who had come from every village of Galilee and from Judea and Jerusalem, were sitting there. And the power of the Lord was present for him to heal the sick. Some men came carrying a paralytic on a mat and tried to take him into the house to lay him before Jesus. When they could not find a way to do this because of the crowd, they went up on the roof and lowered him on his mat through the tiles into the middle of the crowd, right in front of Jesus.

When Jesus saw their faith, he said, "Friend, your sins are forgiven."

The Pharisees and the teachers of the law began thinking to themselves, "Who is this fellow who speaks blasphemy? Who can forgive sins but God alone?"

Jesus knew what they were thinking and asked, "Why are you thinking these things in your hearts? Which is easier: to say, 'Your sins are forgiven,' or to say, 'Get up and walk'? But that you may know that the Son of Man has authority on earth to forgive sins...." He said to the paralyzed man, "I tell you, get up, take your mat and go home." Immediately he stood up in front of them, took what he had been lying on and went home praising God. Everyone was amazed and gave praise to God. They were filled with awe and said, "We have seen remarkable things today."

LUKE 5:17-26

Related texts: PSALM 25:1-11; MICAH 7:18; MATTHEW 9:1-8;
MARK 2:1-12

Jesus Controls Storms and Spirits

**THE ONE
MINUTE
BIBLE**

Then Jesus got into the boat and his disciples followed him. Without warning, a furious storm came up on the lake, so that the waves swept over the boat. But Jesus was sleeping. The disciples went and woke him, saying, "Lord, save us! We're going to drown!"

He replied, "You of little faith, why are you so afraid?" Then he got up and rebuked the winds and the waves, and it was completely calm.

The men were amazed and asked, "What kind of man is this? Even the winds and the waves obey him!"

When he arrived at the other side in the region of the Gadarenes, two demon-possessed men coming from the tombs met him. They were so violent that no one could pass that way. "What do you want with us, Son of God?" they shouted. "Have you come here to torture us before the appointed time?"

Some distance from them a large herd of pigs was feeding. The demons begged Jesus, "If you drive us out, send us into the herd of pigs."

He said to them, "Go!" So they came out and went into the pigs, and the whole herd rushed down the steep bank into the lake and died in the water.

MATTHEW 8:23-32

Related texts: DEUTERONOMY 14:8; ISAIAH 65:1-4; MARK 4:35-5:20; LUKE 8:22-39

Faith and Healing

While Jesus was saying this, a ruler came and knelt before him and said, "My daughter has just died. But come and put your hand on her, and she will live." Jesus got up and went with him, and so did his disciples.

Just then a woman who had been subject to bleeding for twelve years came up behind him and touched the edge of his cloak. She said to herself, "If I only touch his cloak, I will be healed."

Jesus turned and saw her. "Take heart, daughter," he said, "your faith has healed you." And the woman was healed from that moment.

When Jesus entered the ruler's house and saw the flute players and the noisy crowd, he said, "Go away. The girl is not dead but asleep." But they laughed at him. After the crowd had been put outside, he went in and took the girl by the hand, and she got up. News of this spread through all that region.

Is any one of you in trouble? He should pray. Is anyone happy? Let him sing songs of praise. Is any one of you sick? He should call the elders of the church to pray over him and anoint him with oil in the name of the Lord. And the prayer offered in faith will make the sick person well; the Lord will raise him up. If he has sinned, he will be forgiven. Therefore confess your sins to each other and pray for each other so that you may be healed. The prayer of a righteous man is powerful and effective.

Matthew 9:18-26; James 5:13-16

THE ONE MINUTE BIBLE

Related texts: Habakkuk 2:4; Matthew 9:27-30; Mark 5:21-43; Luke 7:1-10, 36-50; 8:22-25, 40-56; 17:11-19; 18:35-43

Jesus Responds to Lack of Faith

**THE ONE
MINUTE
BIBLE**

Then Jesus entered a house, and again a crowd gathered, so that he and his disciples were not even able to eat. When his family heard about this, they went to take charge of him, for they said, "He is out of his mind."

And the teachers of the law who came down from Jerusalem said, "He is possessed by Beelzebub! By the prince of demons he is driving out demons."

So Jesus called them and spoke to them in parables: "How can Satan drive out Satan? If a kingdom is divided against itself, that kingdom cannot stand. If a house is divided against itself, that house cannot stand. And if Satan opposes himself and is divided, he cannot stand; his end has come. In fact, no one can enter a strong man's house and carry off his possessions unless he first ties up the strong man. Then he can rob his house. I tell you the truth, all the sins and blasphemies of men will be forgiven them. But whoever blasphemes against the Holy Spirit will never be forgiven; he is guilty of an eternal sin."

He said this because they were saying, "He has an evil spirit."

MARK 3:20-30

Related texts: EXODUS 22:28; PSALM 106:1-37; MATTHEW 12:22-37; 13:53-58; MARK 6:1-6; LUKE 11:14-23; 12:10

320

Jesus Feeds Five Thousand

When Jesus looked up and saw a great crowd coming toward him, he said to Philip, "Where shall we buy bread for these people to eat?" He asked this only to test him, for he already had in mind what he was going to do.

Philip answered him, "Eight months' wages would not buy enough bread for each one to have a bite!"

Another of his disciples, Andrew, Simon Peter's brother, spoke up, "Here is a boy with five small barley loaves and two small fish, but how far will they go among so many?"

Jesus said, "Have the people sit down." There was plenty of grass in that place, and the men sat down, about five thousand of them. Jesus then took the loaves, gave thanks, and distributed to those who were seated as much as they wanted. He did the same with the fish.

When they had all had enough to eat, he said to his disciples, "Gather the pieces that are left over. Let nothing be wasted." So they gathered them and filled twelve baskets with the pieces of the five barley loaves left over by those who had eaten.

After the people saw the miraculous sign that Jesus did, they began to say, "Surely this is the Prophet who is to come into the world."

JOHN 6:5-14

THE ONE MINUTE BIBLE

Related texts: DEUTERONOMY 8:2-3; MATTHEW 14:13-21; MARK 6:32-44; LUKE 9:10-17

Who Is Jesus?

**THE ONE
MINUTE
BIBLE**

When Jesus came to the region of Caesarea Philippi, he asked his disciples, "Who do people say the Son of Man is?"

They replied, "Some say John the Baptist; others say Elijah; and still others, Jeremiah or one of the prophets."

"But what about you?" he asked. "Who do you say I am?"

Simon Peter answered, "You are the Christ, the Son of the living God."

Jesus replied, "Blessed are you, Simon son of Jonah, for this was not revealed to you by man, but by my Father in heaven. And I tell you that you are Peter, and on this rock I will build my church, and the gates of Hades will not overcome it. I will give you the keys of the kingdom of heaven; whatever you bind on earth will be bound in heaven, and whatever you loose on earth will be loosed in heaven." Then he warned his disciples not to tell anyone that he was the Christ.

From that time on Jesus began to explain to his disciples that he must go to Jerusalem and suffer many things at the hands of the elders, chief priests and teachers of the law, and that he must be killed and on the third day be raised to life.

MATTHEW 16:13-21

Related texts: ISAIAH 52:14-15; MARK 8:27-33; LUKE 9:18-22; JOHN 6:67-71

The Transfiguration

After six days Jesus took Peter, James and John with him and led them up a high mountain, where they were all alone. There he was transfigured before them. His clothes became dazzling white, whiter than anyone in the world could bleach them. And there appeared before them Elijah and Moses, who were talking with Jesus.

Peter said to Jesus, "Rabbi, it is good for us to be here. Let us put up three shelters—one for you, one for Moses and one for Elijah." (He did not know what to say, they were so frightened.)

Then a cloud appeared and enveloped them, and a voice came from the cloud: "This is my Son, whom I love. Listen to him!"

Suddenly, when they looked around, they no longer saw anyone with them except Jesus.

As they were coming down the mountain, Jesus gave them orders not to tell anyone what they had seen until the Son of Man had risen from the dead. They kept the matter to themselves, discussing what "rising from the dead" meant.

The Word became flesh and made his dwelling among us. We have seen his glory, the glory of the One and Only, who came from the Father, full of grace and truth.

Mark 9:2-10; John 1:14

**THE ONE
MINUTE
BIBLE**

Related texts: Exodus 40:33-35; Matthew 17:1-9; Luke 9:28-36; Romans 16:25-27; 1 Timothy 1:17; Jude 24-25

Small Faith — Large Results

**THE ONE
MINUTE
BIBLE**

When they came to the crowd, a man approached Jesus and knelt before him. "Lord, have mercy on my son," he said. "He has seizures and is suffering greatly. He often falls into the fire or into the water. I brought him to your disciples, but they could not heal him."

"O unbelieving and perverse generation," Jesus replied, "how long shall I stay with you? How long shall I put up with you? Bring the boy here to me." Jesus rebuked the demon, and it came out of the boy, and he was healed from that moment.

Then the disciples came to Jesus in private and asked, "Why couldn't we drive it out?"

He replied, "Because you have so little faith. I tell you the truth, if you have faith as small as a mustard seed, you can say to this mountain, 'Move from here to there' and it will move. Nothing will be impossible for you."

When they came together in Galilee, he said to them, "The Son of Man is going to be betrayed into the hands of men. They will kill him, and on the third day he will be raised to life." And the disciples were filled with grief.

[Jesus said,] "I tell you the truth, anyone who has faith in me will do what I have been doing. He will do even greater things than these, because I am going to the Father. And I will do whatever you ask in my name, so that the Son may bring glory to the Father."

MATTHEW 17:14-23; JOHN 14:12-13

Related texts: 1 SAMUEL 16:14-23; MARK 9:14-32; LUKE 9:37-45;
ROMANS 4:18-21; 11:1-23; HEBREWS 3:16-19

Jesus Teaches His Disciples to Pray

**THE ONE
MINUTE
BIBLE**

One day Jesus was praying in a certain place. When he finished, one of his disciples said to him, "Lord, teach us to pray, just as John taught his disciples."

He said to them, "When you pray, say:

"'Father,
hallowed be your name,
your kingdom come.
Give us each day our daily bread.
Forgive us our sins,
for we also forgive everyone who sins
against us.
And lead us not into temptation.'"

Then he said to them, "Suppose one of you has a friend, and he goes to him at midnight and says, 'Friend, lend me three loaves of bread, because a friend of mine on a journey has come to me, and I have nothing to set before him.'

"Then the one inside answers, 'Don't bother me. The door is already locked, and my children are with me in bed. I can't get up and give you anything.' I tell you, though he will not get up and give him the bread because he is his friend, yet because of the man's boldness he will get up and give him as much as he needs.

"So I say to you: Ask and it will be given to you; seek and you will find; knock and the door will be opened to you. For everyone who asks receives; he who seeks finds; and to him who knocks, the door will be opened."

LUKE 11:1-10

Related texts: PSALM 89:19-29; ISAIAH 9:6-7; MATTHEW 6:6-13; 7:7-11; REVELATION 3:14-22

THE ONE
MINUTE
BIBLE

Jesus Welcomes Little Children

An argument started among the disciples as to which of them would be the greatest. Jesus, knowing their thoughts, took a little child and had him stand beside him. Then he said to them, "Whoever welcomes this little child in my name welcomes me; and whoever welcomes me welcomes the one who sent me. For he who is least among you all—he is the greatest."

People were bringing little children to Jesus to have him touch them, but the disciples rebuked them. When Jesus saw this, he was indignant. He said to them, "Let the little children come to me, and do not hinder them, for the kingdom of God belongs to such as these. I tell you the truth, anyone who will not receive the kingdom of God like a little child will never enter it." And he took the children in his arms, put his hands on them and blessed them.

At that time Jesus, full of joy through the Holy Spirit, said, "I praise you, Father, Lord of heaven and earth, because you have hidden these things from the wise and learned, and revealed them to little children. Yes, Father, for this was your good pleasure.

"All things have been committed to me by my Father. No one knows who the Son is except the Father, and no one knows who the Father is except the Son and those to whom the Son chooses to reveal him."

Luke 9:46-48; Mark 10:13-16; Luke 10:21-22

Related texts: Psalm 127:3-5; Matthew 18:1-14; 19:13-15;
Mark 9:33-37; Luke 18:15-17

Jesus Heals on the Sabbath

THE ONE
MINUTE
BIBLE

On a Sabbath Jesus was teaching in one of the synagogues, and a woman was there who had been crippled by a spirit for eighteen years. She was bent over and could not straighten up at all. When Jesus saw her, he called her forward and said to her, "Woman, you are set free from your infirmity." Then he put his hands on her, and immediately she straightened up and praised God.

Indignant because Jesus had healed on the Sabbath, the synagogue ruler said to the people, "There are six days for work. So come and be healed on those days, not on the Sabbath."

The Lord answered him, "You hypocrites! Doesn't each of you on the Sabbath untie his ox or donkey from the stall and lead it out to give it water? Then should not this woman, a daughter of Abraham, whom Satan has kept bound for eighteen long years, be set free on the Sabbath day from what bound her?"

When he said this, all his opponents were humiliated, but the people were delighted with all the wonderful things he was doing.

LUKE 13:10-17

Related texts: EXODUS 20:8-11; MATTHEW 12:1-14; MARK 2:23–3:6;
LUKE 6:1-11; 14:1-6; JOHN 5:1-18

327

Jesus Teaches on Divorce and Celibacy

**THE ONE
MINUTE
BIBLE**

Some Pharisees came to Jesus to test him. They asked, "Is it lawful for a man to divorce his wife for any and every reason?"

"Haven't you read," he replied, "that at the beginning the Creator 'made them male and female,' and said, 'For this reason a man will leave his father and mother and be united to his wife, and the two will become one flesh'? So they are no longer two, but one. Therefore what God has joined together, let man not separate."

"Why then," they asked, "did Moses command that a man give his wife a certificate of divorce and send her away?"

Jesus replied, "Moses permitted you to divorce your wives because your hearts were hard. But it was not this way from the beginning. I tell you that anyone who divorces his wife, except for marital unfaithfulness, and marries another woman commits adultery."

The disciples said to him, "If this is the situation between a husband and wife, it is better not to marry."

Jesus replied, "Not everyone can accept this word, but only those to whom it has been given. For some are eunuchs because they were born that way; others were made that way by men; and others have renounced marriage because of the kingdom of heaven. The one who can accept this should accept it."

MATTHEW 19:3-12

Related texts: GENESIS 1:27; 2:24; DEUTERONOMY 24:1-4; MALACHI 2:13-16; MARK 10:2-12; LUKE 16:18

Treasure in Heaven

A certain ruler asked Jesus, "Good teacher, what must I do to inherit eternal life?"

"Why do you call me good?" Jesus answered. "No one is good—except God alone. You know the commandments: 'Do not commit adultery, do not murder, do not steal, do not give false testimony, honor your father and mother.'"

"All these I have kept since I was a boy," he said.

When Jesus heard this, he said to him, "You still lack one thing. Sell everything you have and give to the poor, and you will have treasure in heaven. Then come, follow me."

When he heard this, he became very sad, because he was a man of great wealth. Jesus looked at him and said, "How hard it is for the rich to enter the kingdom of God! Indeed, it is easier for a camel to go through the eye of a needle than for a rich man to enter the kingdom of God."

Those who heard this asked, "Who then can be saved?"

Jesus replied, "What is impossible with men is possible with God."

Peter said to him, "We have left all we had to follow you!"

"I tell you the truth," Jesus said to them, "no one who has left home or wife or brothers or parents or children for the sake of the kingdom of God will fail to receive many times as much in this age and, in the age to come, eternal life."

LUKE 18:18-30

Related texts: EXODUS 20:12-16; DEUTERONOMY 5:16-20; MATTHEW 19:16-30; MARK 10:17-31; 1 CORINTHIANS 13:3

The Bible is alive, it speaks to me.
Martin Luther (1483-1546)
GERMAN THEOLOGIAN AND REFORMER

He rightly reads Scripture who
turns words into deeds.
St. Bernard of Clairvaux (1090-1153)
FRENCH MONK

The Bible holds up before us ideals
that are within sight of the weakest
and the lowliest, and yet so high that
the best and noblest are kept with
their faces turned ever upward.
William Jennings Bryan (1860-1925)
AMERICAN ORATOR AND POLITICIAN

Jesus Visits a Sinner

Jesus entered Jericho and was passing through. A man was there by the name of Zacchaeus; he was a chief tax collector and was wealthy. He wanted to see who Jesus was, but being a short man he could not, because of the crowd. So he ran ahead and climbed a sycamore-fig tree to see him, since Jesus was coming that way.

When Jesus reached the spot, he looked up and said to him, "Zacchaeus, come down immediately. I must stay at your house today." So he came down at once and welcomed him gladly.

All the people saw this and began to mutter, "He has gone to be the guest of a 'sinner.'"

But Zacchaeus stood up and said to the Lord, "Look, Lord! Here and now I give half of my possessions to the poor, and if I have cheated anybody out of anything, I will pay back four times the amount."

Jesus said to him, "Today salvation has come to this house, because this man, too, is a son of Abraham. For the Son of Man came to seek and to save what was lost."

Just as man is destined to die once, and after that to face judgment, so Christ was sacrificed once to take away the sins of many people; and he will appear a second time, not to bear sin, but to bring salvation to those who are waiting for him.

LUKE 19:1-10; HEBREWS 9:27-28

Related texts: EZEKIEL 34:7-16; MARK 2:14-17; LUKE 7:36-47

Jesus Anointed for Burial

**THE ONE
MINUTE
BIBLE**

Six days before the Passover, Jesus arrived at Bethany, where Lazarus lived, whom Jesus had raised from the dead. Here a dinner was given in Jesus' honor. Martha served, while Lazarus was among those reclining at the table with him. Then Mary took about a pint of pure nard, an expensive perfume; she poured it on Jesus' feet and wiped his feet with her hair. And the house was filled with the fragrance of the perfume.

But one of his disciples, Judas Iscariot, who was later to betray him, objected, "Why wasn't this perfume sold and the money given to the poor? It was worth a year's wages." He did not say this because he cared about the poor but because he was a thief; as keeper of the money bag, he used to help himself to what was put into it.

"Leave her alone," Jesus replied. "[It was intended] that she should save this perfume for the day of my burial. You will always have the poor among you, but you will not always have me."

Meanwhile a large crowd of Jews found out that Jesus was there and came, not only because of him but also to see Lazarus, whom he had raised from the dead. So the chief priests made plans to kill Lazarus as well, for on account of him many of the Jews were going over to Jesus and putting their faith in him.

JOHN 12:1-11

Related texts: PSALM 16:9-11; MATTHEW 26:6-13; MARK 14:3-9; LUKE 7:36-50; JOHN 11

The Triumphal Entry

**THE ONE
MINUTE
BIBLE**

As Jesus approached Bethphage and Bethany at the hill called the Mount of Olives, he sent two of his disciples, saying to them, "Go to the village ahead of you, and as you enter it, you will find a colt tied there, which no one has ever ridden. Untie it and bring it here. If anyone asks you, 'Why are you untying it?' tell him, 'The Lord needs it.'"

Those who were sent ahead went and found it just as he had told them. As they were untying the colt, its owners asked them, "Why are you untying the colt?"

They replied, "The Lord needs it."

They brought it to Jesus, threw their cloaks on the colt and put Jesus on it. As he went along, people spread their cloaks on the road.

When he came near the place where the road goes down the Mount of Olives, the whole crowd of disciples began joyfully to praise God in loud voices for all the miracles they had seen:

> "Blessed is the king who comes in the name
> of the Lord!"

"Peace in heaven and glory in the highest!"

Some of the Pharisees in the crowd said to Jesus, "Teacher, rebuke your disciples!"

"I tell you," he replied, "if they keep quiet, the stones will cry out."

LUKE 19:29-40

Related texts: PSALM 118; MATTHEW 21:1-9; MARK 11:1-10;
JOHN 12:12-19

The Parable of the Vineyard

**THE ONE
MINUTE
BIBLE**

Jesus went on to tell the people this parable: "A man planted a vineyard, rented it to some farmers and went away for a long time. At harvest time he sent a servant to the tenants so they would give him some of the fruit of the vineyard. But the tenants beat him and sent him away empty-handed. He sent another servant, but that one also they beat and treated shamefully and sent away empty-handed. He sent still a third, and they wounded him and threw him out.

"Then the owner of the vineyard said, 'What shall I do? I will send my son, whom I love; perhaps they will respect him.'

"But when the tenants saw him, they talked the matter over. 'This is the heir,' they said. 'Let's kill him, and the inheritance will be ours.' So they threw him out of the vineyard and killed him.

"What then will the owner of the vineyard do to them? He will come and kill those tenants and give the vineyard to others."

When the people heard this, they said, "May this never be!"

Jesus looked directly at them and asked, "Then what is the meaning of that which is written:

> "'The stone the builders rejected
>   has become the capstone'?

Everyone who falls on that stone will be broken to pieces, but he on whom it falls will be crushed."

The teachers of the law and the chief priests looked for a way to arrest him immediately, because they knew he had spoken this parable against them. But they were afraid of the people.

Luke 20:9-19

Related texts: Psalm 118; Matthew 21:33-46; Mark 12:1-12

The Last Supper

Then one of the Twelve—the one called Judas Iscariot—went to the chief priests and asked, "What are you willing to give me if I hand him over to you?" So they counted out for him thirty silver coins. From then on Judas watched for an opportunity to hand him over.

On the first day of the Feast of Unleavened Bread, the disciples came to Jesus and asked, "Where do you want us to make preparations for you to eat the Passover?"

He replied, "Go into the city to a certain man and tell him, 'The Teacher says: My appointed time is near. I am going to celebrate the Passover with my disciples at your house.'" So the disciples did as Jesus had directed them and prepared the Passover.

When evening came, Jesus was reclining at the table with the Twelve. And while they were eating, he said, "I tell you the truth, one of you will betray me."

They were very sad and began to say to him one after the other, "Surely not I, Lord?"

Jesus replied, "The one who has dipped his hand into the bowl with me will betray me. The Son of Man will go just as it is written about him. But woe to that man who betrays the Son of Man! It would be better for him if he had not been born."

Then Judas, the one who would betray him, said, "Surely not I, Rabbi?"

Jesus answered, "Yes, it is you."

MATTHEW 26:14-25

Related texts: PSALM 41:9; PROVERBS 11:13; MARK 14:10-25; LUKE 22:3-23; JOHN 13–17

Faithless Friends

**THE ONE
MINUTE
BIBLE**

"You will all fall away," Jesus told them, "for it is written:

"'I will strike the shepherd,
and the sheep will be scattered.'

But after I have risen, I will go ahead of you into Galilee."

Peter declared, "Even if all fall away, I will not."

"I tell you the truth," Jesus answered, "today—yes, tonight—before the rooster crows twice you yourself will disown me three times."

But Peter insisted emphatically, "Even if I have to die with you, I will never disown you." And all the others said the same.

They went to a place called Gethsemane, and Jesus said to his disciples, "Sit here while I pray." He took Peter, James and John along with him, and he began to be deeply distressed and troubled. "My soul is overwhelmed with sorrow to the point of death," he said to them. "Stay here and keep watch."

Going a little farther, he fell to the ground and prayed that if possible the hour might pass from him. "*Abba,* Father," he said, "everything is possible for you. Take this cup from me. Yet not what I will, but what you will."

Then he returned to his disciples and found them sleeping. "Simon," he said to Peter, "are you asleep? Could you not keep watch for one hour? Watch and pray so that you will not fall into temptation. The spirit is willing, but the body is weak."

MARK 14:27-38

Related texts: ZECHARIAH 13:7; MARK 14:26-42; LUKE 22:31-46; JOHN 13:36-38

Betrayal and Denial

While Jesus was still speaking a crowd came up, and the man who was called Judas, one of the Twelve, was leading them. He approached Jesus to kiss him, but Jesus asked him, "Judas, are you betraying the Son of Man with a kiss?"

Then seizing him, they led him away and took him into the house of the high priest. Peter followed at a distance. But when they had kindled a fire in the middle of the courtyard and had sat down together, Peter sat down with them. A servant girl saw him seated there in the firelight. She looked closely at him and said, "This man was with him."

But he denied it. "Woman, I don't know him," he said.

A little later someone else saw him and said, "You also are one of them."

"Man, I am not!" Peter replied.

About an hour later another asserted, "Certainly this fellow was with him, for he is a Galilean."

Peter replied, "Man, I don't know what you're talking about!" Just as he was speaking, the rooster crowed. The Lord turned and looked straight at Peter. Then Peter remembered the word the Lord had spoken to him: "Before the rooster crows today, you will disown me three times." And he went outside and wept bitterly.

LUKE 22:47-48, 54-62

Related texts: PSALM 42; MATTHEW 26:47-56, 69-75;
MARK 14:43-53, 66-72; JOHN 18:2-12, 25-27

Jesus Is Sentenced to Death

**THE ONE
MINUTE
BIBLE**

The chief priests and the whole Sanhedrin were looking for evidence against Jesus so that they could put him to death, but they did not find any. Many testified falsely against him, but their statements did not agree.

Then some stood up and gave this false testimony against him: "We heard him say, 'I will destroy this man-made temple and in three days will build another, not made by man.'" Yet even then their testimony did not agree.

Then the high priest stood up before them and asked Jesus, "Are you not going to answer? What is this testimony that these men are bringing against you?" But Jesus remained silent and gave no answer.

Again the high priest asked him, "Are you the Christ, Son of the Blessed One?"

"I am," said Jesus. "And you will see the Son of Man sitting at the right hand of the Mighty One and coming on the clouds of heaven."

The high priest tore his clothes. "Why do we need any more witnesses?" he asked. "You have heard the blasphemy. What do you think?"

They all condemned him as worthy of death. Then some began to spit at him; they blindfolded him, struck him with their fists, and said, "Prophesy!" And the guards took him and beat him.

MARK 14:55-65

Related texts: EXODUS 20:16; DANIEL 7:13-14; MATTHEW 26:59-67; MARK 14:55-65; LUKE 23:63-71; JOHN 18:19-24

Jesus Is Crucified

When they came to the place called the Skull, there they crucified Jesus, along with the criminals—one on his right, the other on his left. Jesus said, "Father, forgive them, for they do not know what they are doing." And they divided up his clothes by casting lots.

THE ONE MINUTE BIBLE

The people stood watching, and the rulers even sneered at him. They said, "He saved others; let him save himself if he is the Christ of God, the Chosen One."

One of the criminals who hung there hurled insults at him: "Aren't you the Christ? Save yourself and us!"

But the other criminal rebuked him. "Don't you fear God," he said, "since you are under the same sentence? We are punished justly, for we are getting what our deeds deserve. But this man has done nothing wrong."

Then he said, "Jesus, remember me when you come into your kingdom."

Jesus answered him, "I tell you the truth, today you will be with me in paradise."

It was now about the sixth hour, and darkness came over the whole land until the ninth hour, for the sun stopped shining. And the curtain of the temple was torn in two. Jesus called out with a loud voice, "Father, into your hands I commit my spirit." When he had said this, he breathed his last.

The centurion, seeing what had happened, praised God and said, "Surely this was a righteous man."

LUKE 23:33-35, 39-47

Related texts: PSALM 22; MATTHEW 27; MARK 15; LUKE 23; JOHN 18:28-19:42

The Resurrection

**THE ONE
MINUTE
BIBLE**

Early on the first day of the week, while it was still dark, Mary Magdalene went to the tomb and saw that the stone had been removed from the entrance. So she came running to Simon Peter and the other disciple, the one Jesus loved, and said, "They have taken the Lord out of the tomb, and we don't know where they have put him!"

So Peter and the other disciple started for the tomb. Both were running, but the other disciple outran Peter and reached the tomb first. He bent over and looked in at the strips of linen lying there but did not go in. Then Simon Peter, who was behind him, arrived and went into the tomb. He saw the strips of linen lying there, as well as the burial cloth that had been around Jesus' head. The cloth was folded up by itself, separate from the linen. Finally the other disciple, who had reached the tomb first, also went inside. He saw and believed. (They still did not understand from Scripture that Jesus had to rise from the dead.)

On the evening of that first day of the week, when the disciples were together, with the doors locked for fear of the Jews, Jesus came and stood among them and said, "Peace be with you!" After he said this, he showed them his hands and side. The disciples were overjoyed when they saw the Lord.

JOHN 20:1-9, 19-20

Related texts: PSALM 16:9-11; ISAIAH 53:9-12; MATTHEW 28; MARK 16; LUKE 24; JOHN 20–21

Alive in Christ

See to it that no one takes you captive through hollow and deceptive philosophy, which depends on human tradition and the basic principles of this world rather than on Christ.

For in Christ all the fullness of the Deity lives in bodily form, and you have been given fullness in Christ, who is the head over every power and authority. In him you were also circumcised, in the putting off of the sinful nature, not with a circumcision done by the hands of men but with the circumcision done by Christ, having been buried with him in baptism and raised with him through your faith in the power of God, who raised him from the dead.

When you were dead in your sins and in the uncircumcision of your sinful nature, God made you alive with Christ. He forgave us all our sins, having canceled the written code, with its regulations, that was against us and that stood opposed to us; he took it away, nailing it to the cross. And having disarmed the powers and authorities, he made a public spectacle of them, triumphing over them by the cross.

Therefore do not let anyone judge you by what you eat or drink, or with regard to a religious festival, a New Moon celebration or a Sabbath day. These are a shadow of the things that were to come; the reality, however, is found in Christ.

COLOSSIANS 2:8-17

THE ONE
MINUTE
BIBLE

Related texts: ISAIAH 1:11-14; ACTS 2:22-36; ROMANS 6:1-11; 1 CORINTHIANS 15:12-58

Jesus Returns to the Father

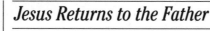

**THE ONE
MINUTE
BIBLE**

In my former book, Theophilus, I wrote about all that Jesus began to do and to teach until the day he was taken up to heaven, after giving instructions through the Holy Spirit to the apostles he had chosen. After his suffering, he showed himself to these men and gave many convincing proofs that he was alive. He appeared to them over a period of forty days and spoke about the kingdom of God. On one occasion, while he was eating with them, he gave them this command: "Do not leave Jerusalem, but wait for the gift my Father promised, which you have heard me speak about. For John baptized with water, but in a few days you will be baptized with the Holy Spirit."

So when they met together, they asked him, "Lord, are you at this time going to restore the kingdom to Israel?"

He said to them: "It is not for you to know the times or dates the Father has set by his own authority. But you will receive power when the Holy Spirit comes on you; and you will be my witnesses in Jerusalem, and in all Judea and Samaria, and to the ends of the earth."

After he said this, he was taken up before their very eyes, and a cloud hid him from their sight.

They were looking intently up into the sky as he was going, when suddenly two men dressed in white stood beside them. "Men of Galilee," they said, "why do you stand here looking into the sky? This same Jesus, who has been taken from you into heaven, will come back in the same way you have seen him go into heaven."

ACTS 1:1-11

Related texts: 1 CHRONICLES 16:8, 23-31; PSALMS 67; 72; ISAIAH 45:22-23; 49:6; LUKE 24:50-53

The Gift of the Holy Spirit

**THE ONE
MINUTE
BIBLE**

When the day of Pentecost came, the believers were all together in one place. Suddenly a sound like the blowing of a violent wind came from heaven and filled the whole house where they were sitting. They saw what seemed to be tongues of fire that separated and came to rest on each of them. All of them were filled with the Holy Spirit and began to speak in other tongues as the Spirit enabled them.

Now there were staying in Jerusalem God-fearing Jews from every nation under heaven. When they heard this sound, a crowd came together in bewilderment, because each one heard them speaking in his own language. Utterly amazed, they asked: "Are not all these men who are speaking Galileans? Then how is it that each of us hears them in his own native language? Parthians, Medes and Elamites; residents of Mesopotamia, Judea and Cappadocia, Pontus and Asia, Phrygia and Pamphylia, Egypt and the parts of Libya near Cyrene; visitors from Rome (both Jews and converts to Judaism); Cretans and Arabs—we hear them declaring the wonders of God in our own tongues!" Amazed and perplexed, they asked one another, "What does this mean?"

Some, however, made fun of them and said, "They have had too much wine."

ACTS 2:1-13

Related texts: LEVITICUS 23:4-16; MATTHEW 3:1-12;
JOHN 14:15-26; 15:26-27; 16:12-15

Peter's First Sermon

**THE ONE
MINUTE
BIBLE**

Then Peter stood up with the Eleven, raised his voice and addressed the crowd: "Fellow Jews and all of you who live in Jerusalem, let me explain this to you; listen carefully to what I say. These men are not drunk, as you suppose. It's only nine in the morning! No, this is what was spoken by the prophet Joel:

"'In the last days, God says,
I will pour out my Spirit on all people.
Your sons and daughters will prophesy,
your young men will see visions,
your old men will dream dreams.
Even on my servants, both men and women,
I will pour out my Spirit in those days,
and they will prophesy.
And everyone who calls
on the name of the Lord will be saved.'

"Men of Israel, listen to this: Jesus of Nazareth was a man accredited by God to you by miracles, wonders and signs, which God did among you through him, as you yourselves know. This man was handed over to you by God's set purpose and foreknowledge; and you, with the help of wicked men, put him to death by nailing him to the cross. But God raised him from the dead, freeing him from the agony of death, because it was impossible for death to keep its hold on him."

Peter replied, "Repent and be baptized, every one of you, in the name of Jesus Christ for the forgiveness of your sins. And you will receive the gift of the Holy Spirit."

Acts 2:14-18, 21-24, 38

Related texts: Ezekiel 36:16-28; 39:21-29; Joel 2:28-32; Romans 10:1-13

Peter Heals a Crippled Beggar

**THE ONE
MINUTE
BIBLE**

One day Peter and John were going up to the temple at the time of prayer—at three in the afternoon. Now a man crippled from birth was being carried to the temple gate called Beautiful, where he was put every day to beg from those going into the temple courts. When he saw Peter and John about to enter, he asked them for money. Peter looked straight at him, as did John. Then Peter said, "Look at us!" So the man gave them his attention, expecting to get something from them.

Then Peter said, "Silver or gold I do not have, but what I have I give you. In the name of Jesus Christ of Nazareth, walk." Taking him by the right hand, he helped him up, and instantly the man's feet and ankles became strong. He jumped to his feet and began to walk. Then he went with them into the temple courts, walking and jumping, and praising God. When all the people saw him walking and praising God, they recognized him as the same man who used to sit begging at the temple gate called Beautiful, and they were filled with wonder and amazement at what had happened to him.

The priests and the captain of the temple guard and the Sadducees came up to Peter and John while they were speaking to the people. They were greatly disturbed because the apostles were teaching the people and proclaiming in Jesus the resurrection of the dead. They seized Peter and John, and because it was evening, they put them in jail until the next day. But many who heard the message believed, and the number of men grew to about five thousand.

ACTS 3:1-10; 4:1-4

Related texts: JEREMIAH 37:15; 38:6; MATTHEW 15:29-31; 21:1-16; JOHN 5; 14:12-14

Obey God Before People

**THE ONE
MINUTE
BIBLE**

When the rulers, elders and teachers of the law saw the courage of Peter and John and realized that they were unschooled, ordinary men, they were astonished and they took note that these men had been with Jesus. But since they could see the man who had been healed standing there with them, there was nothing they could say. So they ordered them to withdraw from the Sanhedrin and then conferred together. "What are we going to do with these men?" they asked. "Everybody living in Jerusalem knows they have done an outstanding miracle, and we cannot deny it. But to stop this thing from spreading any further among the people, we must warn these men to speak no longer to anyone in this name."

Then they called them in again and commanded them not to speak or teach at all in the name of Jesus. But Peter and John replied, "Judge for yourselves whether it is right in God's sight to obey you rather than God. For we cannot help speaking about what we have seen and heard."

After further threats they let them go. They could not decide how to punish them, because all the people were praising God for what had happened. For the man who was miraculously healed was over forty years old.

On their release, Peter and John went back to their own people and reported all that the chief priests and elders had said to them.

ACTS 4:13-23

Related texts: JEREMIAH 20:9; MATTHEW 5:10-12; ACTS 5:17-42

Stephen Is Martyred for His Testimony

THE ONE
MINUTE
BIBLE

So the word of God spread. The number of disciples in Jerusalem increased rapidly, and a large number of priests became obedient to the faith.

Now Stephen, a man full of God's grace and power, did great wonders and miraculous signs among the people. Opposition arose, however, from members of the Synagogue of the Freedmen (as it was called)—Jews of Cyrene and Alexandria as well as the provinces of Cilicia and Asia. These men began to argue with Stephen, but they could not stand up against his wisdom or the Spirit by whom he spoke.

Then they secretly persuaded some men to say, "We have heard Stephen speak words of blasphemy against Moses and against God."

So they stirred up the people and the elders and the teachers of the law. They seized Stephen and brought him before the Sanhedrin.

But Stephen, full of the Holy Spirit, looked up to heaven and saw the glory of God, and Jesus standing at the right hand of God. "Look," he said, "I see heaven open and the Son of Man standing at the right hand of God."

At this they covered their ears and, yelling at the top of their voices, they all rushed at him, dragged him out of the city and began to stone him. Meanwhile, the witnesses laid their clothes at the feet of a young man named Saul.

While they were stoning him, Stephen prayed, "Lord Jesus, receive my spirit." Then he fell on his knees and cried out, "Lord, do not hold this sin against them." When he had said this, he fell asleep.

ACTS 6:7-12; 7:55-60

Related texts: LEVITICUS 24:10-16; MARK 13:9-13; JOHN 16:1-4; ACTS 7:1-54; 8:1-4

Saul Meets Jesus

**THE ONE
MINUTE
BIBLE**

And Saul was there, giving approval to Stephen's death.

On that day a great persecution broke out against the church at Jerusalem, and all except the apostles were scattered throughout Judea and Samaria. Godly men buried Stephen and mourned deeply for him. But Saul began to destroy the church. Going from house to house, he dragged off men and women and put them in prison.

Those who had been scattered preached the word wherever they went.

Meanwhile, Saul was still breathing out murderous threats against the Lord's disciples. He went to the high priest and asked him for letters to the synagogues in Damascus, so that if he found any there who belonged to the Way, whether men or women, he might take them as prisoners to Jerusalem. As he neared Damascus on his journey, suddenly a light from heaven flashed around him. He fell to the ground and heard a voice say to him, "Saul, Saul, why do you persecute me?"

"Who are you, Lord?" Saul asked.

"I am Jesus, whom you are persecuting," he replied. "Now get up and go into the city, and you will be told what you must do."

The men traveling with Saul stood there speechless; they heard the sound but did not see anyone. Saul got up from the ground, but when he opened his eyes he could see nothing. So they led him by the hand into Damascus. For three days he was blind, and did not eat or drink anything.

ACTS 8:1-4; 9:1-9

Related texts: DANIEL 8:26-27; LUKE 1:18-20; ACTS 22:1-21; 26:1-29

Saul Begins to Preach About Jesus

In Damascus there was a disciple named Ananias. The Lord called to him in a vision, "Ananias!"

"Yes, Lord," he answered.

The Lord told him, "Go to the house of Judas on Straight Street and ask for a man from Tarsus named Saul, for he is praying. In a vision he has seen a man named Ananias come and place his hands on him to restore his sight."

"Lord," Ananias answered, "I have heard many reports about this man and all the harm he has done to your saints in Jerusalem. And he has come here with authority from the chief priests to arrest all who call on your name."

But the Lord said to Ananias, "Go! This man is my chosen instrument to carry my name before the Gentiles and their kings and before the people of Israel."

Then Ananias went to the house and entered it. Placing his hands on Saul, he said, "Brother Saul, the Lord—Jesus, who appeared to you on the road as you were coming here—has sent me so that you may see again and be filled with the Holy Spirit." Immediately, something like scales fell from Saul's eyes, and he could see again. He got up and was baptized, and after taking some food, he regained his strength.

Saul spent several days with the disciples in Damascus. At once he began to preach in the synagogues that Jesus is the Son of God.

ACTS 9:10-15, 17-20

THE ONE MINUTE BIBLE

Related texts: GENESIS 20; NUMBERS 12; 1 CORINTHIANS 15:1-11; GALATIANS 1:11-24

**THE ONE
MINUTE
BIBLE**

The First Missionary Journey

In the church at Antioch there were prophets and teachers: Barnabas, Simeon called Niger, Lucius of Cyrene, Manaen (who had been brought up with Herod the tetrarch) and Saul. While they were worshiping the Lord and fasting, the Holy Spirit said, "Set apart for me Barnabas and Saul for the work to which I have called them." So after they had fasted and prayed, they placed their hands on them and sent them off.

The two of them, sent on their way by the Holy Spirit, went down to Seleucia and sailed from there to Cyprus. When they arrived at Salamis, they proclaimed the word of God in the Jewish synagogues. John was with them as their helper.

They traveled through the whole island until they came to Paphos. There they met a Jewish sorcerer and false prophet named Bar-Jesus, who was an attendant of the proconsul, Sergius Paulus. The proconsul, an intelligent man, sent for Barnabas and Saul because he wanted to hear the word of God. But Elymas the sorcerer (for that is what his name means) opposed them and tried to turn the proconsul from the faith. Then Saul, who was also called Paul, filled with the Holy Spirit, looked straight at Elymas and said, "You are a child of the devil and an enemy of everything that is right! You are full of all kinds of deceit and trickery. Will you never stop perverting the right ways of the Lord? Now the hand of the Lord is against you. You are going to be blind, and for a time you will be unable to see the light of the sun."

Immediately mist and darkness came over him, and he groped about, seeking someone to lead him by the hand. When the proconsul saw what had happened, he believed, for he was amazed at the teaching about the Lord.

ACTS 13:1-12

Related texts: NUMBERS 27:22-23; DEUTERONOMY 34:9; MATTHEW 19:13-15; LUKE 4:40; ACTS 6:1-6; 8:5-25; 1 TIMOTHY 4:11-14

Paul and Barnabas Among the Gentiles

In Lystra there sat a man crippled in his feet, who was lame from birth and had never walked. He listened to Paul as he was speaking. Paul looked directly at him, saw that he had faith to be healed and called out, "Stand up on your feet!" At that, the man jumped up and began to walk.

Then some Jews came from Antioch and Iconium and won the crowd over. They stoned Paul and dragged him outside the city, thinking he was dead. But after the disciples had gathered around him, he got up and went back into the city. The next day he and Barnabas left for Derbe.

They preached the good news in that city and won a large number of disciples. Then they returned to Lystra, Iconium and Antioch, strengthening the disciples and encouraging them to remain true to the faith. "We must go through many hardships to enter the kingdom of God," they said. Paul and Barnabas appointed elders for them in each church and, with prayer and fasting, committed them to the Lord, in whom they had put their trust.

From Attalia they sailed back to Antioch, where they had been committed to the grace of God for the work they had now completed. On arriving there, they gathered the church together and reported all that God had done through them and how he had opened the door of faith to the Gentiles. And they stayed there a long time with the disciples.

ACTS 14:8-10, 19-23, 26-28

Related texts: EXODUS 17:1-4; NUMBERS 14:1-10; 1 SAMUEL 30:6; JOHN 8:31-59; ACTS 7:52-60; 14:1-7; ROMANS 1:1-17; EPHESIANS 2:11-22

In Everything Give Thanks

**THE ONE
MINUTE
BIBLE**

Give thanks to the LORD, call on his name;
  make known among the nations what he has done.
Sing to him, sing praise to him;
  tell of all his wonderful acts.

Come, let us sing for joy to the LORD;
  let us shout aloud to the Rock of our salvation.
Let us come before him with thanksgiving
  and extol him with music and song.
For the LORD is the great God,
  the great King above all gods.
In his hand are the depths of the earth,
  and the mountain peaks belong to him.
The sea is his, for he made it,
  and his hands formed the dry land.

Come, let us bow down in worship,
  let us kneel before the LORD our Maker;
for he is our God
  and we are the people of his pasture,
  the flock under his care.

  Be joyful always; pray continually; give thanks in
all circumstances, for this is God's will for you in
Christ Jesus.

1 CHRONICLES 16:8-9; PSALM 95:1-7a; 1 THESSALONIANS 5:16-18

Related texts: NEHEMIAH 12:27-43; PSALMS 77; 135:1-7; 148;
LUKE 22:14-19

Give Thanks for God's Provision

Give thanks to the LORD, for he is good;
    his love endures forever.
Let the redeemed of the LORD say this—
    those he redeemed from the hand of the foe,
those he gathered from the lands,
    from east and west, from north and south.

Some wandered in desert wastelands,
    finding no way to a city where they could settle.
They were hungry and thirsty,
    and their lives ebbed away.
Then they cried out to the LORD in their trouble,
    and he delivered them from their distress.
He led them by a straight way
    to a city where they could settle.
Let them give thanks to the LORD for his unfailing love
    and his wonderful deeds for men,
for he satisfies the thirsty
    and fills the hungry with good things.

Let them give thanks to the LORD for his unfailing love
    and his wonderful deeds for men.
Let them sacrifice thank offerings
    and tell of his works with songs of joy.

PSALM 107:1-9, 21-22

Related texts: 2 CHRONICLES 20:14-26; PSALMS 104; 118; 145;
MATTHEW 6:25-34

Give Thanks to God Among His People

**THE ONE
MINUTE
BIBLE**

A psalm. For giving thanks.

Shout for joy to the Lord, all the earth.
    Worship the Lord with gladness;
    come before him with joyful songs.
Know that the Lord is God.
    It is he who made us, and we are his;
    we are his people, the sheep of his pasture.

Enter his gates with thanksgiving
    and his courts with praise;
    give thanks to him and praise his name.
For the Lord is good and his love endures forever;
    his faithfulness continues through all generations.

Let the peace of Christ rule in your hearts, since as members of one body you were called to peace. And be thankful. Let the word of Christ dwell in you richly as you teach and admonish one another with all wisdom, and as you sing psalms, hymns and spiritual songs with gratitude in your hearts to God. And whatever you do, whether in word or deed, do it all in the name of the Lord Jesus, giving thanks to God the Father through him.

Psalm 100; Colossians 3:15-17

Related texts: 2 Chronicles 6:41; Psalms 65; 84; 96; Ephesians 5:18-20; 3 John 11

Give Thanks to God for His Enduring Love

Give thanks to the LORD, for he is good.
> *His love endures forever.*

Give thanks to the God of gods.
> *His love endures forever.*

Give thanks to the Lord of lords:
> *His love endures forever.*

**THE ONE
MINUTE
BIBLE**

We always thank God, the Father of our Lord Jesus Christ, when we pray for you, because we have heard of your faith in Christ Jesus and of the love you have for all the saints—the faith and love that spring from the hope that is stored up for you in heaven and that you have already heard about in the word of truth, the gospel that has come to you. All over the world this gospel is bearing fruit and growing, just as it has been doing among you since the day you heard it and understood God's grace in all its truth.

I always thank my God as I remember you in my prayers, because I hear about your faith in the Lord Jesus and your love for all the saints. I pray that you may be active in sharing your faith, so that you will have a full understanding of every good thing we have in Christ. Your love has given me great joy and encouragement, because you, brother, have refreshed the hearts of the saints.

PSALM 136:1-3; COLOSSIANS 1:3-6; PHILEMON 1:4-7

Related texts: 1 CHRONICLES 16:34-36; 2 CHRONICLES 5–7; PSALMS 118:1-4; 136:4-26; 2 CORINTHIANS 9:10-15

Receive God's Good Gifts with Thanksgiving

**THE ONE
MINUTE
BIBLE**

The Spirit clearly says that in later times some will abandon the faith and follow deceiving spirits and things taught by demons. Such teachings come through hypocritical liars, whose consciences have been seared as with a hot iron. They forbid people to marry and order them to abstain from certain foods, which God created to be received with thanksgiving by those who believe and who know the truth. For everything God created is good, and nothing is to be rejected if it is received with thanksgiving, because it is consecrated by the word of God and prayer.

If you point these things out to the brothers, you will be a good minister of Christ Jesus, brought up in the truths of the faith and of the good teaching that you have followed. Have nothing to do with godless myths and old wives' tales; rather, train yourself to be godly. For physical training is of some value, but godliness has value for all things, holding promise for both the present life and the life to come.

This is a trustworthy saying that deserves full acceptance (and for this we labor and strive), that we have put our hope in the living God, who is the Savior of all men, and especially of those who believe.

Command and teach these things.

1 TIMOTHY 4:1-11

Related texts: 1 CHRONICLES 16:4-14; ROMANS 8:18-28; 14;
1 CORINTHIANS 10

Give Thanks to God in Heaven

At once I was in the Spirit, and there before me was a throne in heaven with someone sitting on it. And the one who sat there had the appearance of jasper and carnelian. A rainbow, resembling an emerald, encircled the throne. Surrounding the throne were twenty-four other thrones, and seated on them were twenty-four elders. They were dressed in white and had crowns of gold on their heads. From the throne came flashes of lightning, rumblings and peals of thunder. Before the throne, seven lamps were blazing. These are the seven spirits of God. Also before the throne there was what looked like a sea of glass, clear as crystal.

In the center, around the throne, were four living creatures, and they were covered with eyes, in front and in back. Day and night they never stop saying:

"Holy, holy, holy
is the Lord God Almighty,
who was, and is, and is to come."

Whenever the living creatures give glory, honor and thanks to him who sits on the throne and who lives for ever and ever, the twenty-four elders fall down before him who sits on the throne, and worship him who lives for ever and ever. They lay their crowns before the throne and say:

"You are worthy, our Lord and God,
to receive glory and honor and power,
for you created all things,
and by your will they were created
and have their being."

REVELATION 4:2-6, 8b-11

Related texts: EXODUS 24:1-11; ISAIAH 6; PSALMS 103:20-22; 148;
MARK 10:17-18

Let Everything Praise the LORD!

**THE ONE
MINUTE
BIBLE**

Praise the LORD.

Praise God in his sanctuary;
  praise him in his mighty heavens.
Praise him for his acts of power;
  praise him for his surpassing greatness.
Praise him with the sounding of the trumpet,
  praise him with the harp and lyre,
praise him with tambourine and dancing,
  praise him with the strings and flute,
praise him with the clash of cymbals,
  praise him with resounding cymbals.

Let everything that has breath praise the LORD.

Praise the LORD.

Do not get drunk on wine, which leads to debauchery. Instead, be filled with the Spirit. Speak to one another with psalms, hymns and spiritual songs. Sing and make music in your heart to the Lord, always giving thanks to God the Father for everything, in the name of our Lord Jesus Christ.

PSALM 150; EPHESIANS 5:18-20

Related texts: EXODUS 15:1-21; 1 CHRONICLES 15–16; COLOSSIANS 3:16-17

Jews and Gentiles Are One in Christ

THE ONE MINUTE BIBLE

Surely you have heard about the administration of God's grace that was given to me for you, that is, the mystery made known to me by revelation, as I have already written briefly. In reading this, then, you will be able to understand my insight into the mystery of Christ, which was not made known to men in other generations as it has now been revealed by the Spirit to God's holy apostles and prophets. This mystery is that through the gospel the Gentiles are heirs together with Israel, members together of one body, and sharers together in the promise in Christ Jesus.

I became a servant of this gospel by the gift of God's grace given me through the working of his power. Although I am less than the least of all God's people, this grace was given me: to preach to the Gentiles the unsearchable riches of Christ, and to make plain to everyone the administration of this mystery, which for ages past was kept hidden in God, who created all things. His intent was that now, through the church, the manifold wisdom of God should be made known to the rulers and authorities in the heavenly realms, according to his eternal purpose which he accomplished in Christ Jesus our Lord. In him and through faith in him we may approach God with freedom and confidence.

EPHESIANS 3:2-12

Related texts: ISAIAH 49:1-6; ACTS 15; GALATIANS 3:25-29; EPHESIANS 2:11-22

Spiritual Gifts

**THE ONE
MINUTE
BIBLE**

Now about spiritual gifts, brothers, I do not want you to be ignorant. You know that when you were pagans, somehow or other you were influenced and led astray to mute idols. Therefore I tell you that no one who is speaking by the Spirit of God says, "Jesus be cursed," and no one can say, "Jesus is Lord," except by the Holy Spirit.

There are different kinds of gifts, but the same Spirit. There are different kinds of service, but the same Lord. There are different kinds of working, but the same God works all of them in all men.

Now to each one the manifestation of the Spirit is given for the common good. To one there is given through the Spirit the message of wisdom, to another the message of knowledge by means of the same Spirit, to another faith by the same Spirit, to another gifts of healing by that one Spirit, to another miraculous powers, to another prophecy, to another distinguishing between spirits, to another speaking in different kinds of tongues, and to still another the interpretation of tongues. All these are the work of one and the same Spirit, and he gives them to each one, just as he determines.

The body is a unit, though it is made up of many parts; and though all its parts are many, they form one body. So it is with Christ. For we were all baptized by one Spirit into one body—whether Jews or Greeks, slave or free—and we were all given the one Spirit to drink.

1 Corinthians 12:1-13

Related texts: Exodus 31:1-6; 35:30—36:2; Romans 12:1-8; 1 Corinthians 13–14; Ephesians 4:1-16; Hebrews 2:1-4; 1 Peter 4:7-11

*I believe that the intention of Holy Writ
was to persuade men of the truths necessary
to salvation; such as neither science nor
other means could render credible, but
only the voice of the Holy Spirit.*

Galileo (1564-1642)
ITALIAN ASTRONOMER

*I feel that a comprehensive study of the Bible
is a liberal education for anyone. Nearly all
of the great men of our country have been
well versed in the teachings of the Bible.*

Franklin D. Roosevelt (1882-1945)
UNITED STATES PRESIDENT

*I have found in the Bible words for my
inmost thoughts, songs for my joy, utterance
for my hidden griefs and pleading for
my shame and feebleness.*

Samuel Taylor Coleridge (1772-1834)
ENGLISH POET

Future Hope, Future Reward

**THE ONE
MINUTE
BIBLE**

Now we know that if the earthly tent we live in is destroyed, we have a building from God, an eternal house in heaven, not built by human hands. Meanwhile we groan, longing to be clothed with our heavenly dwelling, because when we are clothed, we will not be found naked. For while we are in this tent, we groan and are burdened, because we do not wish to be unclothed but to be clothed with our heavenly dwelling, so that what is mortal may be swallowed up by life. Now it is God who has made us for this very purpose and has given us the Spirit as a deposit, guaranteeing what is to come.

Therefore we are always confident and know that as long as we are at home in the body we are away from the Lord. We live by faith, not by sight. We are confident, I say, and would prefer to be away from the body and at home with the Lord. So we make it our goal to please him, whether we are at home in the body or away from it. For we must all appear before the judgment seat of Christ, that each one may receive what is due him for the things done while in the body, whether good or bad.

2 CORINTHIANS 5:1-10

Related texts: ECCLESIASTES 12; JOHN 11:20-27; ROMANS 14:1-13; PHILIPPIANS 1:20-26; 1 CORINTHIANS 15:35-54

Sealed for Salvation

**THE ONE
MINUTE
BIBLE**

Praise be to the God and Father of our Lord Jesus Christ, who has blessed us in the heavenly realms with every spiritual blessing in Christ. For he chose us in him before the creation of the world to be holy and blameless in his sight. In love he predestined us to be adopted as his sons through Jesus Christ, in accordance with his pleasure and will—to the praise of his glorious grace, which he has freely given us in the One he loves.

In him we have redemption through his blood, the forgiveness of sins, in accordance with the riches of God's grace that he lavished on us with all wisdom and understanding. And he made known to us the mystery of his will according to his good pleasure, which he purposed in Christ, to be put into effect when the times will have reached their fulfillment—to bring all things in heaven and on earth together under one head, even Christ.

In him we were also chosen, having been predestined according to the plan of him who works out everything in conformity with the purpose of his will, in order that we, who were the first to hope in Christ, might be for the praise of his glory. And you also were included in Christ when you heard the word of truth, the gospel of your salvation. Having believed, you were marked in him with a seal, the promised Holy Spirit, who is a deposit guaranteeing our inheritance until the redemption of those who are God's possession—to the praise of his glory.

EPHESIANS 1:3-14

Related texts: PSALM 113; ROMANS 8:29-39; EPHESIANS 2:4-10; REVELATION 3:5; 13:8; 17:8; 20:15

Humility and Glory

If you have any encouragement from being united with Christ, if any comfort from his love, if any fellowship with the Spirit, if any tenderness and compassion, then make my joy complete by being like-minded, having the same love, being one in spirit and purpose. Do nothing out of selfish ambition or vain conceit, but in humility consider others better than yourselves. Each of you should look not only to your own interests, but also to the interests of others.

Your attitude should be the same as that of Christ Jesus:

THE ONE MINUTE BIBLE

Who, being in very nature God,
    did not consider equality with God something
        to be grasped,
but made himself nothing,
    taking the very nature of a servant,
    being made in human likeness.
And being found in appearance as a man,
    he humbled himself
    and became obedient to death—
        even death on a cross!
Therefore God exalted him to the highest place
    and gave him the name that is above
        every name,
that at the name of Jesus every knee should bow,
    in heaven and on earth and under the earth,
and every tongue confess that Jesus Christ
        is Lord,
    to the glory of God the Father.

PHILIPPIANS 2:1-11

Related texts: ISAIAH 45:22-25; JOHN 13:1-15; ROMANS 14:11-12; 1 CORINTHIANS 15:20-28; PHILIPPIANS 2:19-21; 1 PETER 5:5-6

To Know Christ

**THE ONE
MINUTE
BIBLE**

If anyone else thinks he has reasons to put confidence in the flesh, I have more: circumcised on the eighth day, of the people of Israel, of the tribe of Benjamin, a Hebrew of Hebrews; in regard to the law, a Pharisee; as for zeal, persecuting the church; as for legalistic righteousness, faultless.

But whatever was to my profit I now consider loss for the sake of Christ. What is more, I consider everything a loss compared to the surpassing greatness of knowing Christ Jesus my Lord, for whose sake I have lost all things. I consider them rubbish, that I may gain Christ and be found in him, not having a righteousness of my own that comes from the law, but that which is through faith in Christ—the righteousness that comes from God and is by faith. I want to know Christ and the power of his resurrection and the fellowship of sharing in his sufferings, becoming like him in his death, and so, somehow, to attain to the resurrection from the dead.

Not that I have already obtained all this, or have already been made perfect, but I press on to take hold of that for which Christ Jesus took hold of me. Brothers, I do not consider myself yet to have taken hold of it. But one thing I do: Forgetting what is behind and straining toward what is ahead, I press on toward the goal to win the prize for which God has called me heavenward in Christ Jesus.

PHILIPPIANS 3:4b-14

Related texts: PSALM 18:30-33; MATTHEW 5:43-48; MARK 8:34-37; ACTS 22:1-21; COLOSSIANS 1:24; HEBREWS 12:1-3

The Supremacy of Christ

THE ONE
MINUTE
BIBLE

Christ is the image of the invisible God, the firstborn over all creation. For by him all things were created: things in heaven and on earth, visible and invisible, whether thrones or powers or rulers or authorities; all things were created by him and for him. He is before all things, and in him all things hold together. And he is the head of the body, the church; he is the beginning and the firstborn from among the dead, so that in everything he might have the supremacy. For God was pleased to have all his fullness dwell in him, and through him to reconcile to himself all things, whether things on earth or things in heaven, by making peace through his blood, shed on the cross.

Once you were alienated from God and were enemies in your minds because of your evil behavior. But now he has reconciled you by Christ's physical body through death to present you holy in his sight, without blemish and free from accusation—if you continue in your faith, established and firm, not moved from the hope held out in the gospel. This is the gospel that you heard and that has been proclaimed to every creature under heaven, and of which I, Paul, have become a servant.

COLOSSIANS 1:15-23

Related texts: GENESIS 1:26; JOHN 1:1-18; ROMANS 5:9-11; 2 CORINTHIANS 5:17-21; COLOSSIANS 2:9-10; HEBREWS 1:1-3

Meeting the Lord in the Air

**THE ONE
MINUTE
BIBLE**

Brothers, we do not want you to be ignorant about those who fall asleep, or to grieve like the rest of men, who have no hope. We believe that Jesus died and rose again and so we believe that God will bring with Jesus those who have fallen asleep in him. According to the Lord's own word, we tell you that we who are still alive, who are left till the coming of the Lord, will certainly not precede those who have fallen asleep. For the Lord himself will come down from heaven, with a loud command, with the voice of the archangel and with the trumpet call of God, and the dead in Christ will rise first. After that, we who are still alive and are left will be caught up together with them in the clouds to meet the Lord in the air. And so we will be with the Lord forever. Therefore encourage each other with these words.

Now, brothers, about times and dates we do not need to write to you, for you know very well that the day of the Lord will come like a thief in the night. While people are saying, "Peace and safety," destruction will come on them suddenly, as labor pains on a pregnant woman, and they will not escape.

But you, brothers, are not in darkness so that this day should surprise you like a thief.

1 THESSALONIANS 4:13-18; 5:1-4

Related texts: DANIEL 12:1-3; MATTHEW 24; 2 PETER 3; REVELATION 3:1-6

Work Is Good

In the name of the Lord Jesus Christ, we command you, brothers, to keep away from every brother who is idle and does not live according to the teaching you received from us. For you yourselves know how you ought to follow our example. We were not idle when we were with you, nor did we eat anyone's food without paying for it. On the contrary, we worked night and day, laboring and toiling so that we would not be a burden to any of you. We did this, not because we do not have the right to such help, but in order to make ourselves a model for you to follow. For even when we were with you, we gave you this rule: "If a man will not work, he shall not eat."

We hear that some among you are idle. They are not busy; they are busybodies. Such people we command and urge in the Lord Jesus Christ to settle down and earn the bread they eat. And as for you, brothers, never tire of doing what is right.

If anyone does not obey our instruction in this letter, take special note of him. Do not associate with him, in order that he may feel ashamed. Yet do not regard him as an enemy, but warn him as a brother.

2 THESSALONIANS 3:6-15

THE ONE MINUTE BIBLE

Related texts: GENESIS 1:26-30; 2:15; 1 CORINTHIANS 9; 2 CORINTHIANS 12:12-18; 1 THESSALONIANS 2:1-12

Godliness and Contentment

**THE ONE
MINUTE
BIBLE**

If anyone teaches false doctrines and does not agree to the sound instruction of our Lord Jesus Christ and to godly teaching, he is conceited and understands nothing. He has an unhealthy interest in controversies and quarrels about words that result in envy, strife, malicious talk, evil suspicions and constant friction between men of corrupt mind, who have been robbed of the truth and who think that godliness is a means to financial gain.

But godliness with contentment is great gain. For we brought nothing into the world, and we can take nothing out of it. But if we have food and clothing, we will be content with that. People who want to get rich fall into temptation and a trap and into many foolish and harmful desires that plunge men into ruin and destruction. For the love of money is a root of all kinds of evil. Some people, eager for money, have wandered from the faith and pierced themselves with many griefs.

Command those who are rich in this present world not to be arrogant nor to put their hope in wealth, which is so uncertain, but to put their hope in God, who richly provides us with everything for our enjoyment. Command them to do good, to be rich in good deeds, and to be generous and willing to share. In this way they will lay up treasure for themselves as a firm foundation for the coming age, so that they may take hold of the life that is truly life.

1 TIMOTHY 6:3-10, 17-19

Related texts: PSALM 112:4; PROVERBS 11:24-26; 14:31; 19:17; 22:9; 28:8; LUKE 12:13-34; 16:1-15; PHILIPPIANS 4:10-14

The Profit of the Scriptures

**THE ONE
M I N U T E
B I B L E**

But mark this: There will be terrible times in the last days. People will be lovers of themselves, lovers of money, boastful, proud, abusive, disobedient to their parents, ungrateful, unholy, without love, unforgiving, slanderous, without self-control, brutal, not lovers of the good, treacherous, rash, conceited, lovers of pleasure rather than lovers of God—having a form of godliness but denying its power. Have nothing to do with them.

You, however, know all about my teaching, my way of life, my purpose, faith, patience, love, endurance, persecutions, sufferings—what kinds of things happened to me in Antioch, Iconium and Lystra, the persecutions I endured. Yet the Lord rescued me from all of them. In fact, everyone who wants to live a godly life in Christ Jesus will be persecuted, while evil men and impostors will go from bad to worse, deceiving and being deceived.

But as for you, continue in what you have learned and have become convinced of, because you know those from whom you learned it, and how from infancy you have known the holy Scriptures, which are able to make you wise for salvation through faith in Christ Jesus. All Scripture is God-breathed and is useful for teaching, rebuking, correcting and training in righteousness, so that the man of God may be thoroughly equipped for every good work.

2 TIMOTHY 3:1-5, 10-17

Related texts: ISAIAH 40:6-8; MATTHEW 5:10-12; ACTS 14;
2 CORINTHIANS 4; 12:1-10; 1 PETER 1:23–2:3

Jesus: Our High Priest

**THE ONE
MINUTE
BIBLE**

Therefore, since we have a great high priest who has gone through the heavens, Jesus the Son of God, let us hold firmly to the faith we profess. For we do not have a high priest who is unable to sympathize with our weaknesses, but we have one who has been tempted in every way, just as we are—yet was without sin. Let us then approach the throne of grace with confidence, so that we may receive mercy and find grace to help us in our time of need.

During the days of Jesus' life on earth, he offered up prayers and petitions with loud cries and tears to the one who could save him from death, and he was heard because of his reverent submission. Although he was a son, he learned obedience from what he suffered and, once made perfect, he became the source of eternal salvation for all who obey him and was designated by God to be high priest in the order of Melchizedek.

For this reason he had to be made like his brothers in every way, in order that he might become a merciful and faithful high priest in service to God, and that he might make atonement for the sins of the people. Because he himself suffered when he was tempted, he is able to help those who are being tempted.

HEBREWS 4:14-16; 5:7-10; 2:17-18

Related texts: GENESIS 14:18-20; PSALM 110; MATTHEW 4:1-11

Heroes of Faith: Part 1

**THE ONE
MINUTE
BIBLE**

Now faith is being sure of what we hope for and certain of what we do not see. This is what the ancients were commended for.

By faith we understand that the universe was formed at God's command, so that what is seen was not made out of what was visible.

By faith Abel offered God a better sacrifice than Cain did. By faith he was commended as a righteous man, when God spoke well of his offerings. And by faith he still speaks, even though he is dead.

By faith Enoch was taken from this life, so that he did not experience death; he could not be found, because God had taken him away. For before he was taken, he was commended as one who pleased God. And without faith it is impossible to please God, because anyone who comes to him must believe that he exists and that he rewards those who earnestly seek him.

By faith Noah, when warned about things not yet seen, in holy fear built an ark to save his family. By his faith he condemned the world and became heir of the righteousness that comes by faith.

By faith Abraham, when called to go to a place he would later receive as his inheritance, obeyed and went, even though he did not know where he was going.

Hebrews 11:1-8

Related texts: Genesis 1; 4:1-16; 5:23-24; 6–8; 12; Jude 14-15

Heroes of Faith: Part 2

**THE ONE
MINUTE
BIBLE**

By faith Abraham, even though he was past age—and Sarah herself was barren—was enabled to become a father because he considered him faithful who had made the promise. And so from this one man, and he as good as dead, came descendants as numerous as the stars in the sky and as countless as the sand on the seashore.

By faith Abraham, when God tested him, offered Isaac as a sacrifice. He who had received the promises was about to sacrifice his one and only son, even though God had said to him, "It is through Isaac that your offspring will be reckoned." Abraham reasoned that God could raise the dead, and figuratively speaking, he did receive Isaac back from death.

By faith Moses, when he had grown up, refused to be known as the son of Pharaoh's daughter. He chose to be mistreated along with the people of God rather than to enjoy the pleasures of sin for a short time. He regarded disgrace for the sake of Christ as of greater value than the treasures of Egypt, because he was looking ahead to his reward. By faith he left Egypt, not fearing the king's anger; he persevered because he saw him who is invisible.

These were all commended for their faith, yet none of them received what had been promised. God had planned something better for us so that only together with us would they be made perfect.

HEBREWS 11:11-12, 17-19, 24-27, 39-40

Related texts: GENESIS 21–22; EXODUS 2–3; HEBREWS 10:36-39

Wisdom in Trials

Consider it pure joy, my brothers, whenever you face trials of many kinds, because you know that the testing of your faith develops perseverance. Perseverance must finish its work so that you may be mature and complete, not lacking anything. If any of you lacks wisdom, he should ask God, who gives generously to all without finding fault, and it will be given to him. But when he asks, he must believe and not doubt, because he who doubts is like a wave of the sea, blown and tossed by the wind. That man should not think he will receive anything from the Lord; he is a double-minded man, unstable in all he does.

Blessed is the man who perseveres under trial, because when he has stood the test, he will receive the crown of life that God has promised to those who love him.

When tempted, no one should say, "God is tempting me." For God cannot be tempted by evil, nor does he tempt anyone; but each one is tempted when, by his own evil desire, he is dragged away and enticed. Then, after desire has conceived, it gives birth to sin; and sin, when it is full-grown, gives birth to death.

JAMES 1:2-8, 12-15

Related texts: JOB 1–42; MATTHEW 6:9-13; 21:18-22;
1 CORINTHIANS 10:12-13

Controlling the Tongue

**THE ONE
MINUTE
BIBLE**

Not many of you should presume to be teachers, my brothers, because you know that we who teach will be judged more strictly. We all stumble in many ways. If anyone is never at fault in what he says, he is a perfect man, able to keep his whole body in check.

When we put bits into the mouths of horses to make them obey us, we can turn the whole animal. Or take ships as an example. Although they are so large and are driven by strong winds, they are steered by a very small rudder wherever the pilot wants to go. Likewise the tongue is a small part of the body, but it makes great boasts. Consider what a great forest is set on fire by a small spark. The tongue also is a fire, a world of evil among the parts of the body. It corrupts the whole person, sets the whole course of his life on fire, and is itself set on fire by hell.

All kinds of animals, birds, reptiles and creatures of the sea are being tamed and have been tamed by man, but no man can tame the tongue. It is a restless evil, full of deadly poison.

With the tongue we praise our Lord and Father, and with it we curse men, who have been made in God's likeness. Out of the same mouth come praise and cursing. My brothers, this should not be. Can both fresh water and salt water flow from the same spring? My brothers, can a fig tree bear olives, or a grapevine bear figs? Neither can a salt spring produce fresh water.

JAMES 3:1-12

Related texts: PSALM 12; PROVERBS 6:16-19; 10:18-21, 31-32; 12:17-19, 22

The Promise of Salvation

Praise be to the God and Father of our Lord Jesus Christ! In his great mercy he has given us new birth into a living hope through the resurrection of Jesus Christ from the dead, and into an inheritance that can never perish, spoil or fade—kept in heaven for you, who through faith are shielded by God's power until the coming of the salvation that is ready to be revealed in the last time.

THE ONE MINUTE BIBLE

In this you greatly rejoice, though now for a little while you may have had to suffer grief in all kinds of trials. These have come so that your faith—of greater worth than gold, which perishes even though refined by fire—may be proved genuine and may result in praise, glory and honor when Jesus Christ is revealed. Though you have not seen him, you love him; and even though you do not see him now, you believe in him and are filled with an inexpressible and glorious joy, for you are receiving the goal of your faith, the salvation of your souls.

Concerning this salvation, the prophets, who spoke of the grace that was to come to you, searched intently and with the greatest care, trying to find out the time and circumstances to which the Spirit of Christ in them was pointing when he predicted the sufferings of Christ and the glories that would follow. It was revealed to them that they were not serving themselves but you, when they spoke of the things that have now been told you by those who have preached the gospel to you by the Holy Spirit sent from heaven. Even angels long to look into these things.

1 PETER 1:3-12

Related texts: ISAIAH 52:13-53:12; ZECHARIAH 13:7-9; HEBREWS 1–2; JAMES 1

Living Stones and the Cornerstone

**THE ONE
MINUTE
BIBLE**

Therefore, rid yourselves of all malice and all deceit, hypocrisy, envy, and slander of every kind. Like newborn babies, crave pure spiritual milk, so that by it you may grow up in your salvation, now that you have tasted that the Lord is good.

As you come to him, the living Stone—rejected by men but chosen by God and precious to him—you also, like living stones, are being built into a spiritual house to be a holy priesthood, offering spiritual sacrifices acceptable to God through Jesus Christ. For in Scripture it says:

> "See, I lay a stone in Zion,
>   a chosen and precious cornerstone,
>   and the one who trusts in him
>   will never be put to shame."

Now to you who believe, this stone is precious. But to those who do not believe,

> "The stone the builders rejected
>   has become the capstone,"

and,

> "A stone that causes men to stumble
>   and a rock that makes them fall."

They stumble because they disobey the message—which is also what they were destined for.

But you are a chosen people, a royal priesthood, a holy nation, a people belonging to God, that you may declare the praises of him who called you out of darkness into his wonderful light. Once you were not a people, but now you are the people of God; once you had not received mercy, but now you have received mercy.

1 Peter 2:1-10

Related texts: Psalms 34; 118:22-29; Isaiah 28:16-17;
380 | Matthew 16:13-19; Luke 20:9-19; Hebrews 5:11-14

The Morning Star

We did not follow cleverly invented stories when we told you about the power and coming of our Lord Jesus Christ, but we were eyewitnesses of his majesty. For he received honor and glory from God the Father when the voice came to him from the Majestic Glory, saying, "This is my Son, whom I love; with him I am well pleased." We ourselves heard this voice that came from heaven when we were with him on the sacred mountain.

And we have the word of the prophets made more certain, and you will do well to pay attention to it, as to a light shining in a dark place, until the day dawns and the morning star rises in your hearts. Above all, you must understand that no prophecy of Scripture came about by the prophet's own interpretation. For prophecy never had its origin in the will of man, but men spoke from God as they were carried along by the Holy Spirit.

Your word is a lamp to my feet
and a light for my path.

I, Jesus, have sent my angel to give you this testimony for the churches. I am the Root and the Offspring of David, and the bright Morning Star.

2 PETER 1:16-21; PSALM 119:105; REVELATION 22:16

THE ONE MINUTE BIBLE

Related texts: JEREMIAH 26; AMOS 3:1-8; ISAIAH 61; MARK 9:2-9; LUKE 1:1-4

Love One Another

**THE ONE
MINUTE
BIBLE**

My dear children, I write this to you so that you will not sin. But if anybody does sin, we have one who speaks to the Father in our defense—Jesus Christ, the Righteous One. He is the atoning sacrifice for our sins, and not only for ours but also for the sins of the whole world.

We know that we have come to know him if we obey his commands. The man who says, "I know him," but does not do what he commands is a liar, and the truth is not in him. But if anyone obeys his word, God's love is truly made complete in him. This is how we know we are in him: Whoever claims to live in him must walk as Jesus did.

Dear friends, I am not writing you a new command but an old one, which you have had since the beginning. This old command is the message you have heard. Yet I am writing you a new command; its truth is seen in him and you, because the darkness is passing and the true light is already shining.

[Jesus said,] "A new command I give you: Love one another. As I have loved you, so you must love one another. By this all men will know that you are my disciples, if you love one another."

1 JOHN 2:1-8; JOHN 13:34-35

Related texts: 1 KINGS 8:46-51; PSALM 119:9-11; JOHN 14:15; HEBREWS 2:17-18; 4:14-16; 7-9; 1 JOHN 3:11-24

The Love of the Father

Do not love the world or anything in the world. If anyone loves the world, the love of the Father is not in him. For everything in the world—the cravings of sinful man, the lust of his eyes and the boasting of what he has and does—comes not from the Father but from the world. The world and its desires pass away, but the man who does the will of God lives forever.

THE ONE MINUTE BIBLE

How great is the love the Father has lavished on us, that we should be called children of God! And that is what we are! The reason the world does not know us is that it did not know him.

Everyone who believes that Jesus is the Christ is born of God, and everyone who loves the father loves his child as well. This is how we know that we love the children of God: by loving God and carrying out his commands. This is love for God: to obey his commands. And his commands are not burdensome, for everyone born of God overcomes the world. This is the victory that has overcome the world, even our faith. Who is it that overcomes the world? Only he who believes that Jesus is the Son of God.

1 JOHN 2:15-17; 3:1; 5:1-5

___

Related texts: DEUTERONOMY 30:11-16; JOHN 15:17-25; 1 JOHN 4:7-21

Antichrists

**THE ONE
MINUTE
BIBLE**

Dear children, this is the last hour; and as you have heard that the antichrist is coming, even now many antichrists have come. This is how we know it is the last hour. They went out from us, but they did not really belong to us. For if they had belonged to us, they would have remained with us; but their going showed that none of them belonged to us.

But you have an anointing from the Holy One, and all of you know the truth. I do not write to you because you do not know the truth, but because you do know it and because no lie comes from the truth. Who is the liar? It is the man who denies that Jesus is the Christ. Such a man is the antichrist—he denies the Father and the Son. No one who denies the Son has the Father; whoever acknowledges the Son has the Father also.

Many deceivers, who do not acknowledge Jesus Christ as coming in the flesh, have gone out into the world. Any such person is the deceiver and the antichrist. Watch out that you do not lose what you have worked for, but that you may be rewarded fully. Anyone who runs ahead and does not continue in the teaching of Christ does not have God; whoever continues in the teaching has both the Father and the Son. If anyone comes to you and does not bring this teaching, do not take him into your house or welcome him. Anyone who welcomes him shares in his wicked work.

1 JOHN 2:18-23; 2 JOHN 7-11

Related texts: PROVERBS 13:5; ISAIAH 44:24-25; JEREMIAH 14:14-15; 2 TIMOTHY 3; 2 PETER 2-3

The Salvation We Share

THE ONE MINUTE BIBLE

Dear friends, although I was very eager to write to you about the salvation we share, I felt I had to write and urge you to contend for the faith that was once for all entrusted to the saints. For certain men whose condemnation was written about long ago have secretly slipped in among you. They are godless men, who change the grace of our God into a license for immorality and deny Jesus Christ our only Sovereign and Lord.

But, dear friends, remember what the apostles of our Lord Jesus Christ foretold. They said to you, "In the last times there will be scoffers who will follow their own ungodly desires." These are the men who divide you, who follow mere natural instincts and do not have the Spirit.

But you, dear friends, build yourselves up in your most holy faith and pray in the Holy Spirit. Keep yourselves in God's love as you wait for the mercy of our Lord Jesus Christ to bring you to eternal life.

Be merciful to those who doubt; snatch others from the fire and save them; to others show mercy, mixed with fear—hating even the clothing stained by corrupted flesh.

To him who is able to keep you from falling and to present you before his glorious presence without fault and with great joy—to the only God our Savior be glory, majesty, power and authority, through Jesus Christ our Lord, before all ages, now and forevermore! Amen.

JUDE 3-4, 17-25

Related texts: AMOS 4:11; ZECHARIAH 3; ACTS 20:28-31; 2 PETER 3; 1 TIMOTHY 4:1-6

The Lᴏʀᴅ's Anointed King

**THE ONE
MINUTE
BIBLE**

Why do the nations conspire
 and the peoples plot in vain?
The kings of the earth take their stand
 and the rulers gather together
against the Lᴏʀᴅ
 and against his Anointed One.
"Let us break their chains," they say,
 "and throw off their fetters."

The One enthroned in heaven laughs;
 the Lord scoffs at them.
Then he rebukes them in his anger
 and terrifies them in his wrath, saying,
"I have installed my King
 on Zion, my holy hill."

 I will proclaim the decree of the Lᴏʀᴅ:

He said to me, "You are my Son;
 today I have become your Father.
Ask of me,
 and I will make the nations your inheritance,
 the ends of the earth your possession.
You will rule them with an iron scepter;
 you will dash them to pieces like pottery."

Therefore, you kings, be wise;
 be warned, you rulers of the earth.
Serve the Lᴏʀᴅ with fear
 and rejoice with trembling.
Kiss the Son, lest he be angry
 and you be destroyed in your way,
for his wrath can flare up in a moment.
 Blessed are all who take refuge in him.

Psᴀʟᴍ 2

Related texts: 2 Sᴀᴍᴜᴇʟ 7; 1 Cʜʀᴏɴɪᴄʟᴇs 17; Mᴀʀᴋ 1:1-11;

David's Son and Lord

**THE ONE
MINUTE
BIBLE**

Of David. A psalm.

The LORD says to my Lord:
  "Sit at my right hand
until I make your enemies
  a footstool for your feet."

The LORD will extend your mighty scepter from Zion;
  you will rule in the midst of your enemies.
Your troops will be willing
  on your day of battle.
Arrayed in holy majesty,
  from the womb of the dawn
  you will receive the dew of your youth.

The LORD has sworn
  and will not change his mind:
"You are a priest forever,
  in the order of Melchizedek."

The Lord is at your right hand;
  he will crush kings on the day of his wrath.
He will judge the nations, heaping up the dead
  and crushing the rulers of the whole earth.
He will drink from a brook beside the way;
  therefore he will lift up his head.

Now there have been many of those priests, since
death prevented them from continuing in office; but
because Jesus lives forever, he has a permanent
priesthood. Therefore he is able to save completely
those who come to God through him, because he always
lives to intercede for them.

Such a high priest meets our need—one who is
holy, blameless, pure, set apart from sinners, exalted
above the heavens.

PSALM 110; HEBREWS 7:23-26

Related texts: GENESIS 14:18-20; MATTHEW 22:41-46;
HEBREWS 5:1-10; 7

Christus Is Born

**THE ONE
MINUTE
BIBLE**

So Joseph also went up from the town of Nazareth in Galilee to Judea, to Bethlehem the town of David, because he belonged to the house and line of David. He went there to register with Mary, who was pledged to be married to him and was expecting a child. While they were there, the time came for the baby to be born, and she gave birth to her firstborn, a son. She wrapped him in cloths and placed him in a manger, because there was no room for them in the inn.

And there were shepherds living out in the fields nearby, keeping watch over their flocks at night. An angel of the Lord appeared to them, and the glory of the Lord shone around them, and they were terrified. But the angel said to them, "Do not be afraid. I bring you good news of great joy that will be for all the people. Today in the town of David a Savior has been born to you; he is Christ the Lord. This will be a sign to you: You will find a baby wrapped in cloths and lying in a manger."

Suddenly a great company of the heavenly host appeared with the angel, praising God and saying,

> "Glory to God in the highest,
>   and on earth peace to men on whom his
>   favor rests."

LUKE 2:4-14

Related texts: 2 SAMUEL 7:8-17; PSALM 89:20-37; ISAIAH 9:6-7; MATTHEW 1:18-25; LUKE 1-2

The Gifts of the Magi

**THE ONE
MINUTE
BIBLE**

After Jesus was born in Bethlehem in Judea, during the time of King Herod, Magi from the east came to Jerusalem and asked, "Where is the one who has been born king of the Jews? We saw his star in the east and have come to worship him."

When King Herod heard this he was disturbed, and all Jerusalem with him. When he had called together all the people's chief priests and teachers of the law, he asked them where the Christ was to be born. "In Bethlehem in Judea," they replied, "for this is what the prophet has written:

"'But you, Bethlehem, in the land of Judah,
    are by no means least among the rulers
        of Judah;
for out of you will come a ruler
    who will be the shepherd of my people Israel.'"

Then Herod called the Magi secretly and found out from them the exact time the star had appeared. He sent them to Bethlehem and said, "Go and make a careful search for the child. As soon as you find him, report to me, so that I too may go and worship him."

After they had heard the king, they went on their way, and the star they had seen in the east went ahead of them until it stopped over the place where the child was. When they saw the star, they were overjoyed. On coming to the house, they saw the child with his mother Mary, and they bowed down and worshiped him. Then they opened their treasures and presented him with gifts of gold and of incense and of myrrh. And having been warned in a dream not to go back to Herod, they returned to their country by another route.

MATTHEW 2:1-12

Related texts: EXODUS 30:22-33; MICAH 5:2-5; MARK 15:16-24;
LUKE 1–2; JOHN 12:1-7; HEBREWS 13:15-21

New Heavens and a New Earth

**THE ONE
MINUTE
BIBLE**

"Behold, I will create
new heavens and a new earth.
The former things will not be remembered,
nor will they come to mind.
But be glad and rejoice forever
in what I will create,
for I will create Jerusalem to be a delight
and its people a joy.
I will rejoice over Jerusalem
and take delight in my people;
the sound of weeping and of crying
will be heard in it no more.

"Never again will there be in it
an infant who lives but a few days,
or an old man who does not live out his years;
he who dies at a hundred
will be thought a mere youth;
he who fails to reach a hundred
will be considered accursed.
They will not toil in vain
or bear children doomed to misfortune;
for they will be a people blessed by the LORD,
they and their descendants with them.
Before they call I will answer;
while they are still speaking I will hear.
The wolf and the lamb will feed together,
and the lion will eat straw like the ox,
but dust will be the serpent's food.
They will neither harm nor destroy
on all my holy mountain,"

says the LORD.

ISAIAH 65:17-20, 23-25

Related texts: GENESIS 3:1-14; ISAIAH 66:22-24; 2 PETER 3:1-14;
REVELATION 21:1-5

Ezekiel Sees the Glory Return to Jerusalem

Then the man brought me to the gate facing east, and I saw the glory of the God of Israel coming from the east. His voice was like the roar of rushing waters, and the land was radiant with his glory. The vision I saw was like the vision I had seen when he came to destroy the city and like the visions I had seen by the Kebar River, and I fell facedown. The glory of the LORD entered the temple through the gate facing east. Then the Spirit lifted me up and brought me into the inner court, and the glory of the LORD filled the temple.

While the man was standing beside me, I heard someone speaking to me from inside the temple. He said: "Son of man, this is the place of my throne and the place for the soles of my feet. This is where I will live among the Israelites forever. The house of Israel will never again defile my holy name—neither they nor their kings—by their prostitution and the lifeless idols of their kings at their high places. When they placed their threshold next to my threshold and their doorposts beside my doorposts, with only a wall between me and them, they defiled my holy name by their detestable practices. So I destroyed them in my anger. Now let them put away from me their prostitution and the lifeless idols of their kings, and I will live among them forever."

EZEKIEL 43:1-9

THE ONE MINUTE BIBLE

Related texts: EZEKIEL 1; 3; 8–11; ZECHARIAH 14; REVELATION 21:1-4

THE ONE MINUTE BIBLE

His Face Was Like the Sun

I, John, your brother and companion in the suffering and kingdom and patient endurance that are ours in Jesus, was on the island of Patmos because of the word of God and the testimony of Jesus. On the Lord's Day I was in the Spirit, and I heard behind me a loud voice like a trumpet, which said: "Write on a scroll what you see and send it to the seven churches: to Ephesus, Smyrna, Pergamum, Thyatira, Sardis, Philadelphia and Laodicea."

I turned around to see the voice that was speaking to me. And when I turned I saw seven golden lampstands, and among the lampstands was someone "like a son of man," dressed in a robe reaching down to his feet and with a golden sash around his chest. His head and hair were white like wool, as white as snow, and his eyes were like blazing fire. His feet were like bronze glowing in a furnace, and his voice was like the sound of rushing waters. In his right hand he held seven stars, and out of his mouth came a sharp double-edged sword. His face was like the sun shining in all its brilliance.

When I saw him, I fell at his feet as though dead. Then he placed his right hand on me and said: "Do not be afraid. I am the First and the Last. I am the Living One; I was dead, and behold I am alive for ever and ever! And I hold the keys of death and Hades.

"Write, therefore, what you have seen, what is now and what will take place later."

REVELATION 1:9-19

Related texts: PSALM 149; DANIEL 7; 2 TIMOTHY 3; HEBREWS 4:12-13;
REVELATION 2–11; 19:11-21

The Saints and the Serpent

And I saw an angel coming down out of heaven, having the key to the Abyss and holding in his hand a great chain. He seized the dragon, that ancient serpent, who is the devil, or Satan, and bound him for a thousand years. He threw him into the Abyss, and locked and sealed it over him, to keep him from deceiving the nations anymore until the thousand years were ended. After that, he must be set free for a short time.

I saw thrones on which were seated those who had been given authority to judge. And I saw the souls of those who had been beheaded because of their testimony for Jesus and because of the word of God. They had not worshiped the beast or his image and had not received his mark on their foreheads or their hands. They came to life and reigned with Christ a thousand years. (The rest of the dead did not come to life until the thousand years were ended.) This is the first resurrection. Blessed and holy are those who have part in the first resurrection. The second death has no power over them, but they will be priests of God and of Christ and will reign with him for a thousand years.

When the thousand years are over, Satan will be released from his prison and will go out to deceive the nations in the four corners of the earth—Gog and Magog—to gather them for battle. In number they are like the sand on the seashore. They marched across the breadth of the earth and surrounded the camp of God's people, the city he loves. But fire came down from heaven and devoured them. And the devil, who deceived them, was thrown into the lake of burning sulfur, where the beast and the false prophet had been thrown. They will be tormented day and night for ever and ever.

REVELATION 20:1-10

Related texts: GENESIS 3:1-15; EZEKIEL 38–39; 1 CORINTHIANS 6:1-3; REVELATION 12-13; 17-19

Judgment Day

**THE ONE
MINUTE
BIBLE**

Then I saw a great white throne and him who was seated on it. Earth and sky fled from his presence, and there was no place for them. And I saw the dead, great and small, standing before the throne, and books were opened. Another book was opened, which is the book of life. The dead were judged according to what they had done as recorded in the books. The sea gave up the dead that were in it, and death and Hades gave up the dead that were in them, and each person was judged according to what he had done. Then death and Hades were thrown into the lake of fire. The lake of fire is the second death. If anyone's name was not found written in the book of life, he was thrown into the lake of fire.

Then I saw a new heaven and a new earth, for the first heaven and the first earth had passed away, and there was no longer any sea. I saw the Holy City, the new Jerusalem, coming down out of heaven from God, prepared as a bride beautifully dressed for her husband. And I heard a loud voice from the throne saying, "Now the dwelling of God is with men, and he will live with them. They will be his people, and God himself will be with them and be their God. He will wipe every tear from their eyes. There will be no more death or mourning or crying or pain, for the old order of things has passed away."

Revelation 20:11-15; 21:1-4

Jesus Is Coming Soon!

**THE ONE
MINUTE
BIBLE**

"Behold, I am coming soon! Blessed is he who keeps the words of the prophecy in this book.

"Behold, I am coming soon! My reward is with me, and I will give to everyone according to what he has done. I am the Alpha and the Omega, the First and the Last, the Beginning and the End.

"Blessed are those who wash their robes, that they may have the right to the tree of life and may go through the gates into the city. Outside are the dogs, those who practice magic arts, the sexually immoral, the murderers, the idolaters and everyone who loves and practices falsehood.

"I, Jesus, have sent my angel to give you this testimony for the churches. I am the Root and the Offspring of David, and the bright Morning Star."

The Spirit and the bride say, "Come!" And let him who hears say, "Come!" Whoever is thirsty, let him come; and whoever wishes, let him take the free gift of the water of life.

He who testifies to these things says, "Yes, I am coming soon."

Amen. Come, Lord Jesus.

The grace of the Lord Jesus be with God's people. Amen.

REVELATION 22:7, 12-17, 20-21

Related texts: PSALMS 1; 37; MATTHEW 16:24-27; LUKE 12:35-40; 1 THESSALONIANS 4:13-5:11; REVELATION 1:1-3

DAILY BIBLE READING PLAN - I

Day	Date	AM	PM	Day	Date	AM	PM
1	Jan 1	Ge 1-2	Mt 1	61	Mar 1	Nu 26-27	Mk 8:22-38
2	Jan 2	Ge 3-5	Mt 2	62	Mar 2	Nu 28-29	Mk 9:1-29
3	Jan 3	Ge 6-8	Mt 3	63	Mar 3	Nu 30-31	Mk 9:30-50
4	Jan 4	Ge 9-11	Mt 4	64	Mar 4	Nu 32-33	Mk 10:1-31
5	Jan 5	Ge 12-14	Mt 5:1-26	65	Mar 5	Nu 34-36	Mk 10:32-52
6	Jan 6	Ge 15-17	Mt 5:27-48	66	Mar 6	Dt 1-2	Mk 11:1-19
7	Jan 7	Ge 18-19	Mt 6	67	Mar 7	Dt 3-4	Mk 11:20-33
8	Jan 8	Ge 20-22	Mt 7	68	Mar 8	Dt 5-7	Mk 12:1-27
9	Jan 9	Ge 23-24	Mt 8	69	Mar 9	Dt 8-10	Mk 12:28-44
10	Jan 10	Ge 25-26	Mt 9:1-17	70	Mar 10	Dt 11-13	Mk 13:1-13
11	Jan 11	Ge 27-28	Mt 9:18-38	71	Mar 11	Dt 14-16	Mk 13:14-37
12	Jan 12	Ge 29-30	Mt 10:1-23	72	Mar 12	Dt 17-19	Mk 14:1-25
13	Jan 13	Ge 31-32	Mt 10:24-42	73	Mar 13	Dt 20-22	Mk 14:26-50
14	Jan 14	Ge 33-35	Mt 11	74	Mar 14	Dt 23-25	Mk 14:51-72
15	Jan 15	Ge 36-37	Mt 12:1-21	75	Mar 15	Dt 26-27	Mk 15:1-26
16	Jan 16	Ge 38-40	Mt 12:22-50	76	Mar 16	Dt 28	Mk 15:27-47
17	Jan 17	Ge 41	Mt 13:1-32	77	Mar 17	Dt 29-30	Mk 16
18	Jan 18	Ge 42-43	Mt 13:33-58	78	Mar 18	Dt 31-32	Lk 1:1-23
19	Jan 19	Ge 44-45	Mt 14:1-21	79	Mar 19	Dt 33-34	Lk 1:24-56
20	Jan 20	Ge 46-48	Mt 14:22-36	80	Mar 20	Jos 1-3	Lk 1:57-80
21	Jan 21	Ge 49-50	Mt 15:1-20	81	Mar 21	Jos 4-6	Lk 2:1-24
22	Jan 22	Ex 1-3	Mt 15:21-39	82	Mar 22	Jos 7-8	Lk 2:25-52
23	Jan 23	Ex 4-6	Mt 16	83	Mar 23	Jos 9-10	Lk 3
24	Jan 24	Ex 7-8	Mt 17	84	Mar 24	Jos 11-13	Lk 4:1-32
25	Jan 25	Ex 9-10	Mt 18:1-20	85	Mar 25	Jos 14-15	Lk 4:33-44
26	Jan 26	Ex 11-12	Mt 18:21-35	86	Mar 26	Jos 16-18	Lk 5:1-16
27	Jan 27	Ex 13-15	Mt 19:1-15	87	Mar 27	Jos 19-20	Lk 5:17-39
28	Jan 28	Ex 16-18	Mt 19:16-30	88	Mar 28	Jos 21-22	Lk 6:1-26
29	Jan 29	Ex 19-21	Mt 20:1-16	89	Mar 29	Jos 23-24	Lk 6:27-49
30	Jan 30	Ex 22-24	Mt 20:17-34	90	Mar 30	Jdg 1-2	Lk 7:1-30
31	Jan 31	Ex 25-26	Mt 21:1-22	91	Mar 31	Jdg 3-5	Lk 7:31-50
32	Feb 1	Ex 27-28	Mt 21:23-46	92	Apr 1	Jdg 6-7	Lk 8:1-21
33	Feb 2	Ex 29-30	Mt 22:1-22	93	Apr 2	Jdg 8-9	Lk 8:22-56
34	Feb 3	Ex 31-33	Mt 22:23-46	94	Apr 3	Jdg 10-11	Lk 9:1-36
35	Feb 4	Ex 34-36	Mt 23:1-22	95	Apr 4	Jdg 12-14	Lk 9:37-62
36	Feb 5	Ex 37-38	Mt 23:23-39	96	Apr 5	Jdg 15-17	Lk 10:1-24
37	Feb 6	Ex 39-40	Mt 24:1-22	97	Apr 6	Jdg 18-19	Lk 10:25-42
38	Feb 7	Lev 1-3	Mt 24:23-51	98	Apr 7	Jdg 20-21	Lk 11:1-28
39	Feb 8	Lev 4-6	Mt 25:1-30	99	Apr 8	Ruth	Lk 11:29-54
40	Feb 9	Lev 7-9	Mt 25:31-46	100	Apr 9	1Sa 1-3	Lk 12:1-34
41	Feb 10	Lev 10-12	Mt 26:1-19	101	Apr 10	1Sa 4-6	Lk 12:35-59
42	Feb 11	Lev 13	Mt 26:20-54	102	Apr 11	1Sa 7-9	Lk 13:1-21
43	Feb 12	Lev 14	Mt 26:55-75	103	Apr 12	1Sa 10-12	Lk 13:22-35
44	Feb 13	Lev 15-17	Mt 27:1-31	104	Apr 13	1Sa 13-14	Lk 14:1-24
45	Feb 14	Lev 18-19	Mt 27:32-66	105	Apr 14	1Sa 15-16	Lk 14:25-35
46	Feb 15	Lev 20-21	Mt 28	106	Apr 15	1Sa 17-18	Lk 15:1-10
47	Feb 16	Lev 22-23	Mk 1:1-22	107	Apr 16	1Sa 19-21	Lk 15:11-32
48	Feb 17	Lev 24-25	Mk 1:23-45	108	Apr 17	1Sa 22-24	Lk 16:1-18
49	Feb 18	Lev 26-27	Mk 2	109	Apr 18	1Sa 25-26	Lk 16:19-31
50	Feb 19	Nu 1-2	Mk 3:1-21	110	Apr 19	1Sa 27-29	Lk 17:1-19
51	Feb 20	Nu 3-4	Mk 3:22-35	111	Apr 20	1Sa 30-31	Lk 17:20-37
52	Feb 21	Nu 5-6	Mk 4:1-20	112	Apr 21	2Sa 1-3	Lk 18:1-17
53	Feb 22	Nu 7	Mk 4:21-41	113	Apr 22	2Sa 4-6	Lk 18:18-43
54	Feb 23	Nu 8-10	Mk 5:1-20	114	Apr 23	2Sa 7-9	Lk 19:1-28
55	Feb 24	Nu 11-13	Mk 5:21-43	115	Apr 24	2Sa 10-12	Lk 19:29-48
56	Feb 25	Nu 14-15	Mk 6:1-32	116	Apr 25	2Sa 13-14	Lk 20:1-26
57	Feb 26	Nu 16-17	Mk 6:33-56	117	Apr 26	2Sa 15-16	Lk 20:27-47
58	Feb 27	Nu 18-20	Mk 7:1-13	118	Apr 27	2Sa 17-18	Lk 21:1-19
59	Feb 28	Nu 21-22	Mk 7:14-37	119	Apr 28	2Sa 19-20	Lk 21:20-38
60	Feb 29	Nu 23-25	Mk 8:1-21	120	Apr 29	2Sa 21-22	Lk 22:1-30
				121	Apr 30	2Sa 23-24	Lk 22:31-53

DAILY BIBLE READING PLAN - I

Day	Date	AM	PM	Day	Date	AM	PM
122	May 1	1Ki 1-2	Lk 22:54-71	183	Jul 1	Job 21-22	Acts 10:1-23
123	May 2	1Ki 3-5	Lk 23:1-26	184	Jul 2	Job 23-25	Acts 10:24-48
124	May 3	1Ki 6-7	Lk 23:27-38	185	Jul 3	Job 26-28	Acts 11
125	May 4	1Ki 8-9	Lk 23:39-56	186	Jul 4	Job 29-30	Acts 12
126	May 5	1Ki 10-11	Lk 24:1-35	187	Jul 5	Job 31-32	Acts 13:1-23
127	May 6	1Ki 12-13	Lk 24:36-53	188	Jul 6	Job 33-34	Acts 13:24-52
128	May 7	1Ki 14-15	Jn 1:1-28	189	Jul 7	Job 35-37	Acts 14
129	May 8	1Ki 16-18	Jn 1:29-51	190	Jul 8	Job 38-39	Acts 15:1-21
130	May 9	1Ki 19-20	Jn 2	191	Jul 9	Job 40-42	Acts 15:22-41
131	May 10	1Ki 21-22	Jn 3:1-21	192	Jul 10	Ps 1-3	Acts 16:1-15
132	May 11	2Ki 1-3	Jn 3:22-36	193	Jul 11	Ps 4-6	Acts 16:16-40
133	May 12	2Ki 4-5	Jn 4:1-30	194	Jul 12	Ps 7-9	Acts 17:1-15
134	May 13	2Ki 6-8	Jn 4:31-54	195	Jul 13	Ps 10-12	Acts 17:16-34
135	May 14	2Ki 9-11	Jn 5:1-24	196	Jul 14	Ps 13-16	Acts 18
136	May 15	2Ki 12-14	Jn 5:25-47	197	Jul 15	Ps 17-18	Acts 19:1-20
137	May 16	2Ki 15-17	Jn 6:1-21	198	Jul 16	Ps 19-21	Acts 19:21-41
138	May 17	2Ki 18-19	Jn 6:22-44	199	Jul 17	Ps 22-24	Acts 20:1-16
139	May 18	2Ki 20-22	Jn 6:45-71	200	Jul 18	Ps 25-27	Acts 20:17-38
140	May 19	2Ki 23-25	Jn 7:1-31	201	Jul 19	Ps 28-30	Acts 21:1-14
141	May 20	1Ch 1-2	Jn 7:32-53	202	Jul 20	Ps 31-33	Acts 21:15-40
142	May 21	1Ch 3-5	Jn 8:1-20	203	Jul 21	Ps 34-35	Acts 22
143	May 22	1Ch 6-7	Jn 8:21-36	204	Jul 22	Ps 36-37	Acts 23:1-11
144	May 23	1Ch 8-10	Jn 8:37-59	205	Jul 23	Ps 38-40	Acts 23:12-35
145	May 24	1Ch 11-13	Jn 9:1-23	206	Jul 24	Ps 41-43	Acts 24
146	May 25	1Ch 14-16	Jn 9:24-41	207	Jul 25	Ps 44-46	Acts 25
147	May 26	1Ch 17-19	Jn 10:1-21	208	Jul 26	Ps 47-49	Acts 26
148	May 27	1Ch 20-22	Jn 10:22-42	209	Jul 27	Ps 50-52	Acts 27:1-25
149	May 28	1Ch 23-25	Jn 11:1-17	210	Jul 28	Ps 53-55	Acts 27:26-44
150	May 29	1Ch 26-27	Jn 11:18-46	211	Jul 29	Ps 56-58	Acts 28:1-15
151	May 30	1Ch 28-29	Jn 11:47-57	212	Jul 30	Ps 59-61	Acts 28:16-31
152	May 31	2Ch 1-3	Jn 12:1-19	213	Jul 31	Ps62-64	Rom 1
				214	Aug 1	Ps65-67	Rom 2
153	Jun 1	2Ch 4-6	Jn 12:20-50	215	Aug 2	Ps 68-69	Rom 3
154	Jun 2	2Ch 7-9	Jn 13:1-17	216	Aug 3	Ps70-72	Rom 4
155	Jun 3	2Ch 10-12	Jn 13:18-38	217	Aug 4	Ps73-74	Rom 5
156	Jun 4	2Ch 13-16	Jn 14	218	Aug 5	Ps75-77	Rom 6
157	Jun 5	2Ch 17-19	Jn 15	219	Aug 6	Ps78	Rom 7
158	Jun 6	2Ch 20-22	Jn 16:1-15	220	Aug 7	Ps79-81	Rom 8:1-18
159	Jun 7	2Ch 23-25	Jn 16:16-23	221	Aug 8	Ps82-84	Rom 8:19-29
160	Jun 8	2Ch 26-28	Jn 17	222	Aug 9	Ps 85-87	Rom 9
161	Jun 9	2Ch 29-31	Jn 18:1-23	223	Aug 10	Ps88-89	Rom 10
162	Jun 10	2Ch 32-33	Jn 18:24-40	224	Aug 11	Ps90-92	Rom 11:1-21
163	Jun 11	2Ch 34-36	Jn 19:1-22	225	Aug 12	Ps93-95	Rom 11:22-36
164	Jun 12	Ezra 1-2	Jn 19:23-42	226	Aug 13	Ps96-98	Rom 12
165	Jun 13	Ezra 3-5	Jn 20	227	Aug 14	Ps99-102	Rom 13
166	Jun 14	Ezra 6-8	Jn 21	228	Aug 15	Ps103-104	Rom 14
167	Jun 15	Ezra 9-10	Acts 1	229	Aug 16	Ps105-106	Rom 15:1-20
168	Jun 16	Neh 1-3	Acts 2:1-13	230	Aug 17	Ps 107-108	Rom 15:21-33
169	Jun 17	Neh 4-6	Acts 2:14-47	231	Aug 18	Ps 109-111	Rom 16
170	Jun 18	Neh 7-8	Acts 3	232	Aug 19	Ps 112-115	1 Cor 1
171	Jun 19	Neh 9-11	Acts 4:1-22	233	Aug 20	Ps 116-118	1 Cor 2
172	Jun 20	Neh 12-13	Acts 4:23-37	234	Aug 21	Ps 119:1-48	1 Cor 3
173	Jun 21	Est 1-3	Acts 5:1-16	235	Aug 22	119:49-104	1 Cor 4
174	Jun 22	Est 4-6	Acts 5:17-42	236	Aug 23	119:105-176	1 Cor 5
175	Jun 23	Est 7-10	Acts 6	237	Aug 24	Ps 120-123	1 Cor 6
176	Jun 24	Job 1-3	Acts 7:1-19	238	Aug 25	Ps 124-127	1 Cor 7:1-24
177	Jun 25	Job 4-6	Acts 7:20-43	239	Aug 26	Ps 128-131	1 Cor 7:25-40
178	Jun 26	Job 7-9	Acts 7:44-60	240	Aug 27	Ps 132-135	1 Cor 8
179	Jun 27	Job 10-12	Acts 8:1-25	241	Aug 28	Ps 136-138	1 Cor 9
180	Jun 28	Job 13-15	Acts 8:26-40	242	Aug 29	Ps 139-141	1 Cor 10:1-13
181	Jun 29	Job 16-18	Acts 9:1-22	243	Aug 30	Ps 142-144	1 Cor 10:14-33
182	Jun 30	Job 19-20	Acts 9:23-43	244	Aug 31	Ps 145-147	1 Cor 11:1-15

DAILY BIBLE READING PLAN - I

Day	Date	AM	PM	Day	Date	AM	PM
245	Sep 1	Ps 148-150	1 Cor 11:16-34	306	Nov 1	Jer 31-32	Titus 2
246	Sep 2	Pr 1-2	1 Cor 12	307	Nov 2	Jer 33-35	Titus 3
247	Sep 3	Pr 3-4	1 Cor 13	308	Nov 3	Jer 36-37	Philem
248	Sep 4	Pr 5-6	1 Cor 14:1-20	309	Nov 4	Jer 38-39	Heb 1
249	Sep 5	Pr 7-8	1 Cor 14:21-40	310	Nov 5	Jer 40-42	Heb 2
250	Sep 6	Pr 9-10	1 Cor 15:1-32	311	Nov 6	Jer 43-45	Heb 3
251	Sep 7	Pr 11-12	1 Cor 15:33-58	312	Nov 7	Jer 46-48	Heb 4
252	Sep 8	Pr 13-14	1 Cor 16	313	Nov 8	Jer 49-50	Heb 5
253	Sep 9	Pr 15-16	2 Cor 1	314	Nov 9	Jer 51-52	Heb 6
254	Sep 10	Pr 17-18	2 Cor 2	315	Nov 10	Lam 1-2	Heb 7
255	Sep 11	Pr 19-20	2 Cor 3	316	Nov 11	Lam 3-5	Heb 8
256	Sep 12	Pr 21-22	2 Cor 4	317	Nov 12	Eze 1-3	Heb 9
257	Sep 13	Pr 23-24	2 Cor 5	318	Nov 13	Eze 4-6	Heb 10:1-23
258	Sep 14	Pr 25-27	2 Cor 6	319	Nov 14	Eze 7-9	Heb 10:24-39
259	Sep 15	Pr 28-29	2 Cor 7	320	Nov 15	Eze 10-12	Heb 11:1-19
260	Sep 16	Pr 30-31	2 Cor 8	321	Nov 16	Eze 13-15	Heb 11:20-40
261	Sep 17	Ecc 1-3	2 Cor 9	322	Nov 17	Eze 16	Heb 12
262	Sep 18	Ecc 4-6	2 Cor 10	323	Nov 18	Eze 17-19	Heb 13
263	Sep 19	Ecc 7-9	2 Cor 11:1-15	324	Nov 19	Eze 20-21	James 1
264	Sep 20	Ecc 10-12	2 Cor 11:16-33	325	Nov 20	Eze 22-23	James 2
265	Sep 21	Song 1-3	2 Cor 12	326	Nov 21	Eze 24-26	James 3
266	Sep 22	Song 4-5	2 Cor 13	327	Nov 22	Eze 27-28	James 4
267	Sep 23	Song 6-8	Gal 1	328	Nov 23	Eze 29-31	James 5
268	Sep 24	Isa 1-3	Gal 2	329	Nov 24	Eze 32-33	1 Pet 1
269	Sep 25	Isa 4-6	Gal 3	330	Nov 25	Eze 34-35	1 Pet 2
270	Sep 26	Isa 7-9	Gal 4	331	Nov 26	Eze 36-37	1 Pet 3
271	Sep 27	Isa 10-12	Gal 5	332	Nov 27	Eze 38-39	1 Pet 4
272	Sep 28	Isa 13-15	Gal 6	333	Nov 28	Eze 40	1 Pet 5
273	Sep 29	Isa 16-18	Eph 1	334	Nov 29	Eze 41-42	2 Pet 1
274	Sep 30	Isa 19-21	Eph 2	335	Nov 30	Eze 43-44	2 Pet 2
275	Oct 1	Isa 22-23	Eph 3	336	Dec 1	Eze 45-46	2 Pet 3
276	Oct 2	Isa 24-26	Eph 4	337	Dec 2	Eze 47-48	1 John 1
277	Oct 3	Isa 27-28	Eph 5	338	Dec 3	Dan 1-2	1 John 2
278	Oct 4	Isa 29-30	Eph 6	339	Dec 4	Dan 3-4	1 John 3
279	Oct 5	Isa 31-33	Phil 1	340	Dec 5	Dan 5-6	1 John 4
280	Oct 6	Isa 34-36	Phil 2	341	Dec 6	Dan 7-8	1 John 5
281	Oct 7	Isa 37-38	Phil 3	342	Dec 7	Dan 9-10	2 John
282	Oct 8	Isa 39-40	Phil 4	343	Dec 8	Dan 11-12	3 John
283	Oct 9	Isa 41-42	Col 1	344	Dec 9	Hos 1-4	Jude
284	Oct 10	Isa 43-44	Col 2	345	Dec 10	Hos 5-8	Rev 1
285	Oct 11	Isa 45-47	Col 3	346	Dec 11	Hos 9-11	Rev 2
286	Oct 12	Isa 48-49	Col 4	347	Dec 12	Hos 12-14	Rev 3
287	Oct 13	Isa 50-52	1 Thess 1	348	Dec 13	Joel 1-3	Rev 4
288	Oct 14	Isa 53-55	1 Thess 2	349	Dec 14	Amos 1-3	Rev 5
289	Oct 15	Isa 56-58	1 Thess 3	350	Dec 15	Amos 4-6	Rev 6
290	Oct 16	Isa 59-61	1 Thess 4	351	Dec 16	Amos 7-9	Rev 7
291	Oct 17	Isa 62-64	1 Thess 5	352	Dec 17	Obad	Rev 8
292	Oct 18	Isa 65-66	2 Thess 1	353	Dec 18	Jonah	Rev 9
293	Oct 19	Jer 1-2	2 Thess 2	354	Dec 19	Mic 1-3	Rev 10
294	Oct 20	Jer 3-4	2 Thess 3	355	Dec 20	Mic 4-5	Rev 11
295	Oct 21	Jer 5-6	1 Tim 1	356	Dec 21	Mic 6-7	Rev 12
296	Oct 22	Jer 7-8	1 Tim 2	357	Dec 22	Nah	Rev 13
297	Oct 23	Jer 9-10	1 Tim 3	358	Dec 23	Hab	Rev 14
298	Oct 24	Jer 11-13	1 Tim 4	359	Dec 24	Zeph	Rev 15
299	Oct 25	Jer 14-16	1 Tim 5	360	Dec 25	Hag	Rev 16
300	Oct 26	Jer 17-19	1 Tim 6	361	Dec 26	Zech 1-3	Rev 17
301	Oct 27	Jer 20-22	2 Tim 1	362	Dec 27	Zech 4-6	Rev 18
302	Oct 28	Jer 23-24	2 Tim 2	363	Dec 28	Zech 7-9	Rev 19
303	Oct 29	Jer 25-26	2 Tim 3	364	Dec 29	Zech 10-12	Rev 20
304	Oct 30	Jer 27-28	2 Tim 4	365	Dec 30	Zech 13-14	Rev 21
305	Oct 31	Jer 29-30	Titus 1	366	Dec 31	Mal	Rev 22

Daily Bible Reading Plan - II

Jan 1	Gen 1-3	Feb 20	Lev 13-14	Apr 10	1Sa 4-7
Jan 2	Gen 4:1–6:8	Feb 21	Lev 15-17	Apr 11	1Sa 8-10
Jan 3	Gen 6:9–9:29	Feb 22	Lev 18-20	Apr 12	1Sa 11-13
Jan 4	Gen 10-11	Feb 23	Lev 21-23	Apr 13	1Sa 14-15
Jan 5	Gen 12-14	Feb 24	Lev 24-25	Apr 14	1Sa 16-17
Jan 6	Gen 15-17	Feb 25	Lev 26-27	Apr 15	1Sa 18-19; Ps 59
Jan 7	Gen 18-19	Feb 26	Nu 1-2	Apr 16	1Sa 20-21;
Jan 8	Gen 20-22	Feb 27	Nu 3-4		Ps 56; 34
Jan 9	Gen 23-24	Feb 28	Nu 5-6	Apr 17	1Sa 22-23;
Jan 10	Gen 25-26				1Ch 12:8-18;
Jan 11	Gen 27-28	Mar 1	Nu 7		Ps 52; 54; 63; 144
Jan 12	Gen 29-30	Mar 2	Nu 8-10	Apr 18	1Sa 24; Ps 57;
Jan 13	Gen 31-32	Mar 3	Nu 11-13		1Sa 25
Jan 14	Gen 33-35	Mar 4	Nu 14-15	Apr 19	1Sa 26-29;
Jan 15	Gen 36-37	Mar 5	Nu 16-18		1Ch 12:1-7; 19-22
Jan 16	Gen 38-40	Mar 6	Nu 19-21	Apr 20	1Sa 30-31; 1Ch 10;
Jan 17	Gen 41-42	Mar 7	Nu 22-24		2Sa 1
Jan 18	Gen 43-45	Mar 8	Nu 25-26	Apr 21	2Sa 2-4
Jan 19	Gen 46-47	Mar 9	Nu 27-29	Apr 22	2Sa 5:1-6:11;
Jan 20	Gen 48-50	Mar 10	Nu 30-31		1Ch 11:1-9; 12:23-
Jan 21	Job 1-3	Mar 11	Nu 32-33		14:17
Jan 22	Job 4-7	Mar 12	Nu 34-36	Apr 23	2Sa 22; Ps 18
Jan 23	Job 8-11	Mar 13	Dt 1-2	Apr 24	1Ch 15-16;
Jan 24	Job 12-15	Mar 14	Dt 3-4		2Sa 6:12-23; Ps 96
Jan 25	Job 16-19	Mar 15	Dt 5-7	Apr 25	Ps 105; 2Sa 7;
Jan 26	Job 20-22	Mar 16	Dt 8-10		1Ch 17
Jan 27	Job 23-28	Mar 17	Dt 11-13	Apr 26	2Sa 8-10;
Jan 28	Job 29-31	Mar 18	Dt 14-17		1Ch 18-19; Ps 60
Jan 29	Job 32-34	Mar 19	Dt 18-21	Apr 27	2Sa 11-12;
Jan 30	Job 35-37	Mar 20	Dt 22-25		1Ch 20:1-3; Ps 51
Jan 31	Job 38-42	Mar 21	Dt 26-28	Apr 28	2Sa 13-14
		Mar 22	Dt 29:1–31:29	Apr 29	2Sa 15-17
Feb 1	Ex 1-4	Mar 23	Dt 31:30–34:12	Apr 30	Ps 3; 2Sa 18-19
Feb 2	Ex 5-8	Mar 24	Jos 1-4		
Feb 3	Ex 9-11	Mar 25	Jos 5-8	May 1	2Sa 20-21; 23:8-23;
Feb 4	Ex 12-13	Mar 26	Jos 9-11		1Ch 20:4-8;11:10-25
Feb 5	Ex 14-15	Mar 27	Jos 12-14	May 2	2Sa 23:24–24:25;
Feb 6	Ex 16-18	Mar 28	Jos 15-17		1Ch 11:26-47;
Feb 7	Ex 19-21	Mar 29	Jos 18-19		21:1-30
Feb 8	Ex 22-24	Mar 30	Jos 20-22	May 3	1Ch 22-24
Feb 9	Ex 25-27	Mar 31	Jos 23–Jdg 1	May 4	Ps 30; 1Ch 25-26
Feb 10	Ex 28-29			May 5	1Ch 27-29
Feb 11	Ex 30-31	Apr 1	Jdg 2-5	May 6	Ps 5-7; 10; 11; 13;
Feb 12	Ex 32-34	Apr 2	Jdg 6-8		17
Feb 13	Ex 35-36	Apr 3	Jdg 9	May 7	Ps 23; 26; 28; 31;
Feb 14	Ex 37-38	Apr 4	Jdg 10-12		35
Feb 15	Ex 39-40	Apr 5	Jdg 13-16	May 8	Ps 41; 43; 46; 55;
Feb 16	Lev 1:1-5:13	Apr 6	Jdg 17-19		61; 62; 64
Feb 17	Lev 5:14-7:38	Apr 7	Jdg 20-21	May 9	Ps 69-71; 77
Feb 18	Lev 8-10	Apr 8	Ruth	May 10	Ps 83; 86; 88; 91;
Feb 19	Lev 11-12	Apr 9	1Sa 1-3		95

Daily Bible Reading Plan - II

May 11	Ps 108; 109; 120; 121; 140; 143; 144	Jun 12	Pr 28-29	Jul 16	Isa 31-35
May 12	Ps 1; 14; 15; 36; 37; 39	Jun 13	Pr 30-31; Ps 127	Jul 17	2Ki 18:1-8; 2Ch 29-31
May 13	Ps 40; 49; 50; 73	Jun 14	Song of Songs	Jul 18	2Ki 17; 18:9-37; 2Ch 32:1-19; Isa 36
May 14	Ps 76; 82; 84; 90; 92; 112; 115	Jun 15	1Ki 11:1-40; Ecc 1-2	Jul 19	2Ki 19; 2Ch 32:20-23; Isa 37
May 15	Ps 8; 9; 16; 19; 21; 24; 29	Jun 16	Ecc 3-7	Jul 20	2Ki 20; 2Ch 32:24-33; Isa 38-39
May 16	Ps 33; 65-68	Jun 17	Ecc 8-12; 1Ki 11:41-43; 2Ch 9:29-31	Jul 21	2Ki 21:1-18; 2Ch 33:1-20; Is 40
May 17	Ps 75; 93; 94; 97-100	Jun 18	1Ki 12; 2Ch 10:1–11:17	Jul 22	Isa 41-43
May 18	Ps 103; 104; 113; 114; 117	Jun 19	1Ki 13-14; 2Ch 11:18–12:16	Jul 23	Isa 44-47
May 19	Ps 119:1-88	Jun 20	1Ki 15:1-24; 2Ch 13-16	Jul 24	Isa 48-51
May 20	Ps 119:89-176	Jun 21	1Ki 15:25–16:34; 2Ch 17; 1Ki 17	Jul 25	Isa 52-57
May 21	Ps 122; 124; 133-136	Jun 22	1Ki 18-19	Jul 26	Isa 58-62
May 22	Ps 138; 139; 145; 148; 150	Jun 23	1Ki 20-21	Jul 27	Isa 63-66
May 23	Ps 4; 12; 20; 25; 32; 38	Jun 24	1Ki 22:1-40; 2Ch 18	Jul 28	2Ki 21:19-26; 2Ch 33:21-34:7; Zephaniah
May 24	Ps 42; 53; 58; 81; 101; 111; 130; 131; 141; 146	Jun 25	1Ki 22:41-53; 2Ki 1; 2Ch 19:1–21:3	Jul 29	Jer 1-3
		Jun 26	2Ki 2-4	Jul 30	Jer 4-6
May 25	Ps 2; 22; 27	Jun 27	2Ki 5-7	Jul 31	Jer 7-9
May 26	Ps 45; 47; 48; 87; 110	Jun 28	2Ki 8-9; 2Ch 21:4–22:9	Aug 1	Jer 10-13
May 27	1Ki 1:1–2:12; 2Sa 23:1-7	Jun 29	2Ki 10-11; 2Ch 22:10–23:21	Aug 2	Jer 14-16
May 28	1Ki 2:13–3:28; 2Ch 1:1-13	Jun 30	Joel	Aug 3	Jer 17-20
May 29	1Ki 5-6; 2Ch 2-3			Aug 4	2Ki 22:1–23:28; 2Ch 34:9–35:19
May 30	1Ki 7; 2Ch 4	Jul 1	2Ki 12-13; 2Ch 24	Aug 5	Nahum; 2Ki 23:29-37; 2Ch 35:20–36:5; Jer 22:10-17
May 31	1Ki 8; 2Ch 5:1-7:10	Jul 2	2Ki 14; 2Ch 25; Jonah		
		Jul 3	Hosea 1-7		
		Jul 4	Hosea 8-14	Aug 6	Jer 26; Habakkuk
Jun 1	1Ki 9:1–10:13; 2Ch 7:11–9:12	Jul 5	2Ki 15:1-7; 2Ch 26; Amos 1-4	Aug 7	Jer 46; 47; 2Ki 24:1-4 + 7; 2Ch 36:6-7; Jer 25; 35
Jun 2	1Ki 4; 10:14-29; 2Ch 1:14-17; 9:13-28; Ps 72	Jul 6	Amos 5-9; 2Ki 15:8-18	Aug 8	Jer 36; 45; 48
Jun 3	Pr 1-3	Jul 7	Isa 1-4	Aug 9	Jer 49:1-33; Dan 1-2
Jun 4	Pr 4-6	Jul 8	2Ki 15:19-38; 2Ch 27; Isa 5-6	Aug 10	Jer 22:18-30; 2Ki 24:5-20; 2Ch 36:8-12; Jer 37:1-2; 52:1-3; 24; 29
Jun 5	Pr 7-9	Jul 9	Micah		
Jun 6	Pr 10-12	Jul 10	2Ki 16; 2Ch 28; Isa 7-8		
Jun 7	Pr 13-15	Jul 11	Isa 9-12	Aug 11	Jer 27; 28; 23
Jun 8	Pr 16-18	Jul 12	Isa 13-16	Aug 12	Jer 50-51
Jun 9	Pr 19-21	Jul 13	Isa 17-22	Aug 13	Jer 49:34-39; 34; Eze 1-3
Jun 10	Pr 22-24	Jul 14	Isa 23-27	Aug 14	Eze 4-7
Jun 11	Pr 25-27	Jul 15	Isa 28-30		

Daily Bible Reading Plan - II

Aug 15	Eze 8-11	Sep 16	Esth 1-4		Mt 13:54-58; 9:35-11:1; 14:1-12; Lk 9:1-10
Aug 16	Eze 12-14	Sep 17	Esth 5-10		
Aug 17	Eze 15-17	Sep 18	Ezr 7-8		
Aug 18	Eze 18-20	Sep 19	Ezr 9-10	Oct 16	Mt 14:13-36; Mk 6:31-56; Lk 9:11-17; Jn 6:1-21
Aug 19	Eze 21-23	Sep 20	Neh 1-5		
Aug 20	2Ki 25:1; 2Ch 36:13; Jer 39:1; 52:4; Eze 24; Jer 21:1-22:9; 32	Sep 21	Neh 6-7		
		Sep 22	Neh 8-10		
		Sep 23	Neh 11-13	Oct 17	Jn 6:22-7:1; Mt 15:1-20; Mk 7:1-23
		Sep 24	Malachi		
		Sep 25	1Ch 1-2		
Aug 21	Jer 30; 31; 33	Sep 26	1Ch 3-5	Oct 18	Mt 15:21-16:20; Mk 7:24-8:30; Lk 9:18-21
Aug 22	Eze 25; 29:1-16; 30; 31	Sep 27	1Ch 6		
		Sep 28	1Ch 7:1-8:27		
Aug 23	Eze 26-28	Sep 29	1Ch 8:28-9:44	Oct 19	Mt 16:21-17:27; Mk 8:31-9:32; Lk 9:22-45
Aug 24	Jer 37:3-39:10; 52:5-30; 2Ki 25:2-21; 2Ch 36:17-21	Sep 30	Jn 1:1-18; Mk 1:1; Lk 1:1-4; 3:23-38; Mt 1:1-17		
				Oct 20	Mt 18; 8:19-22; Mk 9:33-50; Lk 9:46-62; Jn 7:2-10
Aug 25	2Ki 25:22; Jer 39:11-40:6; Lam 1-3	Oct 1	Lk 1:5-80		
		Oct 2	Mt 1:18-2:23; Lk 2	Oct 21	Jn 7:11-8:59
Aug 26	Lam 4-5; Obadiah	Oct 3	Mt 3:1-4:11; Mk 1:2-13; Lk 3:1-23a; 4:1-13; Jn 1:19-34	Oct 22	Lk 10:1-11:36
Aug 27	Jer 40:7-43:30; 2Ki 25:23-26			Oct 23	Lk 11:37-13:21
				Oct 24	Jn 9-10
Aug 28	Eze 33:21-36:38	Oct 4	Jn 1:35-3:36	Oct 25	Lk 13:22-15:32
Aug 29	Eze 37-39	Oct 5	Jn 4; Mt 4:12-17; Mk 1:14-15; Lk 4:14-30	Oct 26	Lk 16:1-17:10; Jn 11:1-54
Aug 30	Eze 32:1-33:20; Dan 3				
Aug 31	Eze 40-42	Oct 6	Mk 1:16-45; Mt 4:18-25; 8:2-4+ 14-17; Lk 4:31-5:16	Oct 27	Lk 17:11-18:17; Mt 19:1-15; Mk 10:1-16
Sep 1	Eze 43-45	Oct 7	Mt 9:1-17; Mk 2:1-22; Lk 5:17-39	Oct 28	Mt 19:16-20:28; Mk 10:17-45; Lk 18:18-34
Sep 2	Eze 46-48				
Sep 3	Eze 29:17-21; Dan 4; Jer 52:31-34; 2Ki 25:27-30; Ps 44	Oct 8	Jn 5; Mt 12:1-21; Mk 2:23-3:12; Lk 6:1-11	Oct 29	Mt 20:29-34; 26:6-13; Mk 10:46-52; 14:3-9; Lk 18:35-19:28; Jn 11:55-12:11
Sep 4	Ps 74; 79; 80; 89	Oct 9	Mt 5; Mk 3:13-19; Lk 6:12-36		
Sep 5	Ps 85; 102; 106; 123; 137				
		Oct 10	Mt 6-7; Lk 6:37-49	Oct 30	Mt 21:1-22; Mk 11:1-26; Lk 19:29-48; Jn 12:12-50
Sep 6	Dan 7-8; 5	Oct 11	Lk 7; Mt 8:1+ 5-13; 11:2-30		
Sep 7	Dan 9; 6				
Sep 8	2Ch 36:22-23; Ezr 1:1-4:5	Oct 12	Mt 12:22-50; Mk 3:20-35; Lk 8:1-21	Oct 31	Mt 21:23-22:14; Mk 11:27-12:12; Lk 20:1-19
Sep 9	Dan 10-12				
Sep 10	Ezr 4:6-6:13; Haggai	Oct 13	Mk 4:1-34; Mt 13:1-53		
		Oct 14	Mk 4:35-5:43; Mt 8:18+23-34; 9:18-34; Lk 8:22-56	Nov 1	Mt 22:15-46; Mk 12:13-37; Lk 20:20-44
Sep 11	Zech 1-6				
Sep 12	Zech 7-8; Ezr 6:14-22; Ps 78			Nov 2	Mt 23:1-39; Mk 12:38-44; Lk 20:45-21:4
Sep 13	Ps 107; 116; 118				
Sep 14	Ps 125; 126; 128; 129; 132; 147; 149	Oct 15	Mk 6:1-30;		
Sep 15	Zech 9-14				

Daily Bible Reading Plan - II

Nov 3	Mt 24:1-31; Mk 13:1-27; Lk 21:5-27	Nov 28 Nov 29 Nov 30	1Cor 9-11 1Cor 12-14 1Cor 15-16
Nov 4	Mt 24:32–26:5+ 14-16; Mk 13:28- 14:2, 10–11; Lk 21:28-22:6	Dec 1 Dec 2	Acts 19:23–20:1; 2Cor 1-4 2Cor 5-9
Nov 5	Mt 26:17-29; Mk 14:12-25; Lk 22:7-38; Jn 13	Dec 3 Dec 4 Dec 5	2Cor 10-13 Rom 1-3 Rom 4-6
Nov 6	Jn 14-16	Dec 6	Rom 7-8
Nov 7	Jn 17:1–18:1; Mt 26:30-46; Mk 14:26-42; Lk 22:39-46	Dec 7 Dec 8 Dec 9	Rom 9-11 Rom 12-15 Rom 16; Acts 20:2-21:16
Nov 8	Mt 26:47-75; Mk 14:43-72; Lk 22:47-65; Jn 18:2-27	Dec 10 Dec 11 Dec 12	Acts 21:17–23:35 Acts 24-26 Acts 27-28
Nov 9	Mt 27:1-26; Mk 15:1-15; Lk 22:66–23:25; Jn 18:28–19:16	Dec 13 Dec 14 Dec 15 Dec 16	Eph 1-3 Eph 4-6 Colossians Philippians
Nov 10	Mt 27:27-56; Mk 15:16-41; Lk 23:26-49; Jn 19:17-30	Dec 17 Dec 18 Dec 19	Philemon; 1Tim 1-3 1Tim 4-6; Titus 2 Timothy
Nov 11	Mt 27:57–28:8; Mk 15:42–16:8; Lk 23:50–24:12; Jn 19:31–20:10	Dec 20 Dec 21 Dec 22 Dec 23	1 Peter Jude; 2 Peter Heb 1:1-5:10 Heb 5:11–9:28
Nov 12	Mt 28:9-20; Mk 16:9-20; Lk 24:13-53; Jn 20:11–21:25	Dec 24 Dec 25 Dec 26	Heb 10-11 Heb 12-13; 2 John; 3 John 1 John
Nov 13	Acts 1-2	Dec 27	Rev 1-3
Nov 14	Acts 3-5	Dec 28	Rev 4-9
Nov 15	Acts 6:1–8:1	Dec 29	Rev 10-14
Nov 16	Acts 8:2–9:43	Dec 30	Rev 15-18
Nov 17	Acts 10-11	Dec 31	Rev 19-22
Nov 18	Acts 12-13		
Nov 19	Acts 14-15		
Nov 20	Gal 1-3		
Nov 21	Gal 4-6		
Nov 22	James		
Nov 23	Ac 16:1–18:11		
Nov 24	1 Thessalonians		
Nov 25	2 Thessalonians; Acts 18:12-19:22		
Nov 26	1Cor 1-4		
Nov 27	1Cor 5-8		

Scripture Index

Scripture Index

Scripture Index

Scripture Index

Scripture Index

Scripture Index

Scripture Index

Scripture Index

Topical Index

Topical Index

Topical Index

Topical Index

Judas 109, 334, 337, 339
judging 162
judgment 13-15, 17, 18, 93, 96, 97, 101,
  115, 117, 134, 169, 191, 193, 194, 195,
  200, 201, 211, 226, 247, 254, 259, 260,
  263, 274, 276, 277, 280-289, 292, 307,
  365, 391, 393, 394
justice 36, 38, 41, 43, 57, 63, 134-136,
  143, 176, 180

K

kindness 83, 84, 146, 173
king 56, 59, 61, 63, 67, 69, 105, 111, 118,
  233, 234, 236, 248, 282, 308, 335, 386,
  389
kingdom 39, 46, 154, 161, 199, 243, 254,
  262, 309, 315, 320, 325, 329, 344
kingdom of God 39, 46, 154, 161, 254,
  309, 315, 320, 325, 329, 344
knowing God 357, 368
Korah 193

L

land 4, 20
last days 373
Last Supper 108, 337
law 130, 133-138, 147-150, 154, 302
Lazarus 224, 334
laziness 371
life 82, 84, 220, 224, 225, 244, 315, 329, 395
light 2, 5, 153, 155, 157, 221
living water 42
Lord's Prayer 159, 325
lost 255, 257
Lot 20
love 3, 47, 48, 59, 75, 76, 81, 84, 88, 114,
  118, 122, 126, 130, 133, 150, 151, 157,
  170, 175, 176, 182, 184, 186, 187, 195,
  196, 202, 216, 219, 240, 282, 287, 315,
  357, 382, 383
loyalty 217
lust 127, 156, 245
lying 129, 205, 211, 213

M

Magi 389
magic 95
majesty 58
Malachi 307
male and female 10
mankind 8, 10, 11

manna 189, 220
marriage 48, 127, 147, 185, 218, 219, 328,
  358
Martha 224, 334
martyrdom 349
Mary Magdalene 112, 342
Mary, mother of Jesus 68, 310, 311, 314,
  388
Mary, sister of Lazarus 224, 334
meditation 69, 204
meekness 41
mercy 43, 68, 82, 175, 380, 385
messianic prophecy 11, 63, 80, 90, 102,
  105-107, 180, 243, 274, 307, 308, 309,
  310, 336, 338, 340, 346, 379, 380, 386,
  387, 389
Micah 277, 285
millennium 393
miracles 62, 93-97, 106, 117, 119, 189,
  221, 267, 314, 316-319, 321, 327, 347,
  348, 352, 353
miracles of Jesus 62, 106, 221, 314, 316-
  319, 321, 327
Miriam 194
missions 344, 352
money 157
Mordecai 304-306
Moses 15, 50-53, 56, 93-95, 97, 101, 115-
  117, 120, 138, 167-170, 190, 191, 192-
  195, 200, 201, 203, 204, 279, 323, 376
mother 68, 140-143, 310, 311, 314, 388
mourning 40
murder 16, 49, 126, 155, 241, 246
music 206
mustard seed 324

N

Nahum 281
names of God 53-63, 67-73, 86, 123, 142,
  146, 177, 244, 348, 381, 391, 392, 395
Naomi 216-219
Nathan 246
nations 55, 56, 59, 120, 150, 361, 362
Nebuchadnezzar 286, 291-293
Nehemiah 299, 300, 302
neighbor 133
new birth 315
New Covenant 108
new heavens and earth 82, 390, 394
new Jerusalem 394
Nicodemus 315

Topical Index

Topical Index

Israel In Old Testament Times

Israel In New Testament Times

The Assyrian Empire

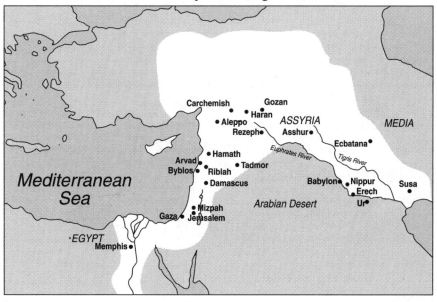

Babylonian & Persian Empires

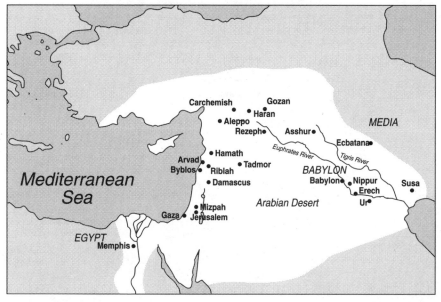

The Roman Empire

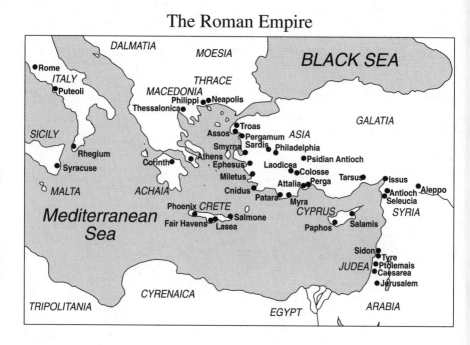

Lands of the Bible Today